The Life of Spirit

Volume Five

The Divine

Workshop

The Divine Workshop

VOLUME V
OF THE LIFE OF SPIRIT

A COLLECTION OF ESSAYS
BY ROBERT R. LEICHTMAN, M.D.
& CARL JAPIKSE

ARIEL PRESS
Atlanta, Georgia

No Royalties Are Paid on This Book

This book is made possible by a gift
to the Publications Fund of Light
by Elizabeth Salt

THE DIVINE WORKSHOP
The Life of Spirit Volume V

ISBN 0-89804-136-8

Table of Contents

A Ceaseless
Flow of Spirit

One of the problems of human thinking is its tendency to categorize. If we think about education, we immediately associate it with schools, teachers, and diplomas. If the conversation turns to science, we conjure up images of research labs and experiments with intricate equipment. Mention business, and the latest activity on Wall Street rushes to the forefront of our thinking. The idea that learning can occur outside of traditional ivied walls is one we rarely consider. The notion that science might have a lot to adapt from the arts—or commerce—is equally remote. We are not accustomed to expanding the boundaries of our categories. In most cases, we would prefer to leave the borders where they are.

Nowhere is the categorization of our thinking more evident than in the life of spirit. For most of us, the mere mention of the word "spirit" immediately conjures up associations with religion—Moses receiving the Ten Commandments, Jesus on the cross, or the Buddha sitting under the bo tree. It would never occur to us to look for evidence of spirit in education or science. Such a concept does not jibe with our categories. The same problem exists with our understanding of inspiration—the process of spirit flowing into our personal awareness. We might be willing to accept that poets and philosophers can be inspired as well as great spiritual leaders. But scientists? Statesmen? Business people? Our categories do not contain that much elasticity!

And yet, if we want to have anything more than a naïve, simplistic view of spirit, we need to stretch our understanding of how we interact with divine life. We need to appreciate that there has been a ceaseless flow of divine intelligence, love, and power into our lives—and the life of civilization—since the dawn of humanity. We also need to recognize that this ceaseless flow does not just single out religion and religious people and dump its entire blessing on them. It flows to every major institution of society—every department of civilization in which creative, dedicated, and intelligent people are laboring to make life on earth more enriched, inspired, and enlightened—and it flows in equal measures. The life of spirit nurtures and guides the development of science and education just as surely as it inspires religion; the love and joy of God lifts up and sustains the progress of business and the arts every bit as much as it supports the good works of the world's temples and churches.

It is sometimes important to remember that God did not create temples and churches; He created humanity. As humanity struggles to define its needs, goals, and basic design, it slowly becomes aware of the necessity to be guided and enriched by spirit. These needs are so diverse they cannot possibly be met by just one institution, whether it be religion or a government. Humanity needs commerce in order to feed and clothe the billions of people alive today. It needs government to organize and protect our efforts. It needs the arts to inspire us to refine consciousness. It needs education to teach us the skills that will let us make our way in life. It needs science to harness the wonderful potential of nature. It needs the healing arts to mend sick bodies.

But the value of these institutions of society is not limited just to providing material needs. Each also speaks to us spiritually, and opens a doorway into the life of spirit, if we choose to pass through it. Science reveals the hidden laws of life, and helps us understand parallels between spirit and earth. Education trains the mind. Government instructs us in basic lessons of cooperation. The arts inspire us to express beauty, joy, and harmony in our daily activities. Business teaches us fundamental principles of tapping the abundance of divine life. Medicine and psychology help us learn and practice the divine laws of health and right human relationships.

A few hundred years ago, it was thought that religion was the only channel to the life of spirit. As a result, the church tried to play too large of a role, and ended up sabotaging its effort. It forgot that its special role in civilization is to teach us the work of stewardship and communing with divine life.

Unfortunately, most of us still think of religion as the sole outlet of the life of spirit. We continue to preserve categories that do not exist. In point of fact, education, the arts, science, government, business, and medicine are designed to be equals with religion in providing channels for the expression of spirit on earth. In some cases, they have actually left religion behind.

Religion will eventually catch up, because the role it is meant to play is of vital importance to civilization. It preserves and disseminates a body of knowledge about the nature of God, our relationship to our Creator, our relationship with each other, and the way to achieve release from the tyranny of materialism and ignorance. Yet organized religion can do little to guarantee our rights and freedoms, even though spirit has an intense interest in promoting liberty. Nor can the church do very much in terms of tapping the hidden energy of the atom, although spirit again is seeking to inspire these developments within science.

In fact, it is harmful and limiting to expect religion to be the sole channel for the expression of spirit through civilization. It is much more appropriate to see it for what it is: one of seven very important human institutions, each of which is designed to express a major facet of the life of spirit on earth. These seven institutions are education, the arts, science, business, government, the healing arts and sciences, and—of course—religion.

It is true that the work of these institutions is often mundane. Yet the needs of humanity are mundane as well as spiritual. We need to be fed, sheltered, and healed. As these needs are met, more subtle ones arise: we need to be educated, protected, and productively employed. It is only when these material needs are satisfied that humanity turns even further inward, and begins to recognize its spiritual needs—its need to learn about divine love and joy, beauty and wisdom, and law and purpose.

At a collective level, these more sublime, spiritual needs could be listed as the need to be liberated from ignorance, chaos, superstition, nihilism, illness, poverty, and exploitation. Surely, education is better prepared than religion to liberate mankind from ignorance. It strives to reveal the presence of divine intelligence within each of us. The arts are better equipped to free humanity from emptiness and disorder, by cultivating a greater attunement to beauty, harmony, and grace. Science is better designed to wipe out superstition and promote the spirit of discovery. The healing arts are better prepared to eliminate illness and teach the principles of health. Business opens the door to the liberation from poverty. Government is best equipped to free us from exploitation and enforce the divine ideal of justice. Religion, too, has its mission to perform—to release us from the chains of nihilism that still imprison most of the race. The major religions of the world are meant to serve as steadfast beacons of the light—the inner meaning and power of divine life.

The confusion lies in the difficulty most people have in contemplating spiritual and mundane aspects of life simultaneously. When these people see businesses dominated by greed, governments controlled by corruption, and the arts seduced by banality, it is hard for them to imagine that these institutions serve any spiritual purpose, let alone respond to divine guidance. To such people, it is just a matter of black and white. Being opposites, the mundane and the spiritual cannot embrace each other; they are eternal foes. Human civilization is the result of resourceful people responding to the obvious needs of mundane life. There is no spiritual element involved at all. Or so they say.

But intelligent people know from their own experience that such materialistic thinking is erroneous, limited by the boundaries of concrete categories. Intelligent people know, from personal experience, that the mundane needs for better education or health can draw forth a greater level of need as well—the need to work with higher possibililties.

Musicians and other creative people are often the first to discover this principle. They cannot hope to play their chosen instrument with skill unless they have devoted themselves to mastering the mundane needs of their craft. Yet even if they have achieved technical perfection through countless hours of drill and rehearsal, their performance may be flat and lifeless unless they are also able to tap and express the exhilarating presence of spirit while they are playing. In such masters, the mundane meets the spiritual, is infused by it, and lifts up the quality of all that they do. To clothe this idea with allegory, it is as though each of us has within our consciousness a divine workshop in which to explore our inner potential for greatness as a human being—as an artist, a business person, a leader, or even a parent or friend. This divine workshop is a level of consciousness in which we can contact and explore spiritual qualities such as love, courage, joy, persistence, wisdom, and patience. We can likewise experiment with new perspectives on life, and learn to heal, reform, renew, and enrich our character and self-expression. In this personal divine workshop, we learn to become creative—to see the experiences of the past and present as the raw materials from which we shape an enlightened self-expression.

The divine workshop of consciousness is not just a temporary phase we pass through on the way to adeptship. It is inherent in our nature, an extension of our will to become the best we can. A mystic might describe it more as an altar of consciousness; a scientist might be more inclined to think of it as a mental laboratory. The allegory can be pictured in many different ways; what counts is our growing awareness that, deep within our consciousness, there is a "place" where our character and self-expression can be refined and enriched.

This work of refining our character is not unlike a master craftsman building elegant furniture in a woodworking shop. He begins by selecting the raw materials he will use for his project. Woods of the highest quality are carefully chosen. He decides on stains, varnishes, and paints. He may even manufacture some of the needed accessories, such as nails, by hand, to meet his specifications. He then begins the work of machining the wood to the proper size and shape, assembling the pieces, and staining and finishing the object. The whole project may require months for a single item, but because he works with assistants or apprentices, his productivity is not restricted by his insistence on quality.

In our case, the raw materials we shape into a better character are our memories, strong feelings, and deeply held beliefs about these experiences. The tools we use to reshape these traits and habits are discernment, persistence, courage, a love of excellence, and self-discipline. Once we have created a new pattern of behavior—say, a deeper trust in divine life—we need to smooth and polish it, varnish it, and add layer after layer of gloss to protect the wood and enhance its beauty. In other words, we need to integrate this new measure of trust into our attitudes to eliminate doubt and discouragement. We must expand our capacity to respond to the guidance and love of the higher self. We must convert trust into a practical attitude toward daily living. And then we must seal and protect our work by adding a new joy of living to achieve the desired level of gloss and shine. It may take us months or years to complete a single project of this magnitude, but like the furniture maker, we have help—the talents, skills, and habits which already serve us day by day.

This divine workshop exists within each of us, and can be discovered through introspection. It is a powerful asset for developing the skills and creativity we need to transcend the hurts of the past, the dangers of the present, and the threats of the future. The workshop contains ideal patterns for every facet of our self-expression—and links us with the power of the higher self to make productive and creative changes in our life energies. As we gain experience working at this level, we will discover that it is possible to transform our resentments, fears, doubts, and disappointments into greater maturity. It is possible to replace anger and depression with tolerance and enthusiasm. It is possible to add new life of spirit to who we are and what we do.

The divine workshop of consciousness is not just allegory, of course—it is a genuine outreach of the inner life. The occasional creative genius who enriches human life by his or her presence and work is actually the outer demonstration of the inner reality. Collectively, these masters and geniuses of their trades, crafts, and sciences form the inspiration and backbone of the key institutions of society. It is therefore right and proper to think of these key institutions as seven great workshops of human life, each representing a major facet of the expression of the divine plan through civilization. In this case, however, the craftsmen are not individuals laboring in private studios, but the whole of the institution of science or the arts or education, laboring within the workshop of humanity.

The raw materials these workshops labor to improve are the struggles and anguishes of the poor and the disadvantaged, the hopes and dreams of our visionaries, the confusion and corruption of our bureaucrats, the ignorance of the uneducated, the crassness of artistic voyeurs, and the pessimism of those enslaved to darkness and bitterness.

These are massive problems, ingrained in millenia of cultural traditions. To transform them, we must learn to use "power tools"—tools which are connected with genuine spiritual power. It is never productive to fight hate with hate—we must heal it with the ceaseless flow of divine love. It is not possible to legislate bigotry out of existence; we must replace it with spiritual respect and cooperation. The problems of modern life seem overwhelming primarily because we are trying to solve them with only human means. This effort is a good beginning, but by itself it cannot succeed. To our human skills and talents, we must add the vitality and strength of divine justice, divine authority, divine beauty, divine nurturing, and spiritual innovativeness.

Above all, however, we must add the divine design for each of these segments of society. It does no good, after all, to build a perfect chair to sit in if the divine design is calling us to get out of our chairs and serve others. It is of little value to preen and polish our feelings, if the divine plan is urging us to train the mind. In terms of civilization, it does little good to indulge the demands of the weak and unskilled, if the divine design for them is to grow strong and become productive. We must therefore resist the temptation to assume that the work of education is just to teach the illiterate people of the world how to read. The divine plan for education embraces the other pole of the spectrum as well—the teaching of skills in excellence, maturity, and thinking to those who are prepared and ready. Such a course of action would serve to lift the whole of society to a greater respect for excellence, maturity, and thinking, thereby benefitting everyone, not just the relative handful being taught.

It is therefore reasonable to see **government** as a divine workshop for integrating new spiritual insights about justice and personal responsibility into society's thinking. It is also reasonable to expect most of these insights to be invoked as we struggle to root out corruption and exploitation from our social structures.

Science can likewise be viewed as a divine workshop for exploring the hidden mysteries of the universe and nature, from the structure of atoms to galaxies. Science has the opportunity—and the responsibility—to translate this new knowledge into helpful inventions and discoveries that enrich society. Many people, especially in recent years, have sought to restrain science's quest for understanding, especially in the fields of atomic energy, the environment, and space exploration. They need to know that they often end up directly opposing the work of the divine design for science; they may well be obstructing human progress, rather than abetting it.

Education is the perfect workshop for receiving and integrating new spiritual ideas about character building and enlightened citizenship, as well as revealing new lessons. Just as the master craftsman in the furniture workshop must at times rely on inexperienced apprentices, our modern educational system is often compromised by "dumbed down" texts and complacent teachers. Nonetheless, even with these conditions, the goal of education remains ceaseless: to teach us how to rise above our intellectual limitations and tap our full inner greatness, individually and collectively.

Commerce performs the work of receiving and integrating new spiritual ideas about productivity, enterprise, and cooperation. While it is true that greed and ambition are often still strong forces in the business world, the collective good produced by commerce far outweighs individual instances of abuse. Indeed, commerce has become one of the strongest factors shaping progress in our modern world.

The workshop of **the arts** provides rich opportunities for receiving and integrating new insights into the relationship of man the microcosm with God the macrocosm, as well as visionary glimpses into the next steps forward in human evolution. All of society thereby benefits from those who labor in this workshop, not just those who love music or great literature. The arts have always been a fertile field for developing creative skills and entertaining divine possibilities.

The healing arts and sciences are a workshop, too— for receiving and integrating new insights into the innate design for health of the human mind and body, and how to activate this divine pattern for healing and renewal. This institution has the profound opportunity of proving the fact of spirit by demonstrating and confirming its healing potential.

The circle of this grand work is completed in the workshop of **religion,** which encourages us to perceive and integrate into our awareness the constant presence of divine life. In spite of the many shortcomings of modern religion, which is often more materialistic than any other institution, it still reminds us of the central importance of our divine connection.

The activities and accomplishments of these seven workshops remind us that the spiritual direction of society is not a capricious event. Just as there is a spiritual plan for our individual life, so also there is a much more elaborate Plan for human civilization. This Plan is created and supervised by the Hierarchy.

The Hierarchy is a vast group of enlightened people who oversee the evolutionary Plan of God for civilization and humanity. Although most of Its members are not incarnate, the Hierarchy does maintain a constant physical presence in every aspect of civilization, with agents of every level of development.

The work of the Hierarchy is directed by the so-called Masters or Adepts of human civilization—the most senior and enlightened members of the race. These are individuals who have transcended their human nature and foibles and have become spiritually focused in divine purpose and perspective. Filled with wisdom and goodwill, they view themselves first as members of the family of God and citizens of the world—not as members of a specific religion, race, or nation. As a result, they guide the activities of the divine workshops with universal insight, archetypal understanding, inclusive love, and the determination to spiritualize humanity.

There is therefore a direct, intimate link between the Hierarchy and the seven primary workshops of human living. As the agents of the Hierarchy interpret the Plan of God, they develop vast programs for reforming human behavior and liberating humanity from the darkness of materialism. These programs then become the inspiration for new work in one or more of the workshops. Occasionally, a Hierarchical agent will incarnate to deliver a specific new burst of creativity and growth in the field in which he or she serves. In most cases, however, the agents laboring in a workshop are guided indirectly, as they struggle to solve humanity's problems in compassionate, intelligent ways.

This is seldom easy work: the road to success is rarely strewn with rose petals scattered by appreciative cherubs. Anyone who has ever struggled with making major changes in his or her life understands that new blasts of inspiration, initiative, and goodwill are almost never translated directly into new maturity, achievement, or enlightenment. It is never as easy as crying "Eureka!"

18.

and then bursting into song and celebration. In fact, the first impact of new spiritual life as it enters our awareness is apt to produce confusion, uncertainty, and conflict.

The same pattern is true for the ceaseless flow of guidance, goodwill, and power into the activities of the seven workshops of civilization. There are two conditions we can always rely upon: first, that the flow of guidance and help from the Hierarchy to these seven workshops never stops, and second, the first inflow of any new idea or energy inevitably creates resistance, leading to struggle and hardship, until enough people become sufficiently acclimated to the new direction that it is finally implemented. This process can easily span thousands of years.

Why is this resistance inevitable? In the individual, it is because the new ideas and forces of spirit must compete with well-established concepts, habits, and attitudes. Our character is not likely to give up its cherished traits without a struggle, and so conflict ensues. In the work of society, the pattern is much the same—only magnified by five or six billion. The new ideas and forces being introduced by the Hierarchy must compete with traditions, customs, and beliefs that nations have fought and died to preserve. They are prone to fight and die for them again, until they are forced to give them up. If immersed in the conflict engendered by this resistance, we are apt to suffer tremendously, either on a personal or a global level. Once we have passed safely through the crisis, however, we begin to see in retrospect that the growth that has occurred makes the discomfort worthwhile. In addition, we come to appreciate that unless the crisis had forced us to abandon old methods of acting in favor of new ones, we would still be stuck in the heart of the problem. The crisis was a necessary part of evoking the right response from us.

The average person never understands the benevolent side of struggle. When hardship arises, he or she gets sucked completely into its pain and misery, identifying with its limitations. Such a person grows only in spite of himself. Intelligent people, however, learn to see the wisdom and compassion within any system that routinely exposes our bad habits and worn-out traits. As a result, they forego the intense personal suffering—and learn to harness the forward momentum of genuine growth.

The inflow of divine life into the major institutions of society occurs in much the same way. An outstanding genius arises in a given field to introduce and define new ideas, only to be met by derision and rejection of his innovations. It could be Joseph Lister introducing his concepts of sterilization to the medical community, or Nikola Tesla shocking the world of science with his revelations about electricity. As has been true with so many others as well, the initial impact of their work was to stir up controversy—and disbelief.

Such resistance is not a minor problem. History has forgotten many geniuses who never survived the initial opposition. Their contributions were destroyed by those who scorned change and resisted progress. And yet, these efforts still made their impact at the level of the divine workshop, and eventually were brought into public awareness by a follower—or possibly even a rival.

Why do we let this opposition occur? The major reason is that we still identify excessively with the suffering and chaos that accompany change. A human personality who takes a step forward in growth due to lessons learned by enduring a scandal often has a hard time focusing on anything but the pain of being embarrassed. Just so, a major segment of society that is forced into redefining its methods in order to meet an external threat may be so preoccupied with the ensuing turmoil that it fails to see the remarkable growth that is occurring.

Until society reverses its standard interpretations of history, and begins to define conflict as a way to promote growth, most of humanity will remain mired in its conflicts and suffering. Most of us will continue to view suffering and conflict as things to avoid, missing entirely the benevolent progress that almost always accompanies them.

In this regard, it needs to be understood that one of the primary ways that change occurs in the divine workshops of society is to intensify selected problem areas until the corruption or distress is so obvious that even average people rebel and clamor for change. This method of change is apparent in the workshop of education today. The goal of education in this country has been so distorted by self-appointed "social engineers" that little effort is presently being made to clean it up. Quite the reverse, it is being allowed to decline to the point where the whole country becomes alarmed by its deterioration, and presses for meaningful reform. Once conditions in any segment of society become so bad that even ordinary citizens are aroused to call for reforms, we can be sure that this is almost certainly evidence of the Hierarchy at work. The Hierarchy has been at work in its divine workshop to nurture our culture and harness a wave of massed support to accept and implement change.

This practice of the Hierarchy implies a heavy responsibility for the rest of us. It is not enough just to pray for world peace; we must start laying the groundwork for genuine world cooperation. It is not enough just to hope that our educational system improves; we must get busy in our communities and do what is necessary to restore good education. It is not just enough to bemoan the size of bureaucracy in our national government; we must plant the seeds that will eventually lead to a public outcry for smaller but more efficient government.

The work that occurs in the seven divine workshops of humanity may be supervised by the Hierarchy, but it is done by people such as ourselves. Each person has been designed by the Creator to become an agent of spiritual light and power. Each of us has the potential to expand our thinking to embrace spiritual ideals. Each of us has the capacity to tap the spiritual well-springs of love and joy. Each of us has the ability to understand that we are meant to follow certain universal laws as part of the vast family of God. We just have to activate these potentials and put them to work in our life.

As we learn this lesson, we start to see that we, too, are part of the ceaseless flow of divine love and light into humanity.

The Divine
Workshop of Education

THE ILLUMINATION OF CONSCIOUSNESS

Human civilization did not just accidentally rise out of the muck of some primeval swamp. It has developed as people in many differing cultures have learned to confront the basic challenges of living and find progressively new and more enlightened ways of meeting them. At first, these lessons were passed on from generation to generation in the form of oral traditions. As civilization matured, these lessons were collected into a basic education—what every intelligent man and woman needs to know. In this way, humanity has moved away from the ignorance and superstition that once held them in the thrall of barbarism. Through education, we have become civilized—and have preserved the contributions and discoveries of past generations, so they can be available still in the present and the future. We have also developed a method for preparing each generation for its particular challenge in preserving and advancing society.

The importance of education in the grand scheme of spiritual evolution cannot be overestimated. An educated public is truly one of the cornerstones of civilization. From the perspective of spirit, awareness is the most important facet of human life. The work of education is to help us discover the difference between sensation and awareness, cultivate the knowledge and skills that make awareness useful, and expand the realm of awareness in which we can act. At its most inspired level, education is meant to be a divine workshop for the illumination of consciousness.

To be sure, humanity has suffered from its share of dark ages, in which ignorance and barbarism have reigned. But we have also been blessed by many golden ages, which have been high points in the flowering of education, from the library of Alexandria, which became the hub of knowledge for the western world, to the Renaissance—and now to modern times. In the West, the power of education was spread by the Roman Empire; in the East, dynasty after dynasty of the Chinese Empire nourished and cultivated it.

Prior to the invention of moveable type by Gutenberg, education was the privilege of the elite. With the advent of printing, however, literacy has spread rapidly throughout the world—and with it, the power to accelerate education. Recent developments in computer technology and the world wide web are making it possible to bring more knowledge and instruction into an individual home than could have been collected at a university one hundred years ago.

In just the past one hundred years, the explosion in educational opportunities has been enormous. In America, night schools and community colleges have sprung up to fill a need for education that cannot be met by standard universities. Adults are becoming much more accustomed to extending their formal education well into their working years—and to pursuing informal education even further. Even vacations are viewed at times as educational opportunities, as cruises or tours visit great centers of art, history, or archaeological digs.

In many ways, the quality of education itself is improving. Textbooks today are far more sophisticated than the McGuffey Reader of one hundred and fifty years ago. Curricula and teaching methods have become more creative, flexible, and progressive. More emphasis is being placed on using education as a springboard for developing social skills and character. Many high schools and colleges feature programs for studying abroad. Others provide for independent study, where the student develops the content of a course on his or her own, under the watchful guidance of a tutor. In these ways, we are moving away from the old "one size fits all" approach to education.

Indeed, educators are beginning to recognize that there are as many as six to nine different kinds of innate intelligence—a radical departure from the usual belief in just three or four basic mental types. To tap the full potential of the human mind, it will be necessary to find teaching techniques to stimulate each type of thinking—even multidimensional thought.

In conjunction with the liberalization of educational methods, modern education is also putting greater emphasis on encouraging creative thinking and innovation. There is a growing rebirth of interest in the study of allegory, symbolism, and archetypes. In fact, the sciences of thinking, logic, and linguistics are experiencing a renaissance that will serve, in due time, to revolutionize all of education.

Not all of these developments are occurring in public schooling, of course. As a rule, the more government controls education, the less effective it becomes. A great many people in the world today hunger for more understanding. If the public system of education does not satisfy their hunger, they will find alternates. And they have. The result is a better informed public, a more rational public, and a more intelligent public.

It is not always easy to see the evidence of the invisible hand of the Hierarchy at work, stimulating new achievements in the teaching of creativity, intuition, symbolic relationships, and rationality. If we look at our large universities, we shall not find it, for all too many of these campuses have become intellectual ghettos that starve out true inquiry, instead of feeding it. But if we look carefully enough, we will find the evidence, especially in small, informal classes, where the original spirit of Plato teaching in a grove has been recreated.

The opportunity for a great education exists as it never has before. But we must learn the secret of obtaining an excellent education. It cannot be bought, absorbed, or even stolen. It must be acquired. It must be learned. We will only become well educated if we are willing to turn our own life and mind into a workshop for exploration and discovery.

HOW EDUCATION SERVES SPIRIT

To most people, the work of education is to teach basic skills of reading, writing, and arithmetic, as well as the core knowledge of math, science, history, geography, and literature. This duty is certainly an indispensable function of education. But if the work of education were limited to this basic responsibility alone, it would be possible to judge education solely in terms of how well it instructs the least prepared members of society.

It is far more informative to examine what education is doing to challenge the best and the brightest members of society. It is at this level that the true creative work of education is accomplished, as it is inspired by the guiding agents of the Hierarchy to introduce new spiritual directions into our lives.

Obviously, the highest functioning of education occurs when it opens our awareness to a fuller and richer participation in life, both the mundane life of earth and the life of spirit as well. There are three primary goals education is striving to achieve in this regard:

1. Create a structure of understanding and a set of tools that will enable people to learn the lessons of emotional control and psychological maturity.

2 Provide a fundamental grasp of the knowledge needed to live a productive life, as well as the skills needed to continue to learn throughout life.

3. Make people aware of the basic principles of civilized, intelligent living—our responsibilities as citizens and children of God.

As time proceeds, a fourth goal will begin to emerge as well: to reveal the nature of the higher self and methods for interacting with it. At present, however, most of the work of spirit in inspiring the divine workshop of education still occurs behind the scenes, beyond the scope of the average person.

If we understand these simple goals and their relevance to the life of spirit, the true meaning of education will become clarified. Let us therefore examine them in detail.

The first goal of education should be to promote maturity. The building of a proper character—the art of living—is the great creative work of men and women, as it affects everything we do as adults. Becoming a mature adult is an essential part of becoming successful as an individual, and is indispensable for the continuity of civilization. Education is the means by which children become adults and—on the larger scale of civilization—barbarians become refined, accountable members of society. In fact, "civility" refers to the basic set of lessons in politeness and grace that lets groups of people cooperate with each other in productive ways.

Teaching civility and maturity involves a great deal beyond self-esteem, however. Reinforcing the self-esteem of students has become the educational rage of the end of the century, but it is not always as beneficial as its advocates proclaim. Teaching a gang member or a drug addict to feel good about himself, after all, may only deepen the criminal, violent elements already present in his or her character. Such instruction does not in any way serve the life of spirit; it obscures it.

The purpose of spirit is served only when education promotes civility and politeness as an expression of a deeper set of values and principles—not just a desire to feel good. Maturity develops as we combine intelligence with enlightened values, emotional control, and rationality. It is not just a desirable byproduct of learning; it should be the number one priority of all education!

In point of fact, no genuine learning can occur in the individual unless his or her education is grounded in a strong base of maturity. As long as we are enslaved by our emotions, for example, we will be excessively swayed by our anger, fear, or doubt, letting our feelings eclipse our mental judgment and distort our perceptions. Clear thought will be rare instead of common, and inconsistent. We will be trapped in a level of imitating other people instead of learning to generate creative interpretations of our own.

Ideally, the right kind of education will help us progress beyond such self-absorbed priorities as popularity, security, comfort, safety, and lust for power, so that we can embrace a more enlightened perspective on life. Collectively, it will likewise help society institutionalize these values in all that it does.

The second goal of education should be to teach a basic curriculum of knowledge and mental skills. This curriculum falls into three cateories:

1. A structure of knowledge and learning skills needed as educated adults. The standard modern curriculum is capable of delivering most of this knowledge in an adequate form. It includes not only basic facts such as the principles of arithmetic, but also the ability to solve the ordinary problems of life and access help as needed.

2. A structure of specialized knowledge and skills needed to help us pursue our careers and family obligations. This body of knowledge might range from the chemistry and physics needed by a rocket scientist to the psychology, intelligence, and maturity needed by a parent in raising children. While many colleges do a good job preparing their students for positions in science and academia, most fail almost completely in providing needed instruction in such vital areas of the adult experience as communications, ethics, conflict resolution, personal organization, cooperation, and leadership.

3. A set of mental skills for exploring the inner dimensions of the mind—the science of awareness and thinking. Once upon a time, these mental skills were considered the core of all education; students were exposed to endless classes in philosophy in an effort to convey these abilities. Over the past one hundred years, however, this element of education

has been dropped almost entirely from formal education; it remains only as an archaic shell, even at the university level. It very much needs to be rediscovered, updated, and returned to our educational agenda. After all, these are the skills that teach us how to keep on learning, once our formal classroom work is finished. They are the skills of self-education. They consist of three elements:

A love of learning—a permanent intellectual curiosity about life and its many wonders. The great threat to learning as an adult is that our motivation may atrophy, or at least become complacent, as we succumb to the arrogant assumption that we know enough or we are too busy too learn anything more. In some cases, we have been so poisoned by the sheer drudgery of overly long academic schedules that we never want to see another book as long as we live.

Such attitudes are unfortunate, for although we may have escaped the formal classroom, life itself continues to be an extended, glorious laboratory in which we are meant to experiment with all manner of energies and issues—and learn. No matter how much we age physically, there is always more to learn to become effective in our career, as a parent, and as a citizen.

The science of learning—the techniques and skills we need to acquire in order to learn the lessons of life easily and efficiently. These skills embrace a wide range of mental functions:

1. Discovering ideas. Where do ideas come from? How do we invoke—or provoke—them? How can we stimulate our thinking to go beyond traditional sources of information and seek out fresh stimuli?

2. Validating the accuracy of facts and ideas. In school, we verify our assumptions by checking the answers at the back of the book. In life, we must develop our own tests to determine if a theory is based on assumptions or facts, or if an idea is based on opinion or reality.

3. Drawing correct conclusions. We must learn skills in deductive and inductive reasoning, in the use of analogy, and in intuitive exploration. We must also learn how to check our conclusions against reality, to make sure they are workable.

4. Understanding symbolic meanings. The educated person should be equally at home dealing with concrete, symbolic, and abstract ideas. Too many "thinkers" are trained only to consider the outer appearances of ideas; they disregard their meaning and power. As a result, their thinking is oddly flat and superficial. As we learn to work symbolically, we are able to establish "thought connections" with larger patterns of meaning.

5. Solving problems. The ability to collect data does not in any way guarantee an ability to use it effectively. We need to learn the skills of applying data to the opportunities, problems, and conditions we face in life.

6. Translating answers and solutions into new behavior and productivity. Learning is never complete until we learn to translate great ideas and plans into great results—and actually precipitate the idea into concrete activities.

Few people graduate from university with all of these skills activated and mastered. It takes a lifetime of proper training and mature application to harness the full range of our mental faculties. It would be healthier to approach education as a life-long proposition, where our schooling prepares us to think, and adult life gives us a productive, creative outlet for growth.

An integrated philosophy of learning—an understanding of knowledge and awareness, why they are important, where they come from, why we need to grow, and what we need to know. It is hard to learn to think effectively unless we know what the roots of ideas and concepts are. A practical illustration of this concept is the difficulty a nihilist would have in learning to interact with archetypal patterns. Being a nihilist, the "thinker" would have no basis for making contact with an Idea that is the abstract essence of a spiritual force such as justice, order, beauty, love, joy, or harmony. Nor would he or she be able to interact with the pure authority of such an Idea, believing instead that all ideas are limited and relative. The ability to entertain the possibility of archetypal Ideas, in other words, is absolutely required before any of us can relate to higher dimensions and power of thought. This philosophy lays the foundation for correct thinking.

Once it is in place, a proper philosophy of learning will also act as a guide for exploring the abstract regions of life. It will help the beginner to recognize that Descartes knew what he was talking about when he stated, "I think, therefore I am," whereas Rousseau and Sartre did not. Far from being profound philosophers, they were more akin to terrorists throwing mental Molotov cocktails to intimidate more serious thinkers.

What should be the basic premises in such a philosophy? It should recognize that the source of all valuable Ideas is the mind of God. From this great Plan for evolution, more specific Ideas, called archetypes, have been generated. These archetypal forces are the blueprints or patterns for everything that has been created in the world, physically, emotionally, and mentally. Ideas that cannot be traced back to an archetypal origin are therefore imperfect and untrustworthy. Learning is the process of following the trail that leads us back to these archetypal forces and patterns, and then discovering how to interact with them and apply them constructively to life.

Walt Whitman called these archetypal ideas "eidólons." Elizabeth Barrett Browning referred to them as "antetypes." Plato called them, simply enough, "Ideas." Even though they are abstract, he regarded them as the true "forms" of thought—the molds or patterns from which concrete ideas and plans derive.

By teaching ourself about ideas and thinking in this way, we learn a tremendous amount about the way ideas are presented to, preserved by, and distorted by society, and how they are transmitted from one era to the next. In the process, we develop a deeper resonance with our cultural myths and the accumulated literature of the past.

Our philosophy of learning also helps us realize that modern education should be teaching us a great deal more than it does. It should be teaching us how to cope with the emotional focus of our modern day, resolve conflicts, and solve problems—while simultaneously instilling in us a fundamental love for learning.

Ultimately, this kind of philosophy of learning should kindle within us an intense curiosity to explore all facets of the divine underpinnings of life, as we have been doing throughout *The Life of Spirit* series. The insights gleaned from this exploration should in turn lead us to a celebration of the divine life in and all around us. If it does, then our personal workshop of learning and exploration will become united with the divine workshop that nurtures the institution of education in civilization.

The third goal of education should be to teach intelligent citizenship. In America, we have the good fortune to live in a free society—a society founded on democratic principles. Our Founding Fathers recognized that such a society could only survive if the citizens were well educated and able to participate intelligently in the processes of government. Education should therefore teach us the meaning of freedom and liberty and the role each of us must play in preserving them. On a global basis, this lesson in citizenship would be adapted country by country. But the basic lessons of freedom, rights, and the dignity of humanity would be common themes of all true education throughout the world, even if excluded by official politics.

The potential for government and politics to corrupt education for its own ends is a powerful reason to always strive to keep government influence in education as minimal as possible. The recent introduction of "political correct-ness" into our educational systems is not in any way a step in the right direction. It has a chilling effect on the develop-ment of thinking skills. At the same time, however, no level of education should ever be allowed to become a captive of anti-government, anti-authority, or anti-social guerrilla warfare. Education in good citizenship should focus on our responsibility to make government work, not a negative recitation of governmental sins and abuses.

The teaching of citizenship should begin with a clear defi-nition of the ideals our country strives to embody: freedom, liberty, goodwill, perseverance, self-sufficiency, innovativeness, and self-discipline. We need to learn how these ideals have inspired our growth as a country—and how they have induced conflict and struggle when we have ignored them. We should likewise be introduced to some of the great issues our country has faced—for example, the effort to establish harmony among the diverse ethnic groups which inhabit the land.

A key element of teaching citizenship lies in inspiring students to cultivate the necessary habits of responsible citizenship—staying informed about the key issues of the day, being alert for possible abuse or corruption in our elected of-ficials, and carefully weighing the real intentions of any group supporting a special interest. We must likewise be alert to the constant, ongoing efforts to misinform and mislead the public about the facts of major events in our national life.

The challenge of educating humanity is a tremendous one. It is not just a simple issue of "Can Johnny read?" It is a far more complex one: "Can Johnny respond to his spiritual design for greatness, and help others do the same?" The seeds have been sown, and the growing season is well underway. If we hope to cooperate with spirit, we need to advance spirit's goals for enriching education on earth.

PROBLEMS IN EDUCATION

Because the primary mission of education is to eliminate human ignorance, the work of teaching and learning is not as simple as it may at first appear. The purpose of education is to awaken the human mind, and not every self-appointed academic expert is eager to see the human mind aroused. Many of them, in fact, would much prefer to keep it in a coma, easily swayed by the emotional messages of their propaganda machines. Education is, in fact, at the heart of a great struggle for the mind and heart of humanity—a battle between the forces of spirit and the forces of the status quo.

The result is great turmoil and conflict in the divine workshop of education. The ideal of the educator as a "master craftsman" is not just ignored by materialists, it is actively reviled. The workshop's "apprentices"—each one of us as we struggle to master the art of living—are often in full revolt. We reject guidance. We may even leave our masterpiece unfinished. If we do complete a project, the end result will often fall short of the intended level of achievement.

The decay in the quality of education over the past one hundred years has been enormous. It is still useful, of course—but it falls far short of the level of achievement education is capable of attaining. While these problems saturate all levels of education, they begin at the top—at the university level. One hundred years ago, most of the colleges and universities in this country were private institutions, often founded by religious denominations. Today, these same institutions have largely traded in their autonomy in exchange for massive funds from the federal government. They have compromised their own charters in pursuit of financing, and as a result, have lost their unique voice and perspective in the educational community. They do what the federal educational bureaucracy tells them to do—a pattern which is now well established all the way through high school and elementary education as well.

As a result, as one recent study warned, we are in danger of becoming a second-class nation—a country of steadily declining academic performance and intellectual skills. It is a trend that is reversible, of course—but herein lies the question of the day. How much worse must our education become before we wake up and demand a return to higher standards? How much longer will it take until we realize that it is our own indifference to growing and learning which is shaping the great educational vacuum in this country?

Some of the most serious problems affecting the quality of education in America today are:

The lowering of academic standards. It is not our purpose to assess blame for the decline in academic achievement over the past fifty years. Some people believe it is the result of uncontrolled experimentation with unproven methods of teaching; others tie it to problems of elitism and racism. A few blame the advent of television, while still others condemn the process of testing for excellence. Some experts relate the decline in academic accomplishments to the rise of unions among teachers. In reality, all of these factors probably contribute to the problem.

Oddly enough, however, parochial and private schools have managed to continue providing quality education during these fifty years without resorting to the lowering of standards. It may be time to stop allowing the public school system to be used as a laboratory for social experimentation and return to the proven methods of teaching which continue to produce effective results whenever used.

Linked with the decline in academic standards is a dilution of thinking and comprehension skills. Students today are far less likely to be able to understand written instructions than they were fifty years ago. Problem solving and creative skills are likewise deteriorating. We are therefore facing an alarming decline in the public's capacity to comprehend the personal, social, and national issues we all must confront. This deficiency creates the possibility that as a nation we will be more vulnerable to the inferior ideas and programs of leaders who are little more than demagogues. It is exacerbated by the fact that life has become even more complex in the last fifty years. We need greater thinking skills than ever—not less.

It will take generations to undo the mischief caused by this decline, leaving huge segments of the institution of education in danger of collapsing under the weight of massive incompetence.

The degeneration of discipline. Just a few decades ago, the most chronic problems among high school students were absenteeism, talking in class, and failure to do homework. Today, the classroom is all too often the scene of shootings, physical assaults on teachers and students, drug dealing and usage, alcoholism, theft, and promiscuity. Many school systems have had to resort to hiring police officers to patrol the hallways of the schools. Education is dealt a lethal blow when forced to operate with so much chaos in the classroom; learning cannot occur in an atmosphere in which respect for basic rights and dignity is missing.

The mystery is why the public school system seems so incapable of solving the problem of poor discipline. Too many schools—even public schools in the so-called "inner city"—have proven that the discipline problem can indeed be solved. The methods that have been proven to work ought to be applied throughout the educational system to insure order. Where discipline is optional, no education occurs.

Bureaucratic bloat and arrogance. It is sad to contemplate the fact that more genuine education occurred in one-room schoolhouses one hundred years ago than in the fancy, elaborate school buildings of our modern times. In an age where everything must be big, we somehow think that auditoriums, football stadiums, and school buses are all part and parcel of the learning process. Huge sums of money are spent every year on educational "extras" that do not advance the quality of learning at any level. It is not only a waste of money, but a distraction from the real work of education.

The biggest waste of all is to be found in the growing structure of educational bureaucracy in every metropolitan school system. Bureaucracies grow like crabgrass. And like the weed, they begin to displace the funds, time, attention, and authority needed for genuine educational activities. Teachers are let go, so that the system can hire another guidance counselor or administrator. Not only does less and less actual teaching occur as a result, but the unnecessary administrators, searching for something to do, arrogate the right of teachers to determine curriculum and style of teaching. As a result, the nation's children have been used as guinea pigs to test all kinds of speculative approaches to teaching, from the "new math" of the 1960's to the "whole language" approach to reading of the 1990's.

Education is not meant to be an experiment; it is meant to be an adventure in learning. This can only occur when an intimate mental relationship is constructed between the teacher and the pupil. The intrusion of any administrator into this process is usually unnecessary and can easily become destructive. The public should insist on the principle of "less is more" when it comes to administration. It works well in private schools; it can work equally well in public education.

The rise of relativism. The changes that have occurred in the standard curriculum over the past one hundred years have often been insidious and dangerous. One hundred years ago, elementary and high school students were routinely taught the great classics of Greek and Roman thought, as well as more modern texts. They examined ethics and philosophy. When they erred, they were disciplined. As a result, they learned the basic lesson that life is governed by universal laws and that all valid thought is based on first principles.

Today, the typical student receives no such foundation in the workings of life or the mind. They are encouraged to form opinions about ideas with their emotions, rather than forge strong convictions about life with clear, rational thought. As a result, whole generations of students have been infected by the mental disease of relativism.

Relativism is the premise that there is no definite truth or reality—only our own interpretations and opinions. There are no universal principles or laws—just subjective observations. In fact, the proponents of relativism go so far as to claim that there is no reality at all, except what we invent in our imagination and speculations.

At first blush, it may seem that the premise of relativism can help us make sense of confusing and irrational times and events. In fact, however, it strands us in our feelings and reactions toward life and prevents us from training the mind to work at objective levels—the level of thought Plato referred to as Ideas. Nor is it necessary to be able to interact directly with archetypes to understand the nature of absolute truth. Each of us is blessed with a rich set of experiences and lessons in the context of our own life. As we learn to examine these events, searching for patterns, we will begin to discover the definitive truth about ourself.

The relativist, by contrast, is taught not to look for an explanation of the patterns of life; he is taught to look only for the source of his misery and discontent, so he can properly assess blame. Relativism gets him off the hook of personal responsibility. And so the relativist believes that if everything is relative, if every event can be interpreted subjectively, then there is no absolute right nor wrong—and hence no rules of conduct, except those we make up for ourselves (and the separate rules we make up for others). In one stroke of irrationality, the relativist denies thousands of years of accumulated wisdom and all ethical responsibility. It is a criminal's wildest dream come true, as it gives him a license to do anything he wants.

It also happens to be a death blow to learning! Relativisim

destroys the intellectual basis for learning and knowledge. It leeches all meaning from the fertile soil of our inquiry and experimentation and—just as perniciously—from the rich resources of culture and civilization. It breeds confusion where once there was clarity.

It is not surprising that relativism has crept into formal educational thinking at this time. Reality has always been the battleground for the war between nonsense and truth. Eventually, the power of archetypal truth will win out over the empty shell of relativism. But in the meantime, relativism has won far too many battles in educational circles—especially at the university level. Relativistic theories have shaped far too much of modern educational policy. As more and more of today's and yesterday's students end up in positions of power and influence in society, they bring their flawed thinking and methods of analysis with them. As a result, modern society as a whole is suffering from an overdose of nonsense—the attitude that everyone has a license to do as they please—and no one has the right to object or interfere.

Some would say, of course, that absolutism is the real curse, not relativism. They claim that relativism promotes openmindedness—a willingness to consider all possibilities. These people miss the point. The goal of learning is not to consider all the possibilities; it is to learn which possibilities will work and which will not. Relativism cripples intellectual curiosity by stating that we can never know the truth, because the truth does not exist. Legitimate thinking, by contrast, embraces truth as knowable and applicable to life.

Intellectual speculation is a valid way of exercising the mind. What really motivated Hamlet? What were the actual causes of World War I? Intelligent people will bring different perspectives to these questions, and each enriches the inquiry as a whole. Yet mere opinion is never an adequate substitute for penetrating and thorough analysis.

Intelligent people who decry the falseness of relativism are immediately accused of being judgmental and narrowminded. All too often, they are held up as examples of bigotry and prejudice by our educational system. And yet, the truth of the matter is just the opposite. The great failing of relativists is that they do not take thinking far enough. They relentlessly ignore input from the realms of meaning—the abstract ideas that reveal the inner connectiveness of all life. It is therefore the relativists who are smallminded, especially as they strive to understand complex issues.

Once a thinker has learned to penetrate to the essence of any abstract idea, he knows how to enter into the realm of truth and meaning. At this level, the concept of relativism disappears, just as a childish fear of monsters disappears once we know the truth.

As long as our educational system continues to support relativism, however, it is, in essence, promoting monsters and ogres. It needs to return to reality.

The disappearance of the liberal arts education. It is a sad fact that most students go to college primarily to secure a good job afterwards—not to learn to think. It is a sadder fact that the liberal arts education is slowly being put on the shelf, even at our most prestigious universities. Technical courses are all the rage, while the study of history and philosophy and other core subjects is slowly fading in popularity.

There is certainly far more that an engineer or scientist must learn about physics and chemistry today than there was one hundred years ago. But much of the "new knowledge" being taught today will be outdated in ten years, so why gut the opportunity for a perfectly good liberal arts education in favor of cramming more and more temporary knowledge into students' heads? The trade-off is not a very favorable one.

The disappearance of the true liberal arts education should concern every intelligent person. Only a good liberal arts education can properly teach the skills of thinking in depth and breadth which are the hallmark of an educated person. The person who specializes in engineering or medicine or government without being exposed in depth to history, philosophy, the arts, and literature will end up being a lopsided thinker. In other words, he will think like a good technician, rather than as a well educated human being.

In fact, the steady decline of the liberal arts education at the college level is a startling indicator that thinking is no longer popular or respected. Sadly, there is mounting evidence that thinking is not even being tolerated.

The study of history, for example, is slowly being poisoned by revisionism. The advent of feminism is a case in point, leading to major revisions in the way we view historical precedences. Since Paul did not assign an equal role to men and women in the early church, all of his writings and teachings have been derided by feminist academics. The idea that it is unfair to use the twentieth century standards of a small group of people to judge the work of someone two thousand years ago boggles the mind, but does not seem to disturb the revisionists, or their adherents. Similar revisionists reject all contributions and ideas of any Founding Father who happened to own slaves—and smear all capitalists as vicious exploiters because a few nineteenth century industrialists used child labor.

Ideas of this nature have been routinely accepted and taught on college campuses across the nation. It has gotten to the point where concerned parents are giving their children crash courses in how to think before sending them off to the intellectual ghettos of feminism, Marxism, and radical "thought"—our universities. If sufficiently prepared, a bright student can survive the ideological indoctrination that a college education now im-poses. The more serious problem is that colleges are supposed to be repositories of the history and culture of humanity. When history is so blatantly diddled by the very people paid to protect and preserve it, we run a substantial risk of losing sight of the truth about our nation, our culture, and our past.

While history is meant to alert us to the dark episodes of human greed and stupidity, it is also meant to be a chronicle of the human capacity to triumph over ignorance, exploitation, and bigotry. Every thinking person needs to learn these les-sons—just as every thinking person needs to be exposed to the study of philosophy, literature, and psychology. A good liberal arts education is essential for producing not only better citizens, but also better lawyers, journalists, nurses, doctors, executives, and government employees.

It is important to understand how fragile public support for the ideal of a liberal arts education actually is—and how easily higher education can be distracted from pursuing its own best interests. It ought to be a priority of every intelligent person to acquire a solid liberal arts education for himself or herself—outside the walls of higher education, if necessary—and to sup-port it as the goal or pinnacle of all educational pursuits.

In the context of a liberal arts education, it may be useful to examine briefly three recent trends in education and expose the damage they have done.

The first trend might be called **culture wars.** It stems from the recent advent of political correctness and multiculturalism on almost every college campus in the United States. As different ethnic groups have challenged a curriculum that they claim teaches the ideas of dead white European males (DWEMs) to the exclusion of all other perspectives, colleges have radically changed their curriculum to avoid being harassed by these groups. As a result, Plato has been replaced by native American thinkers, Shakespeare has been shoved aside for the writings of African tribalists, and history has been revised to demonstrate the importance of gay and lesbian attitudes throughout world culture. Instead of teaching the skills of thinking, these campuses have become "stink tanks," where only popular beliefs that humor or appease these ethnic groups are allowed. As a result, genuine tolerance and fairness are no longer tolerated on many campuses.

Intelligent people, who were lucky enough to get a liberal arts education, recognize these culture wars as just another incarnation of the puritanical and fascist righteousness that sweeps through groups of people generation after generation. The disturbing factor in this latest development is the speed and totality with which most universities are embracing this fanaticism—and the degree to which it is threatening the liberal arts education.

The second alarming trend behind the decline of the liberal arts education is **anti-elitism.** It is bad enough that the educational establishment routinely ignores excellence, genius, and individual achievement in their policies and curriculum, but many educators go even further—they openly condemn these virtues and talents, on the grounds that high achievers reach success only by exploiting or subjugating those who have achieved less. The rationale given by advocates of anti-elitism is that they are determined to democratize education. They claim they want to reach out to everyone. In their view, geniuses already have too many opportunities, so they need to be penalized, not helped, by education—in order to level the playing field.

Tearing down the Acropolis would perhaps create a level field, but who would want to play there? It is the outstanding genius and achievements of ancient Greece that make the Acro-polis a valuable symbol for all humanity. It is already accessible, as a cultural treasure, for any member of humanity who wants to learn about it.

Let it be clearly understood: the proponents of anti-elitism are not interested in fairness or helping the poor and downtrodden. They are promoting class warfare against all achievers. They are merely envious of success and genius, not dedicated to helping anyone else. As such, they should be given no credible voice in modern education.

And yet they are. Anti-elitists sit on curriculum committees across the country. They hold influential jobs in state education departments. Intelligent people must see the motives of these anti-elitists for what they are. The idea that elitism does not belong in education is preposterous. If education does not promote excellence and achievement, what relevance does it have? How can the money spent on it be justified?

The third trend behind the disappearance of the liberal arts education is **anti-Americanism.** The American ideals and values of individuality, personal ambition and responsibility, freedom, self-reliance, and integrity are being attacked. Education is seen by certain people as a huge opportunity to brainwash generation after generation of Americans in their own limited, selfish, sick way of looking at the world. As a result, business people are portrayed as vicious, nasty exploiters who are destroying the environment and are the natural enemy of all workers. Our government is routinely portrayed as the culprit for all suffering and starvation in Africa. Somehow, we are all eventually victims of "the system" in one way or another. The American way of life is held up for scorn, attack, and destruction.

If these challenges were part of a balanced system of self-examination, they might be worthwhile. But they are not. Destruction of the American way of life is the goal and motive of these people. The college classroom is a relatively protected environment in which they have license to spew forth their abuse. The amazing thing is that, being protected by the system of tenure, these people cannot be fired or deprived of their soap-box.

Tenure, a mechanism designed to protect the liberal arts education, is being used deliberately to try to destroy it.

THE WORK OF EDUCATION

As serious as the problems afflicting education are, however, there is no real cause for despair. We know the answers to the problems just listed—they have been taught in schools and universities for thousands of years, at least ever since Plato's time. There is no better cure for fascist, totalitarian, or anti-elitism hysteria than a solid education in thinking skills. There is no better cure for the emotionalism that leads to group neurosis, narrow ideology, militant prejudice, and arrogant bigotry than what Socrates called "the examined life." The foolishness of most of the extremes currently plaguing education will be the stimulus of reform, once the outer expression is challenged by enough people.

The Hierarchical Plan for the evolution of the divine workshop of education is proceeding on schedule. Even though modern schools seem to be in crisis, the symptoms of distress are actually part of the intended cure. One of the most basic lessons of history, after all, is that major reforms can only be precipitated by crisis—and the worse the crisis becomes, the more swift and thorough the reforms will be. Until a genuine crisis occurs, calls for reform in any division of society will tend to be ignored by the masses. Only once large numbers of people have been aroused will it be possible to launch any major corrections.

In other words, the bathetic quality of education in our public schools is intentionally being allowed to sink further, until public indignation comes close enough to outrage to provoke true reforms, not just a superficial reshuffling. In the meantime, the focus of the creative tip of the divine workshop of education has been shifted away from public education in specific and formal education in general. It is now to be found in the various experiments in alternate forms of education which have been quietly pursued by the true leaders of education for decades. Undisturbed by bloated bureaucracies, which stifle creativity and innovation, these programs have often produced remarkable results in education.

Two of the most worthy examples of these experiments in education are the teaching systems founded by Maria Montessori and Rudolf Steiner. These systems have been busy delivering a superior education for more than a hundred years—certainly a record worth imitating. These schools clearly have found the answers to questions the rest of the educational world is still asking—and proven that they work.

As formal education has become more and more ineffective, the business world has also taken on a stronger role in providing training for employees. Much of this training is "job specific"—selling techniques, organization and planning, communication skills, decision making, and effective management. But many businesses are also finding huge gaps in the educational background of new employees. To compensate for what is missing, they have begun to conduct training programs in creative think-ng, problem solving, cooperation, conflict resolution, ethics, and cultural sensitivity. In these areas, the businesses of the private sector are rapidly outpacing our universities and colleges in terms of the quality of education being offered.

The rising role of business in the workshop of education can also be seen in the shift of research and development activities from the college laboratory to the industrial laboratory.

The private sector is likewise beginning to respect and study the nature of intuition and its value in understanding ourselves and solving problems. This body of teaching has been around for decades, typically disguised as self-awareness exercises. As the resistance of the public to these kinds of classes fades, more people are taking a mature interest in the intelligent development of intuition. Even though most of these courses are overly simple—nothing more than exercises of the imagination, in many cases—they represent an important beginning.

With the rise of the computer and the world wide web, the opportunities for independent study are apt to expand rapidly. At present, the development of the computer as an educational tool is still in its infancy, and the results produced so far have been the equivalent of a baby taking his first steps. But the potential for education to become a "cottage industry" is quite real—and exciting.

In order to understand the Hierarchy's plan for education today, we must divorce the idea of teaching and learning from the formal institutions that have assumed responsibility for it. We must appreciate that true learning can occur anywhere and under any circumstances. Schools are meant to show us how to become "master learners"—but it was never intended that we become dependent upon being in school in order to learn.

Ideally, our formal schooling supplies the spark—and each of us as mature adults creates the bonfire. Better education is not just something to support for the benefit of our children—it is something to support for the future of adult civilization! If we wait for professional educators to correct the problems in modern education, we will learn the lesson of patience before anything else. Workable solutions to all of these problems in education already exist. They have been proven.

We just need to decide, as responsible citizens, to settle for nothing less than the best.

SUPPORTING THE PLAN FOR EDUCATION

A common quandary paralyzing the spiritual aspirant is: "I would love to support the Divine Plan, but I have no idea what It is—or how to go about serving It." It is as though the aspirant is waiting for Moses to show up in the midst of a burning bush and present a contract etched in stone, detailing exactly what God expects of us. The actual work of serving the Plan is much different. Once we understand that the major institutions of civilization are the creative wokshops of the life of spirit, we can then see that our own involvement becomes a fertile ground for serving the Plan. Education provides an excellent model for this involvement. Since every spiritual aspirant is meant to be a master learner in life, each one of us has many ongoing opportunities to support the Divine Plan for education. We do not have to be an educator or even a member of our school board. Nor do we have to become an aggressive political activist. We can support the spiritual work of education within the framework of our own intelligent pursuits.

The most important ingredient in serving this plan is to cultivate a deep respect for careful reasoning and genuine creativity, and to encourage this level of respect among our companions in life—our family, friends, colleagues, and fellow citizens. As a people, we need to become excited about exploring all that we do not know. We need to restore intellectual brilliance and achievement as national treasures to be honored and supported. Before we can convince anyone else to support these ideals, however, we must begin demonstrating them in our own lives and learning opportunities.

Once the intellectual standards of society as a whole are raised, academic standards will inevitably follow. It is pointless to blame the educational establishment for failing to exceed the standards of society as a whole. We need to insist, for example, that the news media start reporting on the issues and the intelligent values and principles behind the news—not just the latest gossip. We need to read books and magazines of substance and thoughtfulness, instead of the usual Harlequin romance. We must demand that the movie industry start producing movies of wit and charm again, instead of films that try to outdumb the previous one. We need to support the discussion of mature values in society and "aerobic exercises" for the mind.

We do not have to sit by and quietly watch society sink into the morass of gang culture, rap music, and hip hop banality. We read newspapers and watch television and listen to the radio, too. We count in the ratings, buy movie tickets, and attend concerts. Every time we do so, we cast a vote for an intelligent society—or a superficial one. We can insist that our tastes and intellectual requirements be fulfilled as well—if necessary, by turning off programs that threaten to weaken the mind.

Beyond recognizing our power as a consumer of ideas to influence the intellectual level of society, there are a number of specific ways we can play an active role in supporting the efforts of the divine workshop of education. These include:

We should become a master learner. Life is designed to be a continous series of lessons that open us up to an ever greater field of understanding. Learning is not just something students do; it is the sign of a healthy, intelligent adult as well. Through learning, we push back the barriers and limitations of life that would otherwise limit us. It is therefore of paramount importance to keep our curiosity alive throughout our life, and constantly seek to satisfy our urge to expand our awareness, knowledge, and skills.

In this day of specialization, it is especially important to refresh our thinking with studies that transport us beyond our regular focus. An engineer, in other words, should deliberately take up the study of art, with its rich heritage of symbolism and the creative use of form, in order to prevent the mind from becoming rigid from its daily exposure to formulæ. An artist should take up the study of geology or botany, thereby introducing into the mind a greater appreciation for the way the Master Builder has worked Its genius in physical materials for millenia. A psychologist might take classes studying the great novelists of the last two hundred years, to explore the profundity of the insights of these authors into human nature and behavior. A lawyer or dentist or sales clerk would find it useful to study ancient mythology, thereby learning how the inner worlds of life are organized—and learning as well that our "modern" problems have been challenging humanity for thousands of years.

The goal of this kind of life-long study is not just the acquisition of more knowledge. The true aim is to participate in the grand work of elevating civilized values and tastes, for the benefit of all humanity.

We should sharpen our mental skills. The range of mental skills to be acquired by the intelligent person is vast: logic, deduction, induction, association, abstraction, concentration, and creativity. No matter what level of education we have attained formally, we should never assume that the mind needs no further training. An unused mind atrophies rapidly.

There are many ways these skills can be cultivated and sharpened. Testing mental agility with challenging puzzles is one way; trying to figure out the clues in a good mystery story is another. Local colleges frequently offer classes in basic intellectual skills—or we can read books that will teach us to think. The many books written by Edward de Bono on thinking are an excellent place to begin. It can also be productive to join or form a "study group" of likeminded individuals who will investigate and discuss the deeper meanings of current issues, social values, and ethics.

We should begin exploring the marvelous realms of mythology and archetypal life. Mythology represents the effort of ancient writers to translate the archetypal patterns of life into stories that would enlighten and edify the reader. Because they deal with archetypal energies and events, the ancient myths still contain great wisdom and insight for the modern reader. Studying the mythology of any culture is a powerful way to open up to us the hidden meanings and dimensions of that civilization, be it Greco-Roman, Norse, German, Egyptian, Chinese, or Hindu. The writings of Joseph Campbell are an excellent starting point for the study of mythology, but there is an abundance of material written about myths that goes far beyond Campbell. The writings of psychologist Carl Jung also demonstrate the vital importance of a strong awareness of mythology in sustaining mental vigor and balance. One of the books by Alice Bailey—The Labours of Hercules—relates the myths of the twelve labors of Hercules to both the work of the spiritual aspirant and the study of astrology. It provides an excellent bridge between the symbolism of mythology and the archetypal forces it describes.

The study of mythology raises our sense of being connected with all of life—and with the past and future as well. It is the single most useful way to transcend racial, gender, and cultural chauvinism, because mythology speaks directly to our unconscious. Mythological meanings can often scoot right by our prejudices and assumptions, permitting us to grasp universal themes and forces that we would otherwise ignore—or reject. They reveal to us our place in the grand scheme of things, and help us become more comfortable working with symbolism and abstractions.

We should cultivate creative thinking. Roger von Oech reports that when a teacher draws a dot on the blackboard and asks adults what it is, they inevitably reply: "A dot." When children are asked the same question, their answers are far more imaginative: "a fly squashed on the wall" or "a tiny planet occupied by microscopic people." The imagination is an important stepping stone in building skills in creative thinking; it helps us learn to think "outside of the box" of appearances and traditional solutions to problems. Eventually, the effort to use the imagination to interpret life's phenomena will lead to an ability to be inspired by genuine creative ideas and innovations.

Von Oech's book, *A Whack on the Side of the Head*, is an excellent starting point in cultivating creative thought.

We should refine our mental capacity to solve

problems. The mind is not just a collector of good ideas. It is also meant to be a tool for understanding the relation of ideas—and forces—to each other, and for putting together a plan for harnessing those factors more effectively. As such, it can be trained to become a powerful tool for conflict resolution and problem solving.

The simplest way to approach problem solving is to assume that the problem has an ideal solution known to our higher intelligence. In fact, this ideal solution already exists and has been largely responsible for awaking us to the problem and defining it. If we then think of this ideal solution as a wise sage we can talk to, we can initiate a flow of ideas and insights that will lead us to resolving the problem.

A more sophisticated use of the mind is to train it to discern the different needs, temperaments, and points of view of the people involved in a dispute. In most cases, we will soon realize that the solution to this situation will have to be tailor made; one size will not fit anyone satisfactorily. So we take note of what matters the most to each party. For some, efficiency and reliability may be of paramount importance. For others, dignity and respect for authority may be overriding. As we mentally evaluate all of these requirements, we begin to look for and identify the values, ideals, and goals that everyone can agree on. From that point, we strive to translate these values and priorities into terms that bring agreement instead of further division.

This kind of training in problem solving is one of the best ways to stimulate and exercise the mind. It also demonstrates to others involved the power of the mind to control and regulate the emotions, even in an atmosphere of hurt feelings and damaged egos. It lifts up the noble human mind, and pulls the work of education along with it.

We should study ethics and values. Character building is a vital part of education. The recent neglect of education to address this need has put our culture in peril of huge increases in sociopathic and barbaric thought and behavior. One of the danger signs of this decline is the frightening increase in special interest groups demanding the guarantee of their "rights." Usually, the demand for "rights" is just a blatant grab for unmerited benefits and advantages, but criticism of these power grabs is effectively silenced as being "meanspirited and judgmental." This abuse of the issue of rights could only occur in the cultural vacuum created by the failure of education to teach values.

It is not difficult to find excellent sources for the work of building ethics and values. Every educational system from Plato to one hundred years ago was built on such a core. The essays of Ralph Waldo Emerson are a clarion call for ethics-based thinking. The observations of Henry Thoreau penned by the shores of Walden Pond should convince even the most skeptical that the true classroom is not a building built with public monies, but life itself.

For those who prefer to be entertained while learning to think, the three novels in *The Seventh Sword* series by Dave Duncan are a marvelous description of the importance of character and values as we try to reform society.

In addition to our personal responsibility to expand our own education and learning, there are a number of direct steps we can take, as we play an ever greater role in the workshop of education. These are:

As citizens, we can demand more accountability and higher standards in public schools. Once entrenched in their positions of power, politicians and bureaucrats often tend to stop listening to the public. As a result, the heavy influence of unions, politicians, and other groups often displaces the needs of students as the top priority in making educational policy. This situation will not reverse itself until citizens take action and demand to know why public schools cannot be run as efficiently as private schools. Why do private schools routinely deliver better discipline, better curricula, and better student performance than public schools? If public schools cannot match the results of private schools, why not abolish the public system and let the private one educate everyone?

Whenever the bureaucrats grind out the same old tired excuses, intelligent citizens need to challenge them—vigorously and persistently. It has been well demonstrated that nothing persuades public officials to change their minds more rapidly than twenty or thirty screaming mothers protesting that the local school board is "killing their children's minds."

As a consumer, we need to support books and creative projects that promote the enlightenment of culture and our values. As long as we derive more pleasure from gossiping about movie stars than from feeding and nurturing the mind, our culture will remain mired in pettiness. The choice is ours, and we make it every day, by the way we spend our money. One hundred years ago, the short story—or serial novel—was the most popular literary form in the English-speaking world. Authors like Dickens and Thackeray thrived. Today, there is almost no market for short stories. Why? Because people stopped buying the magazines and journals that printed them. It is not the publishers' fault. The market dried up because readers were seduced by the greater glamour of television.

If we value education, therefore, we must also recognize our responsibility as a consumer to play our part in making sure that the fruits of civilization remain commercially viable.

As intelligent people, we need to study the Great Ideas of human civilization and apply them. Often, our personal needs for insight and understanding are the most compelling reasons why we seek out higher intelligence. Casual curiosity is seldom enough to sustain the effort required to penetrate to higher levels of insight. Fortunately, there is an enormous amount of great literature, from the ancient Hindus and Greeks to the present time, that will guide us in this noble quest. Great ideas can become the seed thoughts that lead us eventually to archetypal understanding. Reading and studying the ideas of the great thinkers of all times and cultures is one of the best ways we can connect ourself with higher intelligence.

As spiritual people, we need to study the divine origins of life and the ability of spirit to assist us. Ultimately, the true work of education is to lead us to an awareness of the universal dimensions of life. The purpose of education is not just to help us, as an individual, become a better, more intelligent person. The purpose of education is to awaken the whole of humanity to discover the rich potential that lies within our minds and creativity.

There are many issues that divide us—issues we debate strongly and feverishly. Education is not meant to be one of them. Learning is a common experience, shared by all. Through a good liberal arts education, we are meant to discover that peoples of all lands share the same basic goals, aspirations, and hopes. Their customs may vary greatly, but their human potential does not.

Through the education of a lifetime, we are likewise meant to discover that feelings and customs vary greatly from person to person. A proper education teaches us to respect these differences, not enlarge them. It also helps us realize that we must not take pride in these differences. Eventually, it teaches us to see the common aspirations and devotion that unites us all.

At the level of spirit, the whole of humanity is educated as One. Each of us is charged with sharing this education with the rest of the world in our own way, with our own vision. As we pursue this goal, individually and collectively, the goals of the divine workshop of education will be achieved.

And the light of learning will burn brightly on earth, casting out the shadows that have held us in ignorance.

The Divine
Workshop of The Arts

THE WITNESS OF WHAT IS

No human institution, not even religion, reveals the breath and presence of divine life as clearly and as completely as the arts, both the fine arts and the performing arts. The arts are the ideal vehicle for lifting up the human imagination to behold divine possibilities and realities, and then, in response to our curiosity, deliver a fresh charge of creative ideas and inspiration directly to mass consciousness. Elizabeth Barrett Browning, in her poem Aurora Leigh, proclaims that "Art's the witness of what Is behind this show." Throughout the generations, artists, writers, and musicians have transcended the mundane levels of human living to deal directly with universal and archetypal forces and themes. As they have translated these divine energies into poems, essays, paintings, sculptures, and symphonies, they have found it possible to communicate important divine messages to the rest of us in ways that we are able to comprehend, as we register their inspiration in our own minds and hearts. Browning continues:

> We stand here, we,
> If genuine artists, witnessing for God's
> Complete, consummate, undivided work;
> That every natural flower which grows upon the earth
> Implies a flower upon the spiritual side,
> Substantial, archetypal, all aglow
> With blossoming causes.

The work of art, in other words, is to communicate these "blossoming causes" so that we become aware of and responsive to them. These messages are not delivered by Western Union telegram, of course. They are embedded in grand stories of heroism or encased in the mythological themes of opera and drama. They are pronounced in poetry, proclaimed in reflective essays, and unveiled in great exhibitions of painting and sculpture.

Because of the eternal nature of the message of great art, these masterpieces tend to endure much longer than a telegram would; they continue to inspire humanity for generation upon generation. As such, they have become the ideal vehicle for instructing humanity in refining its taste and awareness—and in learning to appreciate the creative dimensions of thinking and self-expression. The arts help us learn to transcend the mundane and discover more fully the spiritual realms that lie just beyond our normal, clouded perception. But most of all, the arts provide an unequaled channel for injecting new inspiration into human culture. Repeatedly throughout history, it has been the arts that have been given the mission to launch a major up-grade in the consciousness of civilization, the most notable example being the role of the arts during the Renaissance. The incredible advances made in music, the fine arts, and writing during this time of reawakening served to make it possible for every other institution of civilization to be aroused to a new level of achievement. Once more, Browning captures the inner worth of the arts:

> Thus is Art
> Self-magnified in magnifying a truth
> Which, fully recognized, would change the world
> And shift its morals.

Great art has the capacity to do just this—to shift our polarity from its mundane focus in the material world to a transcendent focus in the life of spirit. Each poem or novel we read, every play or movie we attend, each piece of music we listen to, and every painting we behold in a gallery should lift us out of the shell of physical perception and open the door of our imagination to the inner dimensions of life. It should change our world and shift our morals, by successfully delivering to us yet another message of divine truth.

Sadly, not everything that is labeled "art" performs this function. A famous painting such as "The Cry" conveys despair and pain, not hope and beauty. As a result, it traps us in the seeming futility of physical life, instead of revealing the true causes and purposes of divine life. Other modern art is just plain disgusting. Most modern music provokes irritation instead of sublimity. Popular fiction often appeals only to our lowest impulses and prejudices. Many movies and television dramas stir up only anger and fear.

But even bad art has the power to convey focused ideas and elicit strong emotional reactions, and must be taken into account. In fact, these messages often register strongly in our unconscious minds, even when we consciously reject the piece of art communicating them. This is because the visual and verbal symbols that are the universal media of all arts "speak" directly to the unconscious mind. They bypass the normal filters of our conscious taste, values, and ideals, to impinge with great power on our deepest levels of thought and feeling.

The arts, therefore, play an important role in the unfoldment of the divine workshop of civilization. Their power to exalt—or debase—is enormous. Of equal magnitude is their ability to shape and guide the thinking of large segments of society. More than any other single institution, the arts determine the content and focus of any given human culture.

There are four basic ways the arts are designed to enrich human life:

1. The arts teach us to appreciate subtlety and refinement. Good art of any kind stirs up our imagination to look beyond the obvious and mundane elements of life. Part of the genius of being a great writer, artist, or composer lies in the capacity to perceive the subtle aspects of human character, nature, and our life experiences. When such a genius then translates these insights into the characters of a novel or play, or into the lines and shadows of a portrait, or even into the musical score accompanying a movie, then we are able to see and hear and absorb elements of their more sophisticated observations. The more we are trained to pick up these subtle elements, the more we will perceive them, but even a casual consumer of the arts will be awakened by these inner realities to some degree.

For this reason, every human being can be productively involved in the divine workshop of art—if not as a genius, then as an intelligent individual who recognizes the importance of immersing himself daily in the ennobling richness of inspired music, literature, drama, and fine arts. This enjoyment of art should not be taken for granted, either. If at all possible, it should begin with a study of the arts as a revelation of spiritual elements of life, then proceed to a level where we actually experience some of these spiritual elements while enjoying whatever art form we have chosen. Eventually, this awakened sensitivity can grow even deeper, as we discover that all of our life experiences are filled with subtlety, richness, and nuances of their own, similar to that which we have been able to glimpse only through works of art.

In watching a play such as Hamlet, for instance, we may at first be aware only of the dazzling action and powerful conflicts set in motion by the plot. We may think that Hamlet is driven merely by the passion of his own anger, and see the play as a simple story of retribution. But as we let this drama speak to us as a work of art, we begin to realize that it reveals far more complex interior motives. Hamlet questions his own identity as a human being in order to understand the course of action he must take. Just so, there are often decisions we must make in life that are painful and even terrifying. To the degree that we can plumb the depths of our identity, we can determine an accurate course. Through this progression of observation and understanding, a great work of art can help us come to terms with basic needs of human living. It can show us the connection between the mundane and the spiritual.

Good art likewise teaches us the language of meaning and abstraction. To be good art, the artist or writer or composer must extract abstract qualities and concepts from the phenomena of life and highlight them in his or her works. It would be simplistic to say that Monet painted flowers, even though he did; he captured the abstract essence of radiant goodwill and transposed it into brilliant paintings. It would be equally naïve to state that Dali painted bizarre objects; he painted living symbols that point to an inner spiritual richness and invite us to share the canvas with them.

The artist may or may not be aware consciously of abstracting these inner qualities and revealing them to us; genius is a force that operates unconsciously with both ease and success. Indeed, the actual intent of the artist is often overshadowed by the unconscious dimensions of talent that seize control of the creative process. Yet as we behold a painting by Monet or Dali, the depth with which each artist created touches us with a resonant chord, triggering unconscious insights and realizations that gradually trickle into our values and attitudes, if we are open to them. In this way, the creative cycle of inspiration is completed.

2. The arts teach us the language of symbolism. Although Homer wrote in ancient Greek and we read in modern English, the symbolism of the Odyssey speaks to us loudly and clearly, needing no translation. This is because symbols are a kind of universal language that unite the whole human race. Reading Homer—or admiring the genius of the sculptures of Michelangelo—is a universal activity that cuts across the gaps of culture, language, custom, and time.

Each creative master works with his or her own set of symbols. Robert Frost frequently used the common experiences of farming as the principal symbols of his poems: stone walls that make for good neighbors, snowy evenings that blank out the imperfections of life, and even changes in the weather. Other poets and writers draw their metaphors and symbols from parables and legends. Richard Wagner likewise based many of his great operas on heroic myths. Tchaikovsky's *1812 Overture* draws its symbolism from the Napoleanic wars. DeBussy drew inspiration from the sea—as did the poet John Masefield. A true artistic masterpiece is usually a complex collection of symbols—written, visual, or audible—woven into a tapestry of light or sound, plot or action. The result is a carefully constructed expression of insight which is the living force just behind the finished painting, sculpture, concerto, opera, poem, or novel.

As we interact with any work of creativity, we should strive to tap into this inner construction of inspiration as well as the physical manifestation of it. This inner construction is the template from which the outer form was created. As such, it is linked directly to the original divine archetypes that inspired the artist. Moreover, it contains the full measure of creative power with which this genius worked. Being able to attune our mind and imagination to this inner symbolic construction greatly enriches our enjoyment of the physical work of art. It also helps us learn that art is an important door to the multidimensional nature of life.

Many people, of course, ignore the great works of art because they do not understand them, let alone appreciate them. They scoff at the notion that a great painting or novel has any value to them and their lives. This might be true if the end product of creativity was nothing but the physical form. But since the finished masterpiece includes an inner symbolic construction as well as the outer form, even people who pay no attention to it will be affected and enriched by it, at least to a degree. The inspired forces embodied in the inner construction are able to speak directly to the unconscious mind, and it does so, even if we never attend a play or visit an art museum or read a book. The very presence of art within our cultural milieu has a beneficial impact on each of us at unconscious levels, refining our sense of taste, civilization, and awareness.

This impact of great art can be of practical value, too. It means that the uplifting tones of a Bach or a Schubert can relieve despair in nonmusical people as well as in devotees of their art. The poetry of Walt Whitman was not well received nor widely read during his lifetime, yet it became a powerful force defining the character of American culture and changing the timbre of American thought. Few of us have actually seen the Venus de Milo in person, yet all of us have been affected by it in terms of our artistic values.

There is another way that art's inner symbolic construction affects us. The act of reading Homer can introduce even atheists to the power of divine order and the forces of destiny. They will still believe themselves to be atheists after reading *The Odyssey*, but the power of this epic will have added ideas and perspectives that will subtly dilute the strength of their atheistic beliefs. In much the same way, a good performance of a play by Ibsen will expand our understanding of the foibles of human nature and the need to cultivate tolerance, patience, and compassion in our relationships, even if we consciously thought of it as nothing but an evening's entertainment.

At first, our interaction with the inner symbolic construction of a creative masterpiece will be limited. We will still think in terms of the discrete forms of the finished masterpiece, rather than its universal themes. Rembrandt, after all, is more widely known for his brilliant use of light and shadow than for his penetrating insight into human nobility and dignity. Alexander Pope is more commonly known for his razor sharp satire than for his revelations about the relationship of humanity to God. As we become familiar with the more subtle levels of symbolism, however, we begin to perceive that the same intelligence and beauty that guided Renoir also guided Rembrandt; they just worked in different styles. So also, the same joy of living that inspired Bach likewise inspired Mahler, even though they delivered the message musically in unique ways. Shakespeare, Ibsen, and Tolstoy all touched the human potential to overcome the great suffering that can occur in life, even though they selected widely differing plots, characters, and settings to convey this message.

We, too, can learn to work with these same symbolic forces, and the proper study of art can help us develop this highly useful ability—the ability to recognize and respond to archetypal forces and think about them (interact with them) at abstract levels. Indeed, developing this ability to think abstractly ought to be the end goal of any study of the arts, be it music, theater, literature, or the fine arts.

The sure sign that our study of art is leading us in this direction is the emerging capacity to link concrete events with their divine archetypal correspondences. As we confront a personal tendency to become angry, for example, we begin to see that our problem is not too much anger but rather not enough compassion and goodwill. So, we link ourself with the divine force of goodwill at its abstract level, harnessing its power to act with tolerance and forgiveness in our daily experience.

These lessons may even be tied in with the direct inspiring impact of a work of art. And so, if we learn to recognize the power of joy breaking through suffering and tragedy in a symphony by Mahler or Tchaikovsky, we should be able to awaken our own latent powers of courage and joy to express in daily life. As we learn to interact with the inspiration and idealism symbolically captured by a Thomas Cole landscape, we should be able to activate a stronger measure of idealism for our personal use.

Once this ability to tap archetypal forces is developed, no matter how indirect or minimal it may be, we have gained the potential to be directly inspired by our innate spiritual wisdom, plus the full realm of divine archetypes. We are thereby prepared to engage in the effective use of inspiration and genuine creativity. Ultimately, the ability to work in these ways is part of the destiny of all mankind. Hence, the arts play an enormous role in the proper unfoldment of human talents and awareness.

3. The arts instruct us in holistic thinking and integration. Our lives are filled with experiences and events, many of which confuse us. We suffer divisive conflicts. These conflicts exist only because we do not know how to reconcile warring elements—but most of us do not yet understand this point. We need help in discovering our untrained potential for harmonizing the divisive forces. The arts can be a powerful tool for learning the lessons of integration.

Perhaps we are at odds with life itself. Reading a novel such as *Moby Dick* or attending a performance of *King Lear* might well shock us into realizing the pointlessness of trying to oppose life itself. The impact of a performance of *Much Ado About Nothing* might be far gentler, yet equally revolutionary, if it led us to realize that we were placing far too much importance on assumptions and superficial elements of life.

The arts are designed to help us in these ways. Good art, like most of the problems of life, is complex. We are constantly drawn back to a great painting to view it again and again; we will often be motivated to reread a great novel many times. We cannot wear out a masterpiece such as *The Magic Flute* or *Romeo and Juliet*, no matter how many times we view it. The art form is so complex and rich with meaning and subtlety that we never tire of it. Our mind and heart and imagination are constantly finding new resonances within such great works. Each time we revisit a great work, we find new relevance in it—new ways to harness its power to help us integrate our own consciousness.

The "secret" behind the power of art to help us in this way is threefold:

1. Good art "broadcasts" its symbolic messages on several wavelengths—emotional, mental, and spiritual.

2. Good art reveals to us new measures of insight, gratitude, yearning, courage, or joy, by stimulating a deep, inspired response that we rarely encounter in mundane experiences.

3. Good art helps us pause and put things into perspectives that we rarely or never consider. It encourages us to look at the larger picture of life and to consider the possibility of universal themes. It likewise helps us see the way the different elements of life are meant to relate to one another.

In these ways, art presents to us a symbolic microcosm that can be associated to some theme of life or another, quite possibly one of our own. The story of the prodigal son, for instance—as depicted in Rembrandt's classic painting—reveals the capacity of divine compassion, patience, and forgiveness to redeem our rebelliousness and ignorant egotism. It also symbolizes the terrible grief and guilt we bring upon ourself through our unfettered greed and lust for the "good life." Rembrandt encapsulates the story of humankind in one image—the image of the suffering we bring upon ourself and how this gradually opens us to become receptive to divine love, wisdom, and patience.

In this way, a single painting can express a complex archetypal idea in all of its component parts. The overriding theme of the prodigal son is the transformation and growth in maturity that occurs as a result of human struggle. But each stage of this process is also important: the wayward child, the moment of realization, the trip homeward, and the forgiving parent.   Each aspect will speak to us at different stages of our personal odyssey.

One of the great pitfalls of humanity is its tendency to become isolated in narrow ideas, ideologies, and beliefs. This problem is compounded by a second: the habit of most people to allow contradictory feelings, attitudes, values, and convictions to exist side by side with one another. As a result, the average person is highly volatile as he or she flips from impulse to belief without any apparent pattern. In the individual, these problems create serious internal conflict. In society, they lead to chauvinism and tribalism.

Art has the power to remind us of our universal roots— the power to help us integrate feelings with ideals, ideas with divine patterns, and the individual with the universal.   As such, good art, music, and literature are powerful antidotes for divisiveness, both individually and within the human family. Simply put, they promote the discovery of our creative potential.

Step by step, good art teaches us the lessons of holistic thinking. It teaches us to see how the many tiny pieces and conditions that seem to fight with one another actually fit together in a benevolent, constructive way. It does this by revealing to us the underlying laws and principles which give meaning to seemingly meaningless acts.   In this way, great art serves the divine purpose of inclusiveness.   It enables us to see inner patterns and principles at work within a play or a novel, which in turn help us become adept at recognizing the same factors at play in our life.

One of the great demonstrations of the need for a detached perspective, for example, occurs in Shakespeare's *A Midsummer Night's Dream.*   Puck has been commanded by Oberon, king of the fairies, to make sure that all the mortals fall in love with the correct partner.   But under the spell of youthful infatuation, the would-be lovers repeatedly fall in love with everyone but the right one. This sends Puck into a frenzy, and he complains to Oberon: "Lord, what fools these mortals be." Oberon is not nearly as concerned, because he knows how easily young mortals change their minds. He envisions the end result in his mind, and will not be dissuaded from it. This is the way in which we must learn to deal with unexpected distractions in our life, too.

In this way, we learn to recognize the underlying harmony of life. The role of harmony is obvious in music, but it is present in the other forms of great art as well. It is the central most important tool used in the divine workshop of art.

4. The arts stimulate us to become creative in our life. It is not enough just to live a quiet, peaceful life that harms no one. The challenge of human living is far greater: spirit calls us to discover our divine heritage and learn to express it creatively. This does not mean that we must become an artist or a musician; there are many ways creativity can be expressed. It can inspire the work of business executives, as they strive to develop more enlightened expressions of group cooperation; the labors of housewives, as they juggle the needs of children and household chores with a career; or the efforts of psychologists, as they develop new methods for conflict management. Any effort that brings new life of spirit into the physical plane to reform or to innovate is creative. But most of us do not know how to tap the inspiration that is the vital ingredient of all creative work. It is here that the arts can inspire us. As we perceive and codify the steps involved in interacting with divine archetypes and applying them to the tasks at hand in our life, we too can become creative.

The first step is to learn to look at our world (or our project) from more than one perspective—for instance, through the eyes of others. An entrepreneur, for example, might find it helpful to look at his or her new project or service from the perspective of potential customers. A politician might find it useful to look at a proposal through the eyes of critics and the media. A spiritual reformer would clearly want to look at his or her activities through the eyes of spirit.

To this first step, a second can be added: namely, to learn to recognize the hidden nuances and intangible elements of our life. Instead of becoming bogged down in problems, for example, we can speculate on the ideal creative solution to the conditions at hand. How could beauty or joy or harmony be expressed in the midst of these factors? What innovation would eliminate or reduce these problems?

The creative perspective also needs to include the ability to discern the spiritual significance of our tasks. Shakespeare's creativity, for example, was not just limited to writing brilliant plays. He was also directly involved in consolidating the English language, cementing the role of the English monarchy, and establishing drama as a legitimate art form. Our own efforts to learn and grow, no matter how humble, will also have a similar purpose which holds a key to genuine creative achievement.

The same patterns and perspectives can be perceived in the current upswing of creative activity on the part of groups and nations, as they search for new identities and traditions, new goals, new social institutions, and new distributions of authority. The first result of much of this activity has been an increase in turmoil and uncertainty. But the evidence of new creative energies at work is also abundant, as can be seen in the explosion of courses and books on creative problem solving, negotiations, and the mediation of conflict.

Whether inside or outside of the traditional definitions of the arts, any genuine creative activity that brings heaven to earth is the product of the labors of the divine workshop of art. Creativity is the work and responsibility of all human beings. The great musicians, artists, and writers of any era should be thought of as the visionaries who show us the way—the way we make contact with divine inspiration and integrate it into our own life and activities.

Sometimes, the inspiration comes in unexpected or obscure ways. A good mystery writer may be contributing as much to the work of the arts as a poet, as his or her mysteries stimulate thousands of readers to pay more attention to detail, develop a better model for analysis, and learn to think both deductively and inductively. As literature, it may have a short shelf life at the library, but the impact on humanity may be remarkable.

Another example of a huge contribution from a minor artist would be the drawings of Max Escher. His graphics often depict one scene from two or three different perspectives, indicating that we cannot fully understand anything from a one-dimensional view. He is also a master of depicting the relationship of the formless to the forms, symbolically illustrating the dynamic ebb and flow between the formless and the world of form.

The work of creativity is to open our eyes to the incredible vastness of life around us. It rejects the narrow attitudes of critics and "experts" who would reduce the arts to an ever-smaller circle of the elite. The creative spark burns within all of us. We each have our work to do in the divine workshop of the arts. Through innovation and creativity, we develop a true zest for living. We learn to recognize our birthright and seize it.

THE PROBLEMS OF ART

In terms of reaching the full achievement planned by the Hierarchy, the divine workshop of art is still in its adolescence. The truly inspired geniuses have produced magnificent music, art, and literature that continue to inspire humanity. At the same time, however, there are many other writers, composers, and painters who are doing little more than the equivalent of churning out graffiti, vandalizing canvases, and bombarding humanity with noise.

The mere ability to write, paint, act, or compose does not make one an artist. There has to be a genuine connection with divine inspiration as well. Where this connection is lacking, the effort to be creative may well turn destructive. The problem is not so much a lack of talent, for talent can be learned. Instead, it is an obsession with the dark side of human nature and culture, nurtured by nihilistic and cynical attitudes.

It is certainly within the province of the arts to examine the unredeemed aspects of human life. But while bad art will often wallow in these blemishes and imperfections, great art will always stress the divine connection. It will portray the capacity of the hero to overcome opposition and achieve his or her goals. This may be expressed in highly dramatic terms, as in the Greek myths of Hercules, or in very ordinary terms, as in the quiet elegance of a poem by Emily Dickinson.

It is important to understand this distinction. The great writers of tragedy, from the ancient Greeks to Shakespeare and beyond, have all focused their creative eye on such unpleasant topics as malice, jealousy, and the lust for power. But they do not just dwell on them for cheap thrills; they show the unfortunate consequences of such hubris and the destruction it inevitably generates. In addition, they clearly endorse the spiritual forces which would have prevented the tragedy, had the characters not been blinded to them. The madness of Lear, after all, is juxtaposed with the devotion and goodness of his daughter Cordelia, even while she is being mistreated.

In music, too, composers such as Tchaikovsky and Prokofiev often paint huge canvases of sound that capture the suffocating nature of despair, but always so that the despair can then be shattered and defeated by the inflow of joy and love. In literature, the examples are even more prolific. Somerset Maugham, Taylor Caldwell, and many others have excelled at dramatizing the fierce struggle of individuals battling their own demons of anger, fear, and depression to break through to a personal transformation that leads to inner peace.

In the twentieth century, however, too many artists in all fields have fallen in love with celebrating the dark and seamy side of human life. It is as though they have fallen into a pit of anger, fear, rage, and guilt and are determined to "share" this misery with everyone else! In fact, the performing arts have become so jaded and pessimistic that a director who dares end a movie on an upbeat, optmistic note is critically condemned as naïve or irrelevant. Writers who do not use their novels or poetry to decry the corruption and injustice of the world are derided as lightweights. It seems, at times, that darkness and pessimism have completely polluted the modern artistic consciousness.

In part, this is a sign of the turmoil that society itself is experiencing. To a degree, society has lost its way, and is waiting for a fresh, new definition of it. This new definition will arrive—and will be embraced by the world of art, perhaps even be delivered by it—but until then, we are passing through a phase in which some levels of art itself seem lost.

The unforunate aspect of this problem is that even bad art has an impact on the public. The discerning, intelligent person instantly rejects works of "art" that revel in the dark urges and passions of human nature. The general public, however, is not so discerning. It not only accepts bad art but often even embraces it, especially in music and on television. As a result, "masters" of the cheap thrill, from Martin Scorsese to Guns N Roses, grow rich at the expense of good taste.

In some cases, the glorification of darkness and evil is cleverly disguised as social concern. A movie or book points out what is wrong with society or some segment of it, but without offering constructive solutions or any sign of the divine design. Most of these works, however, are propaganda, not art; they are an attempt to persuade us to adopt a point of view that runs counter to spiritual law. In some cases, it is even more pernicious—it is an attempt to cover up personal flaws by attacking some aspect of society that will be perceived as even more evil or vile than the "artist." This is not a legitimate act of raising anyone's consciousness; it is just an artful deceit.

In the past few years, all too many artists have also succumbed to the rise of "political correctness" as well as pessimism. They are determined to use their music or movies to bully society into conforming to their version of "justice" and "equality." The result has been a very righteous form of indoctrination that offends the genuine spirit of art and creativity.

The underlying danger in this brand of "art" is that, instead of warning us about the problems of human living, it actually adds power to them—by dwelling on them and rubbing our collective noses in them. In this regard, it is the the equivalent of primal scream therapy. According to its advocates, primal scream is designed to dispel our rage by venting it; unfortunately, the expression of rage actually increases it! In the field of art, the incessant harping on the problems of society without offering constructive, intelligent solutions has the same impact: it magnifies our pain and suffering and increases our sense of being trapped.

Bad music is especially pernicious in this regard, largely because it is so omnipresent. Few of us spend hours a day looking at bad art or reading bad poetry, but millions of people spend most of their waking hours listening to destructive popular music, at least in the background. The saturation of our environment with the incessant heavy beat of popular music is no small factor in the decline of civility and the increase in crime and mental illness in society. One critic of the modern music scene has observed that people used to smile and tap their feet while listening to music. Now they sit open-mouthed and stare—or gyrate as though they were having a seizure. Heavy metal virtuosos treat music as warfare. Pop singers reduce love to lust and conjure up not thinking but anxiety, grief, and rage.

In his book *Prophecy in Music*, Albert Roustit writes: "The distinction between music and noise seems to be blurring; melody and words are being replaced by shrieks for which the only accompaniment is a frenetic rhythm...and the result is a kind of hysteria similar to primitive people....To put oneself in a trance under the effect of certain rhythmic excitation is to leave momentarily the civilized state to fall into a savage one, at which point (the unredeemed elements of human nature) can make an appearance too strong for our spirituality to correct."

Scientists who have studied the effect of music on the human body have shown that discordant, inharmonious, and excessively loud music tends to deplete our energy, disorient our feelings, increase irritability, and magnify intolerance, anger, and fear. This is an exact match of the kind of psychological atmosphere in which antisocial and addictive behaviors are spawned.

When scientists observe the impact on people of noble classical music, such as the works of Haydn, Mozart, or Bach, they find the exact reverse. Clarity of thought and memory improves. The emotions become more tranquil and positive. It is easier to express tolerance, gratitude, and joy. Like all forms of good art, most classical music—including the light classics—appear to nourish psychological health and emotional stability, as well as nurturing the mind.

Even bad art will end up serving a worthwhile purpose, however. The day will come when the masses of people wake up to its harmful effect—just as the masses have awakened to the harmful effects of cigarette smoking. Once the truth about bad art is exposed, it will be rejected with as much enthusiasm as it was embraced. In the meanwhile, society is learning yet another lesson in discrimination and discernment.

Each of us needs to realize that the creative arts are meant to be an intimate part of our inner life. If we nurture our need for art with the finest and the best that human creativity has to offer, we will flourish and thrive. Our awareness and responsiveness to life will become more refined—and connected with the life of spirit. But if we pollute ourself with trash, we fail in one of our most basic responsibilities as a human being. We fail to pursue excellence.

Even today, signs are emerging that intelligent people are beginning to see the bankruptcy of rock music, junk art, and trash fiction. As this perception grows, the public will slowly begin to recognize the utter nonsense of it all. The resulting outcry for better forms of popular art will trigger a massive reform throughout all levels of the art world, and the workshop of divine art will return once again to its normal occupation—producing images and portrayals of divine beauty, harmony, and wholeness.

THE SPIRITUAL WORK OF THE ARTS

At times, the subtle influence of the Hierarchy on the divine workshop of art may seem hard to discern. Music, the arts, and literature are so dominated by the crass and the bizarre that it becomes tempting to believe that the Hierarchy is on vacation this century in regards to the arts. Fortunately, this is not so—and never is.

To appreciate the current work of the Hierarchy in terms of the arts, we need to understand that the pace of civilization has been greatly accelerated. The idyllic, pastoral lives of Wordsworth and Frost are now crammed into urban congestion. The pressure of most jobs is far more intense than in past eras. Our schools are plagued with drugs and crime. The political arena is dominated by protest after protest from one special interest group or another. There are greater challenges than ever in dealing with colleagues, friends, and spouses. In America, the melting pot has become a boiling cauldron.

The news makes us aware of all of these assorted pressures, but it is the role of the arts to help us make sense of them. The sudden increase in the pace of life has temporarily created the impression that the arts themselves are foundering, but they are not. They are simply shifting focus in the work they perform.

There may or may not be a Johann Sebastian Bach toiling in obscurity, producing what will eventually be hailed as the great music of the century. But there certainly is an unparalleled opportunity for music lovers to be exposed to the music of Beethoven, Bach, and all the other great composers of centuries gone by. This music is broadcast by radio, performed on television, available on recordings—and played by orchestras in almost every city in the country. In addition, the opportunity to learn to perform music is greater than ever. We are learning what it means to become intelligent consumers of great music.

It is true that the music scene is dominated by rock and roll and country and western, but so what? It is still possible for a Luciano Pavarotti to inspire millions of people worldwide with his operatic recordings and concerts. It is still possible for millions of people worldwide to become familiar with William Shakespeare through movies or stage performances of *Romeo and Juliet, A Midsummer Night's Dream,* and *As You Like It.* It is also possible for millions of viewers to watch excellent presentations of the novels of Jane Austen and Charles Dickens on television. And, thanks to modern print technology and computer innovations, it is possible to expose millions of people to the works of great art as never before.

This accessibility enables the arts to give intelligent people the tools they need to cope with the bewildering complexity of modern life. The primary one of these tools is discernment—the ability to see the subtle hand of the deeper purpose behind the confusion and turmoil of daily events.

Literature, for example, is unequalled in teaching us to discern the inner elements of human nature. By dramatizing the common issues affecting large numbers of people, the works of good authors help us understand these conditions and how to resolve them. In fact, writers are often far more perceptive and accurate than psychologists in describing the foibles and greatness of human nature. Psychologists, after all, spend much of their time reading the works of other psychologists, while writers study human nature itself, unhindered by academic theories. In addition, the good writer is guided by inspiration, and as a consequence is more apt to tap the archetypal patterns of human nature than many psychologists. The psychologist specializes in mental illness and often knows surprisingly little about normal people. Reading a good novel, therefore, may teach us a great deal that can directly help us live our life.

As always, one of the major roles of literature is to expose the hypocrisy and nonsense of self-appointed leaders and experts in every segment of society. While it is true that many modern authors (as well as musicians, actors, and artists) have become advocates for politically correct programs of every kind, there are still a few bright lights who continue to champion equality and liberty. Every age has its share of "emperors without clothing" to expose— and great writers always arise with the skill and insight to do so.

Indeed, part of the role of the arts is always to bring vision to society. This is happening today in specific fields of the arts. In literature, much of this vision is revealed through the works of talented science fiction writers. In music, it lies in the discovery of the power of good music to enrich consciousness as well as entertain. In the fine arts, it lies in the effort to depict fourth dimensional realities in canvases and sculptures. Many of these visions have not yet been fulfilled, but the effort continues.

Society is also beginning to learn that the arts have value beyond simple entertainment. We are beginning to understand the relationship between creativity and healing and between art and integration. In recent decades, there has been a steady increase in our awareness of the value of "right brain thinking"—creativity, innovation, and imagination. Through poetry, drawing, music, and dance, people are being taught to awaken the inner and global aspects of their thinking, and then apply these processes to daily challenges. Their goal is not to produce great works of art, but rather to learn the basics of approaching life from an artistic, creative perspective. In this process, they learn to take the first few, tottering steps toward becoming an artist of life.

Indeed, great strides are being made in tapping the therapeutic powers of excellent music. Music is being intentionally used as therapy to soothe irritation, relieve despondency, invigorate the body, dispel anger, and diffuse fear. At the other end of the spectrum, it is also being used to stimulate clear thinking, build up courage and perseverance, and organize our thoughts. The works of Mozart and J.S. Bach have been found to be exceptionally powerful in this regard. Eventually, it will be found that music of this caliber actually generates a thoughtform that embodies a specific divine force, such as joy, goodwill, peace, or grace. These musical forms can have intense power in unifying groups, exalting consciousness, and aiding spiritual growth.

It is also being discovered that creative writing can be a powerful tool in accelerating personal growth, especially in terms of integrating the events of the past with our current insights—and discerning the patterns which hold the clue to our spiritual purpose. The Hierarchy, naturally, is interested in this development not because it will produce a new wave of diaries, journals, or autobiographies; this kind of glorification of the personal life has little appeal to spirit. Rather, It is stimulating this use of writing for self-discovery in order to encourage more people to seek out the archetypal patterns that create their own "personal myth."

Mythology was the first form of literature, and still remains the symbolic core of all writing. Each culture and nation develops its own mythology to illustrate and explain its roots in the inner life, whether it is a Greek myth about Hercules or an Anglo-Saxon myth about Arthur. Each individual has an intricate mythology, too, that symbolically links the triumphs and tragedies of personal experience with the joy and vision of his or her spiritual design for living. Through the effort to define a personal myth, we learn to view our experiences and trials from a higher, more inclusive level; we integrate our pain with an awareness of the skill, maturity, and intelligence we have gained. In this way, we learn to redefine the struggles of life and see them as essential events in the overall unfoldment of our character and purpose.

Our personal myth will probably never be a great piece of art like *Gulliver's Travels* or *Idylls of the King*. But it can be a most useful way for us to harness the power of literature to propel our own self-understanding.

Obviously, a personal myth can also be discovered through painting, sculpture, or music, if our talents lie in those directions. The creative exploration of music can be an excellent way to stimulate intuitive skills and perception. The practice of art can lead us quickly beyond the exercise of a relaxing hobby into a discovery of the makeup of our own subconscious patterns of self-expression.

The arts as a whole are also in the process of rediscovering the central role of mythology as the heart of inspiration. In movies such as *Star Wars* and *Raiders of the Lost Ark*, we can see early signs of a general return to heroism as a central virtue. As this new trend in the arts unfold, however, the concept of heroism will be expanded and enriched to include noble ideas and ideals as heroes, not just individuals. Already, two great novels by A.E. van Vogt, *The World of Null-A* and *The Players of Null-A*, have made the noble human mind the central hero.

The fine arts and music will likewise do much more to promote the ideals of inclusiveness, goodwill, and divine order. In addition, a whole new set of archetypes are waiting to be revealed by the Hierarchy; it will be the responsibility of the workshop of the arts to interpret these divine forces so that humanity can understand them and tap their integrative powers.

Indeed, only a tiny fragment of the world of spirit has yet been revealed and expressed to humanity. It is the work of the arts to continuously probe these rich inner dimensions, claim them, and reveal them to the rest of us. It is a noble work and an important work—a labor without an end.

As always, however, the most important masterpiece of this great effort is the individual human being—the enlightened spiritual person.

SUPPORTING THE WORK OF THE ARTS

Goethe neatly sums up the responsibility of every intelligent person: "A person should hear a little music, read a little poetry, and see a fine picture every day in order that worldly cares may not obliterate the sense of the beautiful which God has implanted in the human soul." The arts are not just something to be enjoyed. Good art is the great civilizing force of society. It promotes an appreciation of and responsiveness to the noble and refined qualities of spirit. It helps us get on the wavelength of God. Therefore, whenever we, as an individual, take up the study and support of the arts, we are entering into this divine workshop. We are fulfilling one aspect of our spiritual duty.

The impact of our individual effort must not be under-rated. The institution of art is far more than schools of art, museums, libraries, and theaters. It is the combined interest, knowledge, talent, love, and effort of everyone who is involved in creative thinking and living. Therefore, in addition to the traditional venues of art, the work of creativity is also to be found wherever anyone is seeking to introduce greater harmony, beauty, and joy into the home, the office, or the community.

For this reason, anyone who takes the time to educate himself or herself in the language of art can become a true proponent of this divine workhop. The effort to read great literature, listen to superb music, and fill our imagination with outstanding art expands our horizons in healthy ways which enrich humanity as well as ourself. Every class we take that stimulates our imagination promotes the work of art. Every tie we make with writers, musicians, actors, and artists helps us deepen our appreciation of the role they play in enlightening humanity.

Some people would argue that the pursuit of art is a blasphemy so long as anyone is homeless or hungry. What these misguided critics overlook is that without a creative awareness of spirit, every human being is homeless, even if they live in a castle. Without the capacity to integrate divine archetypes into a coherent world view, every human being hungers and thirsts for that which transcends his or her mundane life. Without the ability to work with harmony and beauty, every human being serves a self-imposed sentence in the prison of skepticism, fear, and pessimism. We need the arts to set us free—to realize our full potential as a creative exponent of divine life.

In addition to pursuing our own creative interests, even as a talented amateur, it is important to do all that we can to support good art, literature, and music. This does not mean spending millions to buy an original van Gogh—such silliness does nothing to help civilization flourish. Nor does it mean blindly voting to spend public money to erect some bizarre sculpture of dubious origin in the town square. Genuine support originates in our ability to respect and delight in great works of art, music, literature, and film, and to encourage family and friends to cultivate a similar level of interest and respect. As our own level of interest and support rises, so does the level of sensitivity in all of humanity.

In this regard, it is also important to make sure that our attitude toward creativity and genius is a healthy one. Because artists and writers look at life from alternative perspectives, they are often viewed as suspect by nonartistic people. In our modern society, this suspicion has grown into outright envy and disdain. It is reflected in the obvious fact that a poet cannot make a living by writing poetry, while a baseball player or rock star can earn millions of dollars a year.

It is easy to blame society for these attitudes, but the mores and ethics of society are nothing more than the combined values of individuals. If society is going to learn to honor the arts properly, it must start with intelligent people—intelligent people who insist on the value of refined taste, creative insight, and the inspiration of genius in all that they do. Support-ing these subtle reforms must become a priority in the lives and actions of the spiritual aspirant. Until this occurs, the genius envy of the masses will continue to dilute the impact of the divine workshop of art.

A profound contribution to the arts can be made by sup-porting education in "right brain" skills within the context of our own community—first as private educational projects, and eventually as a part of mainstream, public education. Naturally, this type of support begins by each intelligent, concerned individual making the effort to learn these methods of thinking for himself or herself.

In this regard, one of the beneficial steps to take is to learn to discern the message that great art delivers to us personally. If a poet such as John Keats can be inspired by reading a new translation of Homer, why should we not be inspired by the experiences of life? Art gives us the ability to pierce the unknown:

> Then felt I like some watcher of the skies
> When a new planet swims into his ken;
> Or like stout Cortez when with eagle eyes
> He star'd at the Pacific; and all his men
> Look'd at each other with a wild surmise—
> Silent, upon a peak in Darien.

Whenever we rise above our petty concerns and hear the message of life to us, we add balance and enrichment to our awareness. We grasp new insight into the contrasts and subtle shadings of our life. We sense the larger, spiritual context in which we toil. We discern the real.

But once we have learned to discern the real, yet another responsibility befalls us. We must become a protector of the real as well, by learning to detect bad art—and reject it.

There will, of course, be those self-appointed "experts" who will condemn such attitudes as the bigoted prejudices of a philistine. But art is not a matter of taste—either personal taste or public taste. Bad art has the power to reintroduce barbarism into society, and it has already gained a foothold. Just as fire can be used to heat our homes or burn them down, depending upon how we control it, so also the power and symbols of art can be used either to inspire and uplift or to corrupt and destroy. The raw depiction of violence in movies and video games has corrupted the value system of several generations of youth. The discordance and crudity that course through popular music and its videos has undermined courtesy, self-discipline, patience, and respect in large segments of the population. The silly dramas of soap operas and a good deal of night-time television have legitimized pettiness, personal dishonesty, and lust for power. The unimaginative and uninspired canvases masquerading as modern art in our leading galleries and museums do not just fall short of the mark—they damage consciousness. They promote despair, sterility, and emotional emptiness.

Is it censorship to advocate a return to taste? Of course not. It would be censorship if the state stepped in and prohibited bad art. But when citizens stand up and expose the corrupting influence of bad art, especially on the youth, it is a demonstration of responsibility, not censorship. If intelligent people stop supporting museums that display the equivalent of garbage, they will stop exhibiting it. When the public stops paying to see violent movies, the film studios will stop making them. When the public no longer buys trashy novels, companies will stop publishing them.

In rejecting bad art, we must be sure not to overlook the pernicious influence of political propaganda. Discriminating between good art and propaganda is often a far more difficult call to make than the perception of violence and filth. But the very difficulty of making this choice increases the importance that intelligent people take a stand against the use of art to propagandize. Art is a tool, and a very powerful one. It is often used in negative ways, to undermine civilized values and qualities, to trivialize excellence, to sabotage the work ethic, and to smear the name of tolerance itself. The use of art as propaganda is most obvious in political campaigns, but it is also present in most commercial advertising. Worst of all, it permeates the daily presentation of the news, where words and images are regularly prostituted to serve a hidden agenda.

Ideally, our support of the arts will become a natural expression of our intent to support the best within society, wherever it is found. It should be based on a profound understanding of the dynamic role of good art, literature, and music in elevating our perceptions of life to the inner realms of spirit, and then integrating these new perceptions into our minds and imaginations. In this way, we actually embody the work of art in our own life.

Robert Frost captured this highest meaning of art in one of his sonnets—a story of Eve in the garden.

> He would declare and could himself believe
> That the birds there in all the garden round
> From having heard the daylong voice of Eve
> Had added to their own an oversound,
> Her tone of meaning but without the words.
> Admittedly an eloquence so soft
> Could only have had an influence on birds
> When call or laughter carried it aloft.
> Be that as may be, she was in their song.
> Moreover her voice upon their voices crossed
> Had now persisted in the woods so long
> That probably it never would be lost.
> Never again would birds' songs be the same.
> And to do that to birds was why she came.

Our creative mission is to learn to sing the songs of our Father who created us, and in singing them, to teach the very substance of matter to learn the song. It can only have this influence when we lift our voice aloft—when we seek the inspiration of divine archetypes. But if we persist in learning and singing these songs, through the workshop of art, they will never again be forgotten.

This is the inspired labor of great art.

The Divine
Workshop of Science

THE GREAT IDEAS OF GOD

The story of civilization is a tale of liberation—liberation from ignorance, barbarism, and untold amounts of suffering and hardship. Each institution of society plays its part in this drama of liberation. Education teaches us to think, and the arts refine our awareness. Religion awakens us to the inner realities of spirit. Yet as valuable as these contributions have been, they pale in comparison to the role that has been played by science. Without the knowledge discovered and applied by scientists throughout the ages, humanity would be nothing more than a set of isolated, primitive clans, each one hunting and fishing for its own food, making its own crude clothing, and living in caves or huts. Homes would be lit by candles and heated by wood fires. The only means of traveling would be on foot or horseback. Disease would kill most people before they reached thirty years of age.

It is impressive to reflect on the marvelous contributions and innovations that have been made by science on behalf of society:

In the area of food production, science has helped us increase crop yields and the efficiency of harvesting, processing, preserving, and transporting food. It continues to develop new hybrid grains and vegetables that produce higher yields and are more resistant to disease and drought. These advances have made it possible to eliminate starvation and poor nutrition in vast regions of the earth, and create the legitimate hope that the remaining vestiges of these problems can be eliminated soon.

In the field of communications, science has brought the world much closer together. One hundred years ago, it took hours for a telegaph message to encircle the globe, weeks for distant news to arrive, and months for a person to circumnavigate the earth. Today, thanks to television, radio, the telephone, and—most recently—the world wide web, a message from Singapore can reach us instantly, live news can be broadcast via satellite, or we could catch a jet liner and be there tomorrow. As a result, humanity is better informed and educated than ever before. Science has removed many of the barriers of communication that used to cause isolation, rivalry, and even war.

The same progress has occurred in humanity's transportation of raw materials, goods, and food. A salmon that is caught in the Pacific can be served in an East Coast restaurant two days later. Wheat grown in Kansas can easily be consumed as bread in Korea. These changes were not implemented by the decree of any government. They were made possible by scientific research and development.

Science has done a great deal to penetrate the mysteries of physical disease, mental illness, and the plagues that used to destroy human life by the millions. Part of this improvement is the result of better medical treatments, but much of it also stems from better public hygiene, purer water, insect control, and food handling—all the result of more complete scientific understanding.

Indeed, even the emergence of substantial leisure time is due directly to scientific progress, as the invention of labor saving devices of all kinds has liberated us from the bone-crunching drudgery so common even one hundred years ago.

But not all of the contributions of the divine workshop of science are technological in nature. As it has grown in stature, science has played a major role in internationalizing human civilization. The "language" of science and the scientific method are universal, just as nature's secrets and laws are universal. A new antibiotic discovered in Germany can soon be in use everywhere. A new method of generating electricity from solar radiation, developed in Japan, can soon be adapted for use in most countries. The world wide web is quickly making millions of computer users a nation of their own, able to communicate with each other as though they were a block away.

We routinely take for granted extraordinary discoveries and inventions which, in many ways, overshadow even some of the miracles recorded in the Bible. It may seem astounding that Jesus could feed five thousand people with a few loaves and fish, but is it any less astonishing that modern science can turn a desert into fertile ground and thereby feed millions? It may seem incredible that the Christ could walk on water, but is it any less amazing that men have walked on the moon? The major difference between the miracles and modern science is that few people have been able to duplicate the miracles, while the achievements of science are available for all to use.

These are but a few examples of the effectiveness of the divine workshop of science in fulfilling its primary purpose: to harness the forces of nature to meet human needs. It is the work of science, as a whole, to probe and discover the "secrets of nature," and then put these previously-unknown potentials to work as the master builder of society.

This is no small contribution! We owe a huge debt to science for its role in liberating us from the drudgery, superstition, and austerities of life two and three hundred years ago. Now that we have learned to control it with science, nature is relatively tame and benign. But take away those scientific controls—in meterology, medicine, geology, and virtually every other field—and nature can be cruel, ugly, and lethal. Compare the life of the medieval peasant, whose survival depended upon an all-consuming involvement in providing food, clothing, and shelter, with the life of the average working class American today. The typical blue collar employee works forty hours a week, enjoys three to four weeks of vacation, sends the kids to college, and retires to Florida to play golf. This vast improvement in the comfort level of life is not the result of individual effort and talent. It is primarily the result of the advances made by science, as it has learned to harness the forces and materials of nature for human use. Life today is light years beyond the pastoral life so often extolled by those who are inclined to believe that technology is the root of all modern evil.

And yet, as valuable as all of these technological advances are, there is an even more important aspect to the work of science. The divine workshop of science teaches humanity the scientific way of thinking and reasoning. Moreover, it has taught us this lesson openly—in our factories and marketplaces, in our homes, and through newspapers, magazines, radio, and television. This scientific knowledge and understanding has not just been kept the secret of the university. It has been shared with all, and everyone has learned something of the scientific method of thinking as a result. We do not hire specialists to drive our cars; we learn to operate them ourself—sometimes, even repair and rebuild them ourself. We do not live in an area such as California without learning a significant amount about earthquakes, or in the Midwest without learning about tornados. The new age of computers makes it even more necessary to learn to think scientifically—just to take one out of the box and hook it up to work satisfactorily! We may not grasp the scientific method in its fullest, or apply it consistently, but we have been exposed to it and forced by life to learn something about it.

The result has been the most rapid rise in thinking skills and mental capacity in the whole of human history. It is not the study of history or philosophy that has caused this progress. It is not the increase of leisure time. The enormous spurt forward that has occurred in human mental comprehension is primarily the result of the introduction of the scientific method of thinking as a practical tool for the enjoyment of life, even for the masses.

The scientific method has taught us how to use our God-given mental faculties to:

1. Observe and study the phenomena of life.

2.   Discern and verify facts, while rejecting deception.

3.   Analyze the facts to discover their value and significance.

4.   Develop practical applications for this knowledge.

As a consequence, science has also been responsible for another major achievement: the demystification of the phenomena of life. Science has driven a stake through the heart of ignorant superstition by teaching us to search for causes and verify observable facts. For this reason, we now understand that infectious illnesses are caused by germs, not "bad humors." We have broken the stigma of mental illness, by discovering the subtle biochemical causes of schizophrenia, depression, and hyperactivity. In the process, we have leaped beyond the archaic notion that mental illness stems from moral failure or demonic possession. Perhaps most importantly, science has demonstrated over and over the value of not fearing the unknown, because the unknown may turn out to be something extremely useful, such as a telephone, an airplane, or a computer.

It has not just been scientists who have benefited from the scientific method, in other words. All of us have, because the fruits of the divine workshop of science have become a normal part of modern life. We have all learned, to some degree at least, the value of objective study, reason, analysis, and experimentation in penetrating the fogs of ignorance and illusion. Even if we have no intention of pursuing a career in science, it is a good idea to have this foundation in reasoning. It teaches us how to focus the mind for any pragmatic application. Lacking it, we might possibly become a "saint" in our pursuit of spiritual growth—but we would be only a stupid saint.

Science has shown that no one need be stupid. The mental skills that the master architect and engineer need to build large factories and skyscrapers are also essential—not just useful—in the pursuit of spiritual studies. The spiritual person needs a well-trained capacity to study experiences, discern their meaning, validate conclusions, reason out new solutions, create new behaviors and standards, and revise basic ideas about who we are and what purpose we serve. Science teaches us to think in these ways.

In this regard, however, there is one aspect of life left for science to demystify. There is an inner or mystical core to science that most scientists ignore. It is a tradition in science that mystics study intangible and unknowable forces, while scientists study only observable and tangible forces. This time-worn distinction is not only wrong, but is in fact a barrier to the true work of both science and mysticism.

It is true that science has traditionally had a materialistic focus. But in the past one hundred years, much has happened scientifically to break down this rigid focus. Rœntgen discovered x-rays, that cannot be observed physically, and now these nonmaterial waves have become a keystone in medical diagnosis. Since then, science has discovered many other invisible, nonmaterial forces—television waves, ultrasound, and microwaves—and learned to put them to work. The current work of nuclear physicists with subatomic particles is taking science out of the dense physical dimension of life and into the etheric. Slowly but inevitably, the quest of science for new frontiers is leading it closer and closer to the realm of the mystic, even though many scientists have no appreciation for what is happening.

The truly innovative scientist, in fact, is constantly working with one or more of "the great ideas of God"—using his or her creative skill or intuitive talent to investigate the archetypal patterns of the mind of God to understand the nature of electricity or nuclear energy or physics. When Newton formulated his three great laws of motion, for example, he was translating an archetypal inspiration into practical laws of physics.

It must be understood that scientists do not invent the laws of nature. God determines the laws of nature and embodies them as archetypal patterns. The work of the scientist is to discover these abstract patterns and laws by dint of careful observation, first at the dense physical level, and then at progressively more subtle levels. Science cannot create anything; its task is to discover what already exists in nature—and how to harness it.

The poet Alexander Pope captured this truth about science perfectly in a famous epigram about Sir Isaac Newton:

> Nature and Nature's Laws lay hid in Night:
> God said: Let Newton be! And all was Light!

The discovery of electricity is another good example of the mystical core of science. The phenomena of electricity have always been a part of our life, in the form of lightning and other natural occurrences. They are part of nature. Yet out of the whole span of human history, we have been able to use electricity to light our homes and run our appliances for only one hundred years. Science had to discover what God had already created: the nature and laws of electricity, how to generate it, how to distribute it, and how to use it.

Almost all of the major breakthroughs of science, in fact, are actually "rediscoveries" of the principles and patterns of life. A scientist like Newton or Einstein is observing what already exists at a more subtle level than most scientists are investigating. In this way, the scientist is like a person who discovers an underground cave. The cave has been there for hundreds of thousands of years—it is "new" only in the sense of being new to the current generation of mankind. Once known, it can then be visited by others—perhaps even electrified, to make it more convenient and safe for visitors.

The ultimate role of science is to study and explore all dimensions of life—not just the physical realm. For this reason, the true scientist understands, at least intuitively, that the trained, creative imagination can be just as much a scientific tool for discovery as an expensively equipped laboratory. The tangible observations and experiments of the scientist are often just the prelude for tapping one or more of the Great Ideas of God.

These Great Ideas have always existed. Science is the adventure of employing the human mind to discern them and learn to use them. As such, this begins as a grand journey of discovery—the heart of which is our own self-discovery. To fulfill its commission, the divine workshop of science must relentlessly keep pushing back the frontiers of human knowledge at all levels. When the physical level cannot adequately explain physical phenomena, it becomes necessary to explore the inner levels that esotericists call the etheric plane. When etheric exploration is insufficient to explain observed phenomena, it becomes necessary to push back the frontier even further, to discover yet more subtle realms. And so the process must continue, until science finally reaches the level of causes—the Great Ideas and Laws of God.

It is at the level of causes and laws that we find the hand of divine intelligence at work, supervising and guiding the ongoing unfoldment of creation. When science can tap into this level, then it is able to work directly from divine blueprints—and becomes, at last, a divine builder itself, thereby fulfilling its mission.

In this way, the workshop of science demonstrates more completely than any other institution humanity's capacity to act as a co-Creator with God. Inspired by God's design, science discerns the hidden potentials of nature and translates these potentials into practical devices and resources that help humanity. As science takes each technological step forward, more of the potential of nature is tapped for our use.

Much of what science achieves daily for our benefit—the feeding of billions of people, curing disease, purifying the water supply, and much more—would have been seen as a miracle two hundred years ago. And, in truth, it is a miracle—a miracle that transforms God's Great Ideas into a practical reality here on earth.

THE PROBLEMS OF SCIENCE

Like all of the major institutions of society, science often fails to live up to its noble goals of understanding and mastering nature. New discoveries are inevitably challenged by the guardians of traditional thinking, while entire realms of potential exploration are routinely overlooked by scientific narrowmindness. As a result, scientific breakthroughs come more slowly and painfully than need be.

Some of these problems exist within science, while others exist with the way society restricts or inhibits scientific exploration. The attitude of the Hierarchy toward the development of nuclear energy, for example, is one of keen anticipation. The attitude of the public toward nuclear development, on the other hand, is highly reactionary and charged with irrational fear. Whenever the old and the comfortable become the measuring sticks for the new and unknown, most innovative ideas remain unexplored, untested, and undeveloped.

From society's viewpoint, the lost opportunities are great tragedies that almost no one comprehends. Who is to say, after all, that the intelligent development of nuclear energy might not be a key factor in eliminating the last vestiges of starvation from the planet? When opportunities for growth are spurned and resisted by humanity, society must inevitably suffer the cost.

It therefore behooves us to understand precisely how we cripple modern science in its mission to explore and utilize nature, both from within and without. The major sources of sabotage in the divine workshop of science are:

Professional arrogance. Science, like any human institution, has built up an establishment—a central core of "experts" who are the currently recognized authorities in any given field. Among all too many scientists, there is an unspoken belief that if any new innovations are going to emerge in science, they will be produced by these experts. In other words, the assumption is made that any legitimate breakthrough in a cure for cancer will probably come out of a laboratory of the National Institute of Health. An innovation in energy production will probably come out of a laboratory at the Massachusetts Institute of Technology. The idea that any valuable development could emerge in an independent researcher's "basement laboratory" is instantly rejected as unthinkable. As a result, almost all of the funds for scientific research are funneled toward highly visible, bureaucratically-controlled projects that do more to protect the status quo than contribute significant new knowledge to science.

This is scientific arrogance—and it is lethal to the scientific process. It equates scientific progress with peer recognition and funding, rather than genuine inspiration. It is a system designed to advance personal prestige, not scientific productivity.

Very few scientific breakthroughs occur by thinking in traditional ways. Usually, the process requires "thinking outside the box"—searching for ideas and evidence in new and unusual places, instead of the "obvious." For years, scientists tried to control the insect population of the world with lethal pesticides, but the pesticides damaged the soil and water supplies as well. By going outside the box, they have developed a new strategy—spraying bugs with birth control chemicals.

The ability to go outside the box introduces a higher level of creative thinking to the scientific process. Instead of approaching problems traditonally—starting with a problem and then methodically looking for a solution, scientists who work outside the box learn to take giant leaps of thought. They envision the big picture and the perfect end result of their labors, then work backward, trying to understand what steps must be taken to reach the final goal. In this way, the scientist borrows some of the thinking skills of the artist or writer—and is likely to achieve much more signficant breakthroughs than those using standard approaches.

A good example of a researcher who has worked in this way is John Ott, whose investigations into the nurturing and healing capacity of light are chronicled in his book, *Health and Light.* Through pragmatic experimentation, Ott discovered that the growth of plants and animals is directly affected by exposure to light. He also found that certain deficiencies of light adversely affected human health. Even though his experiments and results were carefully documented, many scientists sniffed openly at his work, labeling it "amateur."

These scientists suffer from what might be called "learned ignorance." They are very impressed with their knowledge of what cannot be done, and have no intention of wasting time exploring ideas they know to be useless and pointless.

The history of science is filled with the sad stories of such learned ignorance. In the nineteenth century, the scientific experts "knew" that it would be dangerous for trains to travel faster than twenty miles an hour, because it would cause passengers to have nosebleeds! These same scientists also "knew" that no aircraft made of wood and metal could ever sustain flight, because it would be too heavy to get off the ground. And even once air transportation became a fact of life, these same experts "knew" that it would be impossible to fly faster than the speed of sound, because the aircraft would explode! Once that belief was shattered, then still other experts "knew" that humanity would never be able to leave earth's gravity to travel to other planets, because we could never achieve escape velocity.

Fortunately, there have always been enough "oddball" scientists—as the experts label them—to ignore the stifling obstacles of accepted scientific thinking. Yet somehow science never learns to recognize the basic trap of smallmindedness and arrogance. Even today, the same inhibitions and vanity afflict the thinking of scientific experts in every university and reseach laboratory around the world.

Scientific arrogance would not be a problem if these experts kept their opinions to themselves. Unfortunately, being "authorities," they are often in a position to deny funding or—even worse, credibility—to the very scientific investigators who are humble and creative enough to look outside the box of the establishment. As a result, this arrogance actively thwarts a good deal of useful scientific research.

Very few people are willing to admit that they are sometimes arrogant and closeminded. Until science finds a way to curb this problem, however, such arrogance will continue to inhibit the true work of the divine workshop of science.

Junk science. The pursuit of science is meant to begin with the objective, honest study of the secrets of nature. Unfortunately, strong economic and political influences can often skew the outcome of "scientific research" to fit the need of its sponsor. This has resulted in the rise of what is called "junk science"—a spurious body of research that proves that all asbestos is dangerous (it is not), that cigarette smoking is safe (it is not), that silicone breast implants cause major health problems (they do not), that certain widely used pesticides are highly toxic (they are not), and that global warming is imminent and will be catastrophic (it is not).

In junk science, greed, fear, and the lust for power replace the true scientific methodology of careful investigation and reasoned interpretation. Some scientists are all too willing to sell out objectivity for funding, fame, and reputation. As Will Rogers once put it, "It isn't what we don't know that hurts us; it is what we know that ain't so that harms us." Junk science harms us—and science as an institution—by substituting false claims and assumptions for verifiable fact, at times even in the face of contradictory evidence. The price tag is often very high. In recent decades, schools across the country were forced by the federal government to remove all asbestos from their buildings—originally installed to meet government requirements for fire protection—on the basis of junk science findings that asbestos caused cancer. In fact, there was no link whatsoever between the kind of asbestos used in schools and the variety that might cause disease. In much the same way, huge corporations providing useful health care products and services have been bankrupted by a hysterical reliance on the findings of junk science research in breast cancer implants.

Worst of all, the blatant prejudice of junk science casts a dark shadow over the whole of science, and increases public distrust of important, meaningful work.

Tinkering. Just as many people who write are not skilled authors and many people who paint are not great artists, so also many people who wear white coats and work in research laboratories are not scientists. They are technicians—people who use scientific apparati to measure and quantify facts. They play an important support role in the work of medicine and science, but all too often the role they play is confused for that of science itself. Nothing could be further from the truth. Science is the work of discovering the unknown but knowable; it may involve weighing and measuring at times, but it goes far beyond the grunt work of "tinkering." It reveals the Great Ideas of God.

Scientists, for example, widely accept as accurate the testing for human intelligence on the basis of language, math, and spatial skills. These tests, however, are not as well constructed as most people believe; they miss many key areas of complex human intelligence. These key areas include kinesthetic intelligence, our coordination and athletic potential; intrapsychic intelligence, our awareness of self and our emotions; interpsychic intelligence, our awareness of the character and idiosyncrasies of others; and creative intelligence, the imagination and intuition. Even though these additional kinds of intelligence are clearly demonstrated by most geniuses and many other clearheaded, intelligent people, they are still largely ignored by the scientific (and educational) community.

The passion to tinker in some small area while ignoring the big picture is a common blind spot that inhibits science from fulfilling more of its promise. Scientific effort should eventually lead to a progressive expansion of our mastery of the phenomena of life. It should be holistic, seeking to draw in as much knowledge about any given subject as possible, from every conceivable realm. Tinkering, by contrast, keeps the scientist-technician stuck in one narrow groove, producing piles of data but no relevant breakthroughs. If, on rare occasion, the work of tinkering does accidentally lead into unknown territory, the technician almost always retreats.

While calibration and technical measurement are indispensable in the application of science—as in making sure of precise doses in powerful drugs or radiation treatments—it is never a substitute for first-rate scientific exploration and experimentation, based on tapping the Great Ideas of God.

Dense materialism. So far, science has mostly limited itself to studying and exploring the dense physical world, ignoring and—at times—even denying the existence of more subtle realms of life and human experience. As a result, much of science has become as focused in physical materialism as it was trapped, just a few centuries ago, in the belief that the earth was the center of the universe. The failure of science to investigate inner psychological and spiritual realms of life, and their connection to the physical plane, represents a tremendous blindness.

To some degree, of course, science has been forced into this posture by ignorant theologians and social scientists who resist the use of scientific methods to acquire a deeper understanding of their fields. If science dares to try to explain any facet of divine life in pragmatic terms, it is immediately condemned by religious ideologues. Still, certain scientists do their share to keep science focused in materialism, by rejecting and condemning any effort to study the sublime and intangible phenomena of life as a legitimate activity of science. They presume that if they cannot see, measure, or quantify anything, it does not exist. Yet true scientists know that we can study and measure intangible forces by their tangible effects and influences. Just as the famous "invisible man" of H.G. Wells left visible footprints that could be studied, so do the many invisible and unmeasurable forces of the subtle realms.

For generations, after all, psychologists have studied the unconscious mind by indirect means—through dreams, Rorschach tests, free association techniques, and patterns of behavioral responses. As a result, they have accumulated a huge body of knowledge about qualities and forces that are not directly visible or measurable.

The day will come when science recognizes that the mind itself can be trained to investigate directly the workings of the subconscious and unconscious minds. Until then, however, it is missing a great deal of understanding by failing to recognize the possibility of studying these dimensions indirectly. At first, physicists had no way to study the interior of atoms except by indirect observation, yet the information gathered in spite of this limitation led to the discovery of techniques for direct observation. There is no question that science can study the invisible and the intangible, if it has a will to do so. It is incongruous that some scientists eagerly accept the latest data from subatomic research, yet reject all information proving the reality and importance of the psychic dimensions of human life.

Ultimately, science must recognize that it is its duty to investigate all aspects of nature, not just selected ones. The practice of ignoring massive dimensions of our life experience calls into question the objectivity and accuracy of every scientific conclusion about life. After all, from the basic blueprints for all life forms to the laws that govern change, the most pivotal forces and ideas of life are rooted in sublime and intangible realms—the very realms science has yet to explore.

The misuse of technology. When Alfred Nobel invented dynamite, he thought only of its constructive uses in helping humanity. He was chagrined when less noble individuals found in dynamite the perfect tool for blowing up railroad tracks, breaking open safes, and creating terror. Science has an enormous power to enrich human life—but it also has the power inadvertently to terrorize society, when its inventions and developments fall into the wrong hands.

It is therefore important for scientists to take responsibility for the innovations and discoveries they make available for use by others. They sometimes need to follow the lead of Nikola Tesla, who reportedly suppressed many of his most remarkable discoveries because they involved a huge potential for misuse.

The ethical ambivalence found in science is nothing more than a reflection of the moral vacuum currently afflicting all of humanity. Until the human race does a better job establishing priorities based on spiritual principles, many useful discoveries will have to be withheld from science—by the Hierarchy.

Not all of the abuses of technology are overtly destructive. Many school systems, for example, are spending an outrageous amount of money acquiring expensive computer and video equipment, instead of investing the money in additional teachers and teacher aides. In the field of health, medications that were intended for cases of severe mental imbalance are now being prescribed for anyone having trouble coping with their marriage or a bad job. The medication works, by numbing their anxieties and fears, but it does nothing to resolve the underlying psychological problems. These people need more self-control and a lifestyle change, not just medication.

Hysterical science. On the other end of the spectrum from the abuse of scientific progress is the use of scientific findings to induce fear in mass consciousness. This is the "Chicken Little" approach to science, where scientific speculation about holes in the ozone layer becomes a dire threat of the end of human civilization as we know it within twenty years—or a weather prediction about the "el niño" currents in the Pacific become hysterical overreactions used by politicians to intimidate the public into rushing into unwarranted programs and changes.

The element that is lacking in this hysterical perversion of science is any kind of regard or respect for the tremendous power of Mother Nature to correct imbalances. Science is meant to be an objective, dispassionate exploration of life as it is. When it is captured and held hostage by hysterical reformers, the sane objectivity of all science is seriously crippled. Science needs to be the work of intelligent people who scrupulously protect the objectivity and integrity of their findings by not letting them become tainted by passion and hidden agendas.

Fear of technology. The worst example of hidden agendas sabotaging the work of science, of course, is to be found in those voices outside of science who arouse a militant fear and loathing of scientific progress in the masses, not through the use of hysterical science but by playing on the insecurities of the public. Some of these voices cloak their campaigns in religious tones; others employ political or even environmental propaganda to camouflage their true motives—a neurotic distrust and jealousy of the high technology lifestyle. They are more committed to telling the rest of us how wrong we are than they are in doing anything positive or constructive. They are, in essence, chronic malcontents and troublemakers who use science as a handy whipping boy.

In the 1980's, they led demonstrations against the use of nuclear reactors to generate energy. Today, they are more apt to be radical environmentalists, trying to save wolves, owls, insects, and tiny fish, at the expense of the welfare of their fellow human beings. Such troublemakers hide behind humanity's universal concern for cleaning up the planet, while insisting that we make sweeping but unnecessary changes in our lifestyle to accommodate their demands. They view science with hostility, since the work of science is to harness the rich potential of nature, not just leave it alone, as they would prefer.

The fear and divisiveness stirred up by such demagogues has spawned far worse problems in mass consciousness than anything science or technology has inadvertently done. The fear of technology can be highly contagious as well as irrational, and much mischief has already occurred in terms of skewing public opinion and common sense on the issues of the environment, science, and nuclear energy. It has actually gotten to the point in California where homeowners are not allowed to protect their property from brush fires, lest they uproot the habitat of an endangered species of rodents.

Fear of rational thinking. Very few people actually think about life, their work, or their goals—probably less than five percent on a regular basis. Many of the nonthinking members of society end up in positions of influence and power, however, because they are able to imitate the thinking process well enough. These people, whether in government, religion, education, or whatever, live in fear that their stupidity, double standards, distortions, and hypocrisy will be exposed. The calm logic and rationality of science is an especially powerful threat to them.

This fear of rationality is a major reason why certain administrators constantly shy away from any scientific testing of the effectiveness of their programs—and why numerous educators fiercely oppose standardized testing of students. It is the explanation why various religious groups suppress any suggestion that their beliefs harm mental health, and why some psychologists are reluctant to subject pet therapies to scientific scrutiny. It is also why some of the so-called "experts" on race issues do not want to hear that their efforts to teach gender and racial cooperation actually end up reinforcing stereotypes and increasing conflict.

There is never any reason for any intelligent person to fear the truth—which is always the goal of scientific pursuit.

Only those who have something to hide, because they are acting with less than integrity, will fear rational thinking. A society that winks its eye at deceptiveness, however, is one in which the true work of science is being crippled.

Fortunately, the scientific method contains within itself the power to correct these problems and overcome them. All it needs is a more consistent effort from the intelligent people in society to view the truth as a friend, even when it exposes our previous assumptions. Science has done yeoman work thus far in clearing away the deceptions and fogs that have troubled humanity for centuries; there is no need for any of us to shirk in supporting it to continue to do the same in the years ahead.

THE CURRENT WORK OF SCIENCE

The work of the divine workshop of science, like all major human institutions, is supported by the Hierarchy. But the interest of the Hierarchy in science is vastly different from that of the average person, who is largely excited by technology, gadgetry, and the challenge of harnessing nature. The Hierarchy, by contrast, is more interested in the pursuit of science as it trains and expands human thinking—and awakens the scientific mind to the need to explore the inner, subtle realms of life, which will of course lead to the scientific discovery of the reality of the soul and God.

There are two facets to the Hierarchy's involvement in modern science. The first focuses on directing science into profitable new areas for investigating the rich possibilities of physical life. The second is aimed at encouraging scientists to begin exploring the inner realms of life.

There are a number of key areas of human living which will be revolutionized by scientific breakthroughs in the coming years. These include:

1. The search for renewable energy sources. We cannot rely on fossil fuels indefinitely; science needs to explore the development and application of alternate kinds of energy production. These include experiments in many diverse technologies, from harnessing the radiation of the sun or tapping the energy within wind currents, to cultivating rapidly growing plants as new sources for combustible fuels.

2. The more efficient use of energy. Major strides are being made in research to build engines and motors that burn energy more efficiently, for use in everything from automobiles to refrigerators. One of the most exciting areas of research in this regard is in the area of the superconductivity of energy.

3. The genetic manipulation of plants and animals to increase food production. Vegetables of all kinds are being genetically improved to create plants that are more disease-resistant and produce a greater harvest. Experiments are likewise being conducted to improve milk production from cows.

4. Genetic treatments for human diseases. Dramatic breakthroughs are occurring which will lead to far better treatments of all kinds of diseases in the future.

5. Improved meteorological predictions of weather trends. Increasing sophistication in predicting the weather helps society in many ways, from agriculture to airplane travel.

6. Greater accessibility to knowledge. Recent breakthroughs with computers and miniaturization have led to an explosion in our ability to package knowledge on compact discs and make them readily accessible to everyone. Medical schools are now using virtual reality simulations to teach anatomy to students.

7. The advent of the world wide web. The creation and expansion of the internet is a project of great importance that will affect virtually every facet of our lives, from the way we approach schooling to the way we perform our work. It will soon be possible, for example, for a sales person in St. Louis to present a new project to buyers in Paris, without ever leav-

ing his or her office.   The ramifications of the internet are tremendous.

Each of these projects represents an area of scientific research in progress, leading to the development and building of new methodologies, devices, and systems.   Even though our personal life may not be touched directly by the investigative activities of science, we benefit directly from the new approaches and practices of banking, farming, transportation, and education that are built on top of the foundation of scientific innovation.

The other key way the Hierarchy influences science is by encouraging individual scientists to become more aware of and responsive to the inner nature of their work.

The highest priority of the Hierarchy in this regard is to use science as a means of strengthening the mental faculties of humanity. As the scientific method spreads to every corner of the globe, it helps the race become more focused in the mind and more competent in the use of our rational faculties. At this stage in human evolution, only a small percentage of humanity is focused in the mind; the vast majority is centered in the emotions.   In other words, most people give more credence to feelings than to understanding, evaluate opportunities and the issues of life through the filter of the emotions rather than the lens of the mind, and rely on their wishes and desires to motivate and direct them, instead of ideas or the spiritual will.

This entrapment in the emotions must change before the human race can fulfill its spiritual destiny. Without ignoring or suppressing the emotions, human beings need to become focused in the mind and its rational skills of perception, evaluation, and direction. This shift from an emotional to a mental focus will enable people to use their emotions wisely instead of blindly, and tap more of their inner design for maturity. It will let them discern cause from effect—a vital step in learning from experience. It will also liberate them from much of the suffering that torments so many people, by helping them discover the larger context and picture into which they fit.

The end result of this evolutionary work is to produce a fully aware, mature spiritual adult who is able to discern and cooperate with the presence of Divine Intelligence. The workshops of education, the arts, and religion certainly make major contributions to this evolutionary thrust, but it is science that plays the central role of teaching people to think rationally and objectively.

The effort to move humanity from its emotional focus to a more mental one has already met with strong resistance. Critics wail that the effort to develop the mind is actually just a disguised plot to kill off the emotions. They insist that only the emotions fully humanize a person—that a rational person is insensitive, cold, and cruel. Then, in a stretch of amazing arrogance, they equate the emotions with creativity and the soul, thereby demeaning the divine life to a mere feeling! Even though such claims are palpably not true, they are highly attractive and persuasive to emotionally-based individuals. So they continue to be embraced by a wide range of "authorities" in the human family.

Still, the evolutionary work of science moves forward. With each passing generation, more and more people are learning to respect the noble human mind and are taking steps, no matter how tentative, in moving from an emotional focus to a mental one. There are four major ways the divine workshop of science spearheads this effort:

1. By exposing the prevalence of propaganda in shaping human thought. Whenever a new quality or activity is introduced, it will be recognized first through its perverse misuse, and only later through its correct application. This is the law of the dominating lower. It is illustrated by the fact that pornography was the first thing that made the internet well known. For the last few centuries, the clever misuse of the mind has been more prevalent than the constructive use of our rational faculties. As a result, we have seen a phenomenal increase in propagandizing—for example, distorting issues, demonizing the opposition, and appealing directly to people's fears. Ideas and principles have been shoved aside. Demagogues and ideologues have had a field day. Truth has been buried in an avalanche of posturing, positioning, and prostituting. A tremendous number of bad ideas have been accepted in its place.

Fortunately, the very falseness of any concept is the seed of its own destruction. The exposure of propaganda is achieved simply by telling the whole story on any issue, warts and all, and then letting common sense rule.

2. By breaking up the elitist control of the dissemination of ideas. In every major institution of society, it has been the habit of the elite to guard the door by which new ideas pass into general knowledge and use, so that not too much information gets into the hands of thinking people. The news media, for example, does more to filter out news than it does to report it. So do the official journals of almost every professional society. In order to get at the truth, it is necessary to develop alternative avenues of inquiry. Fortunately, the recent explosion in use of the internet, e-mail, direct satellite communications, compact disks, and newsletters is reopening the door to a free flow of information. People are once again beginning to dare to tell the truth that the mainstream media ignores.

3. By exposing hypocrisy and double standards. One of the primary ways that the mighty fall is by condemning behavior in others that they routinely engage in themselves. Sooner or later, someone notices the discrepancy and blows the whistle exposing their corrupt behavior and hypocrisy. We are meant to reflect on these exposés, and eliminate any traces of hypocrisy from our own value system and thinking.

4. By raising intellectual standards at all levels. As science has become more firmly established, and brought certain standards and criteria with it, an opposing effort has been launched to loosen rigorous intellectual standards, under the guise of providing opportunity for everyone and respecting all opinions. The result has been the substitution of intellectual dishonesty for integrity and forthrightness. This trend has now reached the point where many "experts" blithely pronounce that women can never be sexists, because they can only be victims of sex, and assert equally that blacks can never be racists, because they are victims of racism.

It is hard to predict how much lower we can go in relaxing intellectual standards, but the bottom of the pit is regrettably within range. It is time for intelligent people to recognize and reaffirm their responsibility to support the highest intellectual standards possible, and not be swayed by the doubletalk of dishonest people.

While it may not seem to be science's responsibility to promote these changes, it is a vital part of its work. Science is the guardian of the knowledge of what is—and ultimately, the doorway to the Great Ideas of God. Any misuse or perversion of the thinking process therefore must be corrected by the shining example of science, as it reveals the full potential of the well-trained human mind.

In addition to shifting the focus of society from the emotions to the mind, the divine workshop of science is also busy subtly extolling the use of scientific objectivity and rationality in every phase of human living. True scientists formulate rational decisions about their projects only after they have made a thorough study and observation of all of the facts and factors involved. Contrast this approach to that of most people as they interact with a problem; feelings, biases, and fears will cancel out rational insight every time. Even normally intelligent people sometimes seem to wear a set of blinders that paralyzes their minds whenever an important personal issue must be decided or resolved.

In truth, scientists likewise set aside their scientific objectivity when it comes to making many personal decisions. There is much to be done before large numbers of humanity make the scientific approach a standard feature of daily living. But the seed has been planted, and is being cultivated by the Hierarchy. It is of vital importance to the future of humanity that this particular seed be protected and fertilized, so that it may grow.

Another important goal of the Hierarchy in using the divine workshop of science to guide humanity is to help us comprehend that all things visible are supported by a greater and divine life, design, and laws. At first, it may seem as if this lesson falls more into the province of religion than science. But religions have never progressed beyond the point of encouraging their followers to believe in God and the divine life. It is the work of science, as it peels back the layers of our ignorance, that will reveal the designs and laws of divine life in such a way that we can understand them. Already, it has accurately defined a number of the laws governing life, even though science as yet has not linked them to a divine origin.

Currently, humanity seems to be comfortable with the notion that all that is required of it is to "accept" the mysteries of life and believe in God. We have even been assured by "experts" that most of these mysteries are forever unknowable.

With mentally lazy attitudes like that, they probably would be unknowable forever! Nonetheless, the Creator has designed us to learn to use the mind to penetrate these mysteries and understand them. Science holds the key to this understanding. As it continues to study and observe the laws it has already codified, it will discover the inner, divine patterns from which they arise. This breakthrough will revolutionize human thinking far more than the whole of the Renaissance. It will reveal the intelligent basis for the whole of nature, from rocks to humans to angels.

As we realize that the Hierarchy is striving to use science in these ways, we will also find that it is quietly training us to become explorers of the divine. Discovering the presence of divine life, with its laws and Great Ideas, will be a revolutionary step for both science and humanity—but it will be just a first step. It will open the door to a whole new possibility—that of translating divine patterns, forces, and laws into activity and form on earth.

This lesson will be learned first through the transformation of our own character and the quality of the work we perform to more fully embody and express divine illumination. Eventually, however, it is meant to spread out and embrace the work of society as a whole. This will only be possible when enough people have learned to adopt the scientific approach to living as their primary focus.

Naturally, the methods of exploring the divine life will vary from person to person, depending upon temperament and training. Some will find it easiest to explore the divine realms of life through their creative activities. Others will sense the spiritual purpose of their work, and seek to honor it. Those who are filled with goodwill and charity will discover the redemptive power of divine inclusiveness. All will realize, however, that their contact with divine life is greatly enriching the quality of their daily work.

But the activities of the divine workshop of science extend even beyond this breakthrough. It is also the job of science to demonstrate that divine revelation is continuous and perfectly natural. Many religious authorities insist that divine revelation ceased two thousand years ago. This is nonsense. The potential for divine revelation, both in our individual lives and in the life of humanity, continues to exist—and can be a daily occurrence, once we learn to make proper contact with divine life.

Science is forever seeking to unlock the secrets of nature—and has been quite successful, as far as it has gone. It just needs to extend its inquiry to every aspect of life—specifically, to the inner psychological and spiritual realms it has tended to overlook and ignore.

This is not as far-fetched as it may seem at first. Scientific investigators could receive revelation consciously, by turning their attention in the right direction. Health professionals would be able to discover the laws of health by carefully observing the inner forms that maintain physical and emotional health. Psychologists could discover the laws governing right human relationships by tapping the inner elements that increase peace of mind and cooperation. Teachers could examine the basic design of the inner impulse to grow by interacting with students intuitively as well as physically. As a result, they would be able to demonstrate conclusively what makes Johnny learn—and what hinders him.

The opportunity to reveal divine life in such pragmatic ways lies well within the grasp of science. It simply needs to outgrow its obsession with the dense material planes of life and begin to discern the divine design for wholeness for each individual—and for society.

One of the most interesting ways that the divine workshop of science is influencing humanity is by demonstrating the universal nature of life. The laws of physics are the same in every culture and every nation. They cannot be changed by popular vote; they must be obeyed. We may choose to disbelieve in the law of gravity, but this belief will not prevent us from falling to the ground if we step off the top of a building.

Science has already demonstrated this principle of universality in terms of physical laws. Eventually, it will also prove its applicability to the emotions and the mind. So far, however, it has not been adequately demonstrated. Indeed, intelligent people often scoff at any accountability to divine life for our thoughts and actions. They have seen too many misdeeds seem to go unpunished to believe otherwise.

Nonetheless, just as boiling water will inevitably scald human skin, if spilled on it, so also overheated emotions will seriously harm our psychological makeup. Because the substance of our emotions is more subtle than the dense physical body, the harm we do in these ways is not always immediately apparent. But it is still quite real. Repeated moments of sadness eventually build into a pattern of depression. Repeated moments of anger lead eventually to a permanent mood of hostility.

Even when this fact of divine life is confirmed by science, as it will be, there will be people who will attempt to lie and cheat in order to avoid having to face their own inner nature. It will take them a bit longer to discover that scientific principles cannot be denied or shortcircuited. In general, however, the whole of humanity will be vastly enriched by the discovery that we are affected just as much by divine laws as we are by laws of physics.

Finally, it is also the privilege of the divine workshop of science to help us discover that each of us individually, and humanity as a whole, has an active and meaningful role to play in the universe. Many good people know this truth intuitively, but rarely activate it in any purposeful or powerful way. They accept their status passively. We cannot manifest our full destiny, however, until we become a creative agent of these divine and universal forces. We must become an explorer of the divine, a scientist of the inner side of life.

It may sound odd to an artist or diplomat or factory worker to think of themselves as a scientist, but this is the ideal model to inspire each of us. The creative scientist must probe beyond what is known to discover what lies behind it. He must then become the divine builder, working directly with the divine laws and designs that govern life on this planet. Just so, each of us must become a discoverer of the inner realms of life, and learn to use the rich treasures and resources we find there.

In other words, the scientist and the mystic must merge within each of us, if we are ever to discover and understand our true role in life. It is not that the scientist should dominate the mystic, or the mystic govern the scientist—but that both halves of the whole respect and cooperate with its companion.

This is the ultimate labor of science, therefore: to help us understand God and the divine laws and designs that guide and direct our evolution. Only science can teach us the full significance of what it means to be in awe of the Creator, and reveal to us the full scope of the work that is yet to be done.

SUPPORTING THE WORK OF SCIENCE

We do not have to be a chemist or a botanist in order to help support these spiritual projects of the divine workshop of science. In fact, some of the most effective contributions to the work of science in the past fifty years have come from people who were not educated as scientists or engaged in scientific work. Just becoming more aware and rational as a thinking person will do much to support the inner workings of science. The linchpin of all scientific work is to think and act in a scientific style. Learning to think in this fashion is not a deep mystery reserved only for rocket scientists and advanced members of esoteric schools. There are a number of ways each of us can lend our support:

1. By learning to think clearly. We should make it a personal goal to learn to recognize the difference between thinking and feeling. Whenever we evaluate an idea or person on the basis of our likes or dislikes, we are using our emotions, not reason. We might occasionally use the mind to generate rationalizations to support our emotionally-based conclusion, but this only plunges us further into confusion. Using the emotions instead of the mind to evaluate life and make decisions is a major way that we preserve prejudices, blind ourself to reality, and create mischief. When we use the mind to think, by contrast, we set aside our personal preferences and penetrate to the heart of the issue, where we can comprehend its meaning and potential—and make relevant conclusions and useful decisions.

Only people who have learned to think clearly can discern and cooperate with the ongoing projects of the divine workshop of science. Emotionally-based people may from time to time receive glimpses of spiritual realities, but they are severely handicapped in understanding them or even relating them properly to their own lives.

2. By learning to observe life carefully. If we are going to think, we need to be able to work with original and accurate information. Emotionally-based people often never hear or see much of what goes on around them, because they are too busy projecting their own assumptions about what is happening. Hostile people frequently hear insults and threats that were never made. Depressed people often think they have been criticized or rejected by others, even though nothing of the sort occurred. Hysterical people often "remember" bizarre events that never transpired. Casual thinkers regularly assume that everything they hear or read in the papers is true, without bothering to verify or crosscheck it.

If we begin the thinking process with distorted information or wholly imaginary events, however, we cannot hope to draw correct conclusions. As obvious as this statement is, it does not deter most everyone from regularly letting their emotions condition what they hear, see, and remember. Day in and day out, they pollute their belief systems with self-serving urges, wishes, cultural traditions, and raw prejudice.

In order to support the work of science, we must therefore master the skill of observing with detachment what actually happens in life, without distorting it emotionally. We must also make sure that we observe thoroughly—and not just jump to conclusions based on partial information.

3. By digesting input completely. Even if we understand all of the relevant facts of a situation, we still may make a snap judgment that sabotages the thinking process.

Some people, of course, are certain that all snap judgments represent divine illumination. More often, however, they turn out to be leaps to judgment that had nothing to do with intelligence, rationality, or the intuition.

Rational thought is still so rare that most people put more thought into purchasing a new piece of furniture than in making a major life decision. We need to digest all of the relevant input before formulating our decision. This is best done by asking ourself a set of probing questions: What do I really need? How will I know when I get it? What could go wrong? What is the best I can reasonably expect? What do I have to do to prepare myself for this change? How might I sabotage the outcome if I am careless? What do I have to do to sustain this new direction, once it appears? What is the creative challenge within this issue? What is the payoff? Are there any downsides? What new responsibilities are implied by choosing this course?

People who opt for divorce after twenty years of marriage because they feel romantically unfulfilled, for example, are listening far too much to their emotions and not enough to rational thought. They are forgetting the commitments they have made, ignoring the strengths of the marriage, and overlooking the impact such a change will make on their spouse, children, and friends. They are flouting the wisdom and love of their own higher self, who set up the marriage in the first place and has used it as a significant element of personal destiny.

A rational person, of course, is not immune from making mistakes. Nonetheless, he will be deceived far less often and would probably avoid a complete disaster. He will be more in tune with the larger picture and context of any specific situation. He will also be less likely to generalize from too little data.

It should be obvious that a lot of the pain and suffering that plague the lives of emotionally-based people are rapidly outgrown as we become more rational in our approach to life. But there are even greater benefits to us as we turn the mind to dealing with national and international issues. If the citizens of this country were suddenly to become rational tomorrow, many politicians currently in office would be recalled immediately. The bloated inefficiency of government bureaucracy would no longer be tolerated; reforms would be demanded. Special treatment of "disadvantaged" groups would be discontinued. The labor unions and management would suddenly recognize that they share common goals.

Most importantly, the capacity to weigh the conditions of life thoughtfully and thoroughly enables us to become receptive to divine guidance and intelligence. The person who is still dominated by the emotions will willingly exchange contact with the soul for a warm feeling. Yet the person who is able to think rationally will gradually become aware of the guidance from the higher self, and learn to rely on it.

4. By working creatively. Far too many people sleep-walk through life. They are passive. They listen but do not hear. They look but do not see. They live but do not grow. Their thinking is controlled entirely by tradition. Their emotions are governed by conventional beliefs. Their behavior is routine and predictable. Such people resemble zombies more than living humans. Their worlds are very small, and they rarely undergo significant change, unless it comes from external sources. They suffer misfortune as much as anyone, but they endure it rather than grow from it.

If we are going to get on the wavelength of divine life, we need to be awake and alert. We need to become more involved in living than just stumbling through the paces. We need to become creative.

Becoming creative is not as difficult as it may seem at first. It simply means that we adopt a lifetstyle based on the fact that we live and move and have our being within a larger, spiritual context—and this divine realm contains all kinds of innovative and creative ideas and forces we can tap to enrich our personal self-expression. We do not have to be content with whining and bitching about problems; we can harness the joy of divine life and express it through everything we do. This is a creative act! Nor do we have to remain depressed because we do not approve of our life. We can tap the optimism and hope of the life of spirit to transform our attitudes—toward work, toward others, and toward life itself. This, too, is a creative act.

In short, we stand ready to participate with the divine presence in active, intelligent, and skillful ways—not just to know, but to do and be in new and useful ways. We become a true scientist in our own life.

5. By learning to cooperate with divine life. It is not enough just to become creative. We must also learn that the universe is alive and intelligent and ready to help us, if we will learn to cooperate with it. Even when we do awaken from the zombie-like state of the uncreative person, there still remains the danger that we will look around us and conclude that the rest of the world is relatively dead—and treat it as such. We will see the starvation and poverty and pessimism that abounds in the world and conclude that the world's problems are insurmountable. We may even conclude that God pretty much botched the whole effort.

If we form such a belief, however, we will be missing the most obvious fact of all: that the universe is alive and well and eager to interact with us. Even though society is caught in the clutches of pessimism, it is still growing. Just because humanity has not eliminated starvation and poverty does not mean that God has botched the effort. It just means our eyes are still sealed shut.

If we open our eyes—intuitively—we will discover that the universe is very much alive, full of dynamic and powerful archetypal forces and ideas, and constantly guiding and directing humanity to create a more perfect society. These archetypal forces are available for our inspection and investigation, and can be used to transform human life into the greatness and glory that is its destiny.

There are a number of other ways we can prove that the universe is alive and creative:

• We can discover the underlying patterns of our own destiny. Instead of wondering why the higher self would let us suffer through the misery of our life, we begin to see these misfortunes and setbacks as marvelous opportunities for new growth and responsibility.

• We can learn to cooperate with divine laws and patterns, instead of seeing how long we can "get away" with immature behavior. As a result, we establish a mature code of ethics and behavior that guides our life.

• We can recognize that the living universe is a resource that can help us cope with problems, heal illnesses, and support us in times of hardship.

• We can activate the support of divine life by initiating new projects, confident that the universe will respond to our creative efforts and help us apply our talents and knowledge in successful ways.

In short, we become a practical scientist, capable of blending intelligence with inspiration.

6. By approaching the future with constructive optimism. Many intellectually developed people affect a cynical, pessimistic attitude toward humanity and its future, which colors the way they think about God and mankind. These people betray their own lack of faith in the Hierarchy and the guidance of God.

In order to support the work of the divine workshop of science, we must become solution-oriented. As long as we are focused primarily in the problems of life—individual or collective—we cannot hope to acquire the long range vision needed to solve the issues facing ourself and society today. We must see clearly that pessimism cripples our capacity to make progress, whereas optimism opens up new possibilities.

The proper perspective begins with being able to discriminate between a problem and a solution in progress. When we are physically ill, for example, our body may vomit in order to expel the source of its trouble. The average person might well define the vomiting as the real problem, but it is not — it is part of the solution. Just so, some of the "problems" of life are actually solutions in progress, when viewed scientifically.

A scandal in government, for example, tends to delight pessimists everywhere, especially in the press, who see it as another confirmation of their dark view of society. Yet the scandal may have been carefully arranged by the Hierarchy as part of an effort to expose corruption and promote honest government. The awakening of the public to the problem is, in fact, a cause for great optimism.

In general, those who intend to work with the Hierarchy must assume that all problems have solutions. But this precept must not be interpreted or applied naïvely. Just as an individual's problems may be buried under many subconscious layers, so also the problems of society as a whole may well involve many strata of underlying issues. Trying to solve the surface problem with a quick-fix cure may well worsen the deeper conflicts.

A problem such as class bigotry cannot be resolved in a single generation, or by a single stroke of legislation, no matter how much starry-eyed idealists think it should be. The solution to a problem of this nature often requires major upheavals in tradition, values, and lifestyle. As such, several generations may well be required to produce true change. For this reason, the programs for social change launched by the Hierarchy are usually designed to embrace several centuries of struggle, debate, and even confrontation.

It is not the responsibility of any individual spiritual person to try to embrace the full Plan of the Hierarchy; it simply would not be possible. Instead, we are meant to concentrate on "our part of the Plan"—for example, protesting the use of junk science to support local projects, working within our own circle to support more rigorous intellectual standards, and demonstrating in our own life the essence of scientific discovery.

7. Solving problems rationally. Most people react to problems with their emotions. They become hysterical. They fear the worst. They choose up sides. They affix blame. None of these emotional reactions will ever resolve a problem, however. Usually, they will make it worse. The only way to solve any problem, personal or societal, is to think it through rationally and analytically. We must set aside emotional factors, personal agendas, old grudges, and grievances in favor of reasoning out what positive steps can be taken to resolve the underlying issues. Instead of just lamenting mistakes and demanding change, we should strive to repair whatever needs to be fixed.

The scientific approach will not work magic, but it at least lifts our efforts to solve problems to a higher plateau. It redefines problems rationally, giving us a starting place. The effort to solve life's problem rationally is therefore an enormous contribution to the whole of the scientific process, and something each spiritual person should make a top priority.

8. Understanding that reason must be added to faith. Religion has spawned a horrible misunderstanding that the intellect interferes with faith. Many popular authorities even today preach that God must be accepted on faith alone, and that reason sabotages this faith.

In actual fact, faith and reason are natural companions. A pessimistic, weak intellect might interfere with faith, but wisdom will only enrich it. The intelligent use of faith adds skill to our use of divine life. Wisdom strengthens faith by adding understanding to it. Faith returns the favor by opening doors that our understanding has not yet discovered.

It only makes sense that the more we comprehend the ways of God, the more we can follow them. The more we understand God's will, the more we can consciously work to fulfill it.

The more we grasp the difference between personal and divine love, the more we can protect ourself from self-deception. It is true that much of God's Creation still remains unknown to us. But this is not because divine life is unknowable. It just remains undiscovered and therefore unknown. Sooner or later, science will penetrate these mysteries, and reveal them.

We are designed to make these discoveries—the noble human mind is God's endowment in us for this precise purpose. But as long as the mind remains earthbound and concrete in its focus, it finds it difficult to work with sublime and abstract ideas—God's Great Ideas. We must therefore train the mind to work abstractly as well as analytically, before we can hope to comprehend the ways of spirit or understand the Plan of the Hierarchy. Many generations have struggled successfully to take these steps, and we will be able to as well.

Our Creator is intelligent and has blessed us with a tremendous potential to expand our awareness beyond the mundane. God wants us to be wise as well as compassionate. God wants us to understand as well as have faith. It is our responsibility to accept this challenge and pursue both wisdom and love. We must make the mind an ally with the heart.

These are the primary ways that we can support the work of science, regardless of our focus in life. The major work of science is to penetrate the mind of God and discover the divine archetypal forces which are the blueprints of human culture and destiny. As each of us learns to work mentally in this way, we become the true spiritual scientist, able to translate the laws and principles of God into ideas and programs for ourself and the whole human family.

The work of the spiritual scientist is to be the master builder for the whole world. Science has already demonstrated a tremendous capacity to embrace this role and fulfill it. Because of science and the scientific method, we can look forward to a future filled with breathtaking new discoveries and technological breakthroughs.

The Divine
Workshop of Commerce

THE ENGINE OF SOCIETY

One of the many names humanity has employed for heaven is the term "Providence." It recognizes that divine life is the source of all good things, and provides for each of us all that we need to prosper. And yet, we often believe that our enjoyment of Providence is somehow postponed. Even though the Christ repeatedly told us that the kingdom of God is at hand, we refuse to see the evidence of it—especially the evidence of Providence. We see only the necessity of enlisting ourselves in the work of business and commerce, sweating and laboring to earn our daily bread. As a result, we often end up resenting the need to work and equate it with drudgery, yearning for the time when we can follow our own wishes.

To many people, in fact, business is almost a polar opposite of anything divine. Commerce deals with money, profit, and materialism. They therefore presume that it breeds selfishness, greed, and ambition. It encourages exploitation, ruthlessness, and corruption. For these reasons, such people view business and commerce with suspicion and distrust. It may be necessary, but in their opinion, it is definitely a necessary evil.

This bias runs throughout society. Television reinforces it in virtually every show it airs. Academics sneer at business with pecksniffian arrogance. Protesters of every stripe and shade accuse it of propagating calamities from nuclear wastes to the destruction of the rain forest. It is small wonder that almost everyone views business and commerce with a jaundiced eye—even many of those who receive their weekly paychecks from the "ogre" of business.

This prejudice against business is most unfortunate, and has crippled human thinking for far too long. Business has not yet cornered the market on greed, selfishness, or exploitation. Greed and corruption are much more evident in government. Selfishness is rampant today in professional educational circles. And who can top the record of organized religion in the field of exploitation?

Yes, business does have its share of problems. It is charged with developing and managing the great abundance of this planet, and so it inevitably suffers from abuse and mismanagement. These abuses, however, pale in comparison to the evils inflicted upon society by other, more respected institutions of society—academia, religion, and even the arts.

If these abuses are no worse, and usually less severe, than those found in the rest of society, then why is business seen in such a prejudicial light? The reason is simple. Because business is involved in harnessing and expanding the tangible wealth of the planet, it has become the object of massive but irrational envy and attack from the truly greedy, selfish, and exploitive elements of society. The "have nots," as they are called, are bitterly jealous of the wealth they presume business to have. And so they attack business and commerce, in the mistaken belief that they are attacking their poverty. In truth, however, they are attacking the only system that can relieve their poverty—the great war horse that generates and distributes wealth to everyone on the planet.

Business, in fact, is the power on earth that enables the other institutions of society to survive. It is business that creates personal and corporate income that is then taxed by the government, and used to finance its projects. It is business that feeds and clothes the human family, and provides enough extra cash to send children through college, fund our great churches, support the arts, and underwrite scientific investigations. It is business that funnels billions of dollars every year into philanthropic activities—everything from feeding the poor and housing the homeless to rewarding great humanitarian and scientific breakthroughs. Take away the productivity of business, and all of the other institutions of society collapse, bankrupt.

Can individuals in business be selfish, mean, and corrupt? Of course—just as they can be in any walk of life. Is business as a whole always fair and just in how it treats human and natural resources? Of course not—it is run by fallible human beings. But does it have a heart, a mind, and a noble soul? Definitely!

The heart of business is its ability—when not constrained by government—to create the jobs that employ the vast population on earth. As a result, each individual has the opportunity to be self-supporting and earn his or her fair portion of abundance.

The mind of business is its ability to create and seize opportunity to take wealth, invest it, and create even more wealth—so that more people can be employed and become self-sufficient.

The soul of business is its power to develop and organize the resources of civilization. Business is always in the forefront of human exploration. It was commerce that spurred Marco Polo and Christopher Columbus to make their journeys into the unknown—and shrink the size of the world. It was commerce that led to the development of diplomatic ties among countries. And today, it is commerce that is leading the way in demonstrating that world cooperation is far more profitable than world conflict and struggle.

Naturally, not everyone agrees with this view of business. But all anyone needs to do is look at the record. Marxist societies eliminate free enterprise and put commerce under the iron fist of the government. The result, time after time, has been unparalleled disaster. By its very nature, bureaucracy, no matter how well trained and intentioned, performs very poorly in creating wealth. The decision-making process of committees and strategic plans blunts the entrepreneurial edge needed to generate wealth. Instead of an explosion of opportunity, government control of business creates an implosion—and all of society suffers with it.

Business is nothing less than the engine that drives the economy upon which all people and nations depend. It is society's vehicle for organizing, creating, and distributing the innate wealth of the earth. It taps the wealth of every level of life on the planet—mineral, vegetable, animal, and human—and finds ways to put this wealth to work for the good of society. It may be science that first discovered the means of harnessing electricity, but it was business that laid the wires and cables that bring electricity to us. It is business that generates the electricity. And it is business that supplies us with computers, vacuum cleaners, radios, televisions, toaster ovens, and countless other devices that run on electricity. Pull the plug on business, and most of the inventions of science would disappear into the dark. Just so, it may be a health researcher who initially discovers a serum that cures a dreaded disease, but it is business that manufactures the medicine and makes it available through our local pharmacy.

In addition to being the driving force behind the economy of mankind, business and commerce serve a number of inner, spiritual purposes. Business demonstrates the workings of the law of increase and the law of compensation. It teaches us the right use of authority, pragmatic organization, productivity, and problem solving. It is, moreover, the only force that can establish economic freedom, which is perhaps the one freedom that truly guarantees individual liberty.

These are the fruits of the divine workshop of business and commerce. If we understand how they enrich the life of humanity, we will comprehend the noble purposes of business more fully—and revise our niggardly attitudes toward it. It may therefore be useful to examine these three great spiritual expressions of commerce more thoroughly.

Business reveals to us the divine laws of increase and compensation. Many people snigger when the word "profit" is mentioned, as though it is somehow vulgar. Some sidewalk philosophers and troublemakers actually argue that profit is exploitative, and that commerce should be based on a goal of "zero return." Yet one of the strongest currents of divine life is the impulse to grow: we are told as early as Genesis "to be fruitful and multiply." Indeed, one of the divine laws governing all of life is the law of increase. We are given the seed. If we plant it, we shall reap abundance. If we hoard it, we shall reap nothing. The seed may be artistic talent, a thirst for scientific discovery, a knack for teaching, or skills in business. If we invest them, we will generate abundance. We take what has been given us, and increase it. No institution in life portrays this law for us more dramatically and consistently than commerce. The profits of commerce throughout the ages have enabled us to create the abundance of our present civilization.

A corollary to the law of increase is the law of compensation, which might also be called the law of accountability. The law of increase applies to any seed we plant—wholesome or rotten. If we sow the seed of bad taste, we will harvest spoiled fruit. If we plant seeds of lies and misinformation, we will harvest confusion and treachery. The law of compensation helps us understand this principle and learn to become accountable for our motives and acts. Nowhere is this principle more regularly illustrated than in business.

Because business generates the wealth of society, it naturally attracts people who wish to get something for next to nothing—people who would rather use manipulation and exploitation than skills and hard work. Some of these people manage to achieve a measure of success, but sooner or later the law of compensation holds them accountable, and they lose it. They may be indicted and convicted for criminal offenses; they may simply be fired. In some cases, they are destroyed by an even more unethical operator; in others, they lose the loyalty of their customer base. The principles of accountability upon which commerce is founded will not tolerate such greed and selfishness for very long.

In this regard, the field of business is an excellent school for those people who naïvely believe that they create their own reality and that everything is relative. It is true that we can exercise free will in choosing how to act; we can be a liar, thief, or extortionist if we wish. But we cannot select the consequences of these actions. The price we must pay for our indiscretions is determined by divine law—the law of compensation.

In other words, if we cheat others, life will eventually exact compensation. The same will occur if we knowingly provide inferior goods or services to others. The liar loses what he has gained by being deceived by others. The provider of inferior goods loses what has been gained by having the true nature of his wares exposed to the world.

The law of compensation is most easily understood as an investment governed by the law of increase. If we provide quality goods and services at a fair price, we can anticipate a reasonable profit on our investment. But if we invest deception, exploitation, or arrogance, we can anticipate a payback commensurate to what we invested—a harvest of trouble and disgrace.

These laws, of course, are basic to all of life—not just business. But the world of commerce reveals them to us far more poignantly and consistently than any other part of society. A person who fails to see how business and commerce are busy teaching us these lessons probably does not yet understand the principles involved. Even among well-educated people, it is easy to misconstrue these laws and rationalize selfish behavior. The work of business in this regard is therefore far from finished.

Business teaches us skills of pragmatic living.

We tend to equate "learning" with education, but many of the practical lessons of life are learned most quickly and effectively within the crucible of business. Every major institution of society could make this claim, of course, but business has one advantage over all the rest. It is driven by the bottom line. A government, church, or school can experiment with unworkable theories for decades, even centuries, before pressure mounts to discard them. In business, unworkable plans and theories are apt to be discarded within a fiscal quarter or two. The lesson is therefore learned quickly—and, sometimes, dramatically.

The right use of authority is a good example of the unique teaching power of business. At first, we might think we can learn more about authority from government than business. Governments do possess great authority. But the flow of power in government affects us more at the community level than at a personal level, unless one of our rights is abridged or trampled on. Few of us, in other words, deal daily with the President of the United States—or even the governor of our state. But if we work in business, we all interact daily with a boss, who represents the authority of the enterprise to us. Our boss may express authority properly to us, motivating us and supporting us to get our work done. In such a case, we learn the right use of authority. Or our boss may abuse his or her authority, confusing us, undermining us, and using us as a scapegoat. In such a case, we learn perhaps even more, as we observe the mischief created by the misuse of authority.

But the real lesson business teaches us about authority is the flip side—how we respond to it. Do we see our boss as a resource of power and authority, to be tapped so that we can act more effectively in our work? If so, we are responding well to authority—we are using it. Or do we resent his power over us and rebel against his guidance, looking for ways to undercut him? If so, we are abusing authority by our immature response to it.

It is the need to respond to authority in the business setting that teaches us these lessons so well. If a legislator abuses his or her power to follow a personal agenda, it seldom affects us directly. Our only opportunity to respond is through the ballot box. But on the job, we must respond to authority every work day of our life.

Another lesson business teaches us is the virtue of productivity. Businesses cannot rest on past achievements; they must continue to provide quality goods and services to their customers, lest they be driven out of business by competitors. Governments do not teach us this lesson—they are a monopoly. They frequently fall short of their promises and goals. On Saturdays throughout the country, it is common to have to wait excessively in line at the post office. Does management make any changes to eliminate this problem? Of course not. Does the postal union? Of course not. Will complaining about it do any good? Of course not. The post office is a government-protected monopoly. Productivity and performance are not among their goals. In the business world, however, such an operation would be the sign of a corporation falling apart.

Business also demonstrates the value of efficiency. If another enterprise can offer the same goods or services at a lesser cost, even loyal customers will flock to it in an instant. So business executives are always looking for ways to increase the margin between the cost of goods and their selling price, without losing position in the market. As a result, they are constantly challenging old, worn-out assumptions and testing new methods of manufacturing. Government, by contrast, has no reason to be efficient. When it needs more money, it raises taxes—on businesses as well as citizens. In the end, this becomes a massive transfer of money from efficiency to inefficiency.

Efficiency and competitiveness demand that employees be well-trained and competent. With the recent decline in education, most businesses are finding that they must take a new role in encouraging employees to continue their education, in order to maintain competence and skill. Business spends billions every year in underwriting education for this reason. It also rewards brilliance and genius in ways that no other institution of society can—in the wallet. In government, brilliance and creativity are usually punished. In education, they are given tenure and then allowed to decay. But in business, creativity and innovation are rewarded. The effort to improve oneself is honored.

The business environment also encourages us to learn to solve problems. Even a day's delay in shipping goods may cause a company to lose thousands of dollars. The failure to follow through on promises and performance may cost a corporation millions of dollars. Business managers and executives continually face a bewildering array of problems: disgruntled customers, rebellious employees, unscheduled delays, uncooperative suppliers, cantankerous unions, and uncooperative weather. Recently, the government has become a major source of problems as well, as it monitors every facet of business Big Brother style, from safety to pollution to political correctness. Somehow, all of these distractions from the basic work of meeting the needs of the customer or client must be solved and fit into an efficient delivery of goods or services.

In these ways, business becomes a workshop in which ordinary men and women learn many of the attributes of important divine archetypes. Every time someone in business becomes more organized, he or she learns something about divine order. Every time someone in business produces an innovation, he or she learns something about the spiritual work of creativity.

Are there inefficient businesses? Sure—but they do not prosper. Are there businesses that fail to innovate? Yes—but they went out of business years ago. Are there businesses that are not accountable to their customers, or take advantage of employees? Of course—but they have joined Ozymandias in the ranks of the obscure. The innate laws and forces that guide business constantly provide the incentives and disincentives which prompt business people to embrace, more and more fully, appropriate divine ideals.

In this way, commerce forms a training ground for the right use of money, power, and the resources of earth. It stimulates innovation. It promotes cooperation and teamwork. It encourages individuals to learn to interact with others, control their reactiveness, and harness their ambition. It rewards those who act with accountability and integrity. All of these accomplishments of business help human beings become more attuned to the best within them—the life of spirit.

Business creates economic freedom. When permitted to operate more or less freely, business serves the spiritual life and humanity in yet another way: it creates and sustains economic freedom. It liberates the individual from slavery to material needs, by enabling people to rise out of poverty.

How does business perform this miracle? It creates jobs, plus the opportunity for advancement. In an agrarian society, most everyone is bound to his farm and working the land. There is no hope for doing much other than laboring hard to survive. In our industrial society, however, the farmer has the opportunity to move to the city and find a job. In the early stages of the Industrial Revolution, the lure of such economic freedom drew more people to the cities than business could support, and much poverty resulted. But gradually, the machinery of commerce has corrected this imbalance. Now, virtually everyone in a western society can find and hold a job—a job that will lead to advancement, allow us to purchase a home, enable us to improve ourselves, send our children to college, and retire to a life of ease. This is economic freedom, and it is created by business—not by government or education or religion or science.

In countries where business is run by the state, of course,

this economic freedom is still just a dream. In these countries, there is often a good deal of rhetoric about how business exploits the average person and how government preserves their equality. Unfortunately, the bond of equality in these countries is poverty.

Some would argue that there is still poverty in America, and that business excludes certain classes of people from this dream of economic freedom. Yet business has not only provided the opportunity for all people to succeed, it has also been active in eliminating sexual and racial discrimination and bias. Prejudice is not good business, and the business world has been successful in leveling the playing field for all to share in prosperity.

The importance of commerce to humanity is obvious. It is not government or the church that establishes the standard of living; it is business. It is not government or even soup kitchens that feed the hungry; it is business. Business supplies the jobs that let everyone be a full and complete citizen of society, if they so desire. Business creates the opportunities that lift up the poor and the downtrodden, and gives them freedom. Business helps us see beyond our personal needs and trains us to the see the value of working together as a group.

THE PROBLEMS OF BUSINESS

The temptations of business are often powerful and difficult for some people to resist. Commerce generates vast sums of wealth; it therefore attracts people who lust for wealth themselves. They devote themselves to attaining it, sometimes legally, sometimes not. Business champions innovation and success; it consequently inspires people with powerful ambitions. Many aspects of business life are also highly competitive; as a result, it appeals to people who love to engage in battle with others. Often, this competitiveness is good for the customer, as it results in lower prices and higher quality. Sometimes, however, it is abused, leading to the corporate equivalent of Macbeth.

Business is notorious for breeding these ills. To be fair, however, these problems must be seen in their true light. None of these flaws is the direct fault of business. They are inherent failings of human character. The seeds of these flaws are already part of the human character before an individual enters business. The business environment simply enables the flaws to grow. This is just common sense. If an ambitious, greedy person entered government instead of business, he or she would quickly gravitate toward an ideal environment for incubating his or her innate flaws. Indeed, the same problems would emerge even if the individual became an artist, a teacher, a prelate, a lawyer, or a doctor. Business does not have any more or less temptation than any other field of human endeavor.

In a sense, the problems of business are akin to the problems of automobiles. Sometimes cars are involved in fatal accidents. But automobiles are not designed to kill people; the accidents are caused by careless driving. Just so, the business world is not designed to induce greed or ambition. But it can be an arena in which these conditions flourish, until they are corrected.

Indeed, business is actually designed to expose the worst of these excesses. Every business is driven by the bottom line—the need to operate at a profit, in order to continue in business. If one key person's greed becomes so huge that it siphons off funds needed for a company to prosper and grow, then eventually this will lead to the demise of the company—and curtail that individual's opportunity for greed.

Nor is the balance sheet the only check and balance. Every business, large or small, is a living organism. Major mismanagement in any department wounds the entire enterprise. The unfair treatment of employees, the exploitation of vendors, contempt for customers, or exorbitant salaries for executives are all examples of policies that ultimately harm the well-being of a company as a whole. Such excesses are similar to the excessive drinking of an alcoholic. Eventually, a price must be paid for this abuse. In the alcoholic, the price is ill health. In a company, it would be discontent among the employees, the inability to acquire supplies, an eroding market base, and an inability to attract outside financing. Most businesses cannot survive long under such conditions, and so they correct the abuses far more quickly than most alcoholics become sober.

Unfortunately, society as a whole has yet to understand this aspect of business. And so, thousands of people enter business every year with twisted motives and selfish goals. As they gain experience in the business world, many of these people adopt more honest and helpful values and attitudes. For some, however, the lesson is much harder.

Business will continue to receive a bad rap for these problems until society itself wakes up and sees the real dynamics of commerce. The essence of business is investment. If an individual invests the best within him or her, he or she will receive the best from business opportunities. On the other hand, if the individual invests selfishness, greed, or treachery, then he or she will reap failure, embarrassment, and perhaps disgrace. One of the oldest platitudes about business expresses this principle quite succinctly: if you want to become wealthy, help others become rich.

To be sure, there are many people in business today who view helpfulness and cooperation as signs of weakness. These are the people who do not bring honesty and integrity with them into their careers. They believe that they can prosper only through manipulation and exploitation. They are always looking for an "edge," forgetting that edges are sharp and cut most deeply into those who possess them.

A more serious problem that business must confront is its innately materialistic focus. By its nature, the business world deals with goods and services. Sometimes this focus becomes too intense.

The simplest sign of the depth of this problem is that almost everyone, when asked why they are in business, replies: "to make a profit." They are overlooking the fact that unless they serve a very human need, there will be no profit. They are also discounting the fact that this human need must ultimately serve the growth of society.

Whenever business focuses solely on profit, it becomes shortsighted. It forgets that it is a member of a community and a nation, let alone a vital part of the human race.

Business and commerce are greatly enriched as its leaders become aware of the larger dimensions of life in which they exist. Fortunately, business has begun making major steps in this direction during this century. It has learned the importance of being a good citizen in their community. It has become concerned about the need for quality education, neighborhood safety, the competence of local government, and the infrastructure of their community. In fact, in many cases, it has discovered that investing time and even money in these concerns has enriched their own profitability.

Another problem that stems from the materialism of business is its blindness to ethics and ethical behavior. There is a tendency to become so absorbed by the bottom line that considerations of morality, decency, helpfulness, and even lawfulness are sometimes displaced by the holy grail of profit. They seldom disappear entirely, of course, but they can definitely be overshadowed by the constant pressure to succeed.

A clear example of this problem is the tendency of the entertainment industry to pander to the lowest common denominator of public taste. Apologists for this behavior reply that the movie moguls are not responsible for this problem—

they are just responding to public demand. It is undeniable that the masses will indeed flock to horror films, just as they will snatch up newspapers and magazines that glorify the latest gossip. It is equally undeniable that bull fights are still hugely popular in Spain, and that gladiators used to kill Christians for the amusement of the masses in ancient Rome. There can be no doubt that millions of people in the United States would pay good money to watch such blood sports again, if society tolerated it. But society has a responsibility to draw the line between good taste and bad taste—never by censoring, but by acting with self-restraint.

Business is a vital part of society. Because it has an investment in the well-being of society, it has perhaps the largest responsibility to act with good taste and restraint. It is fairly easy to understand the ethical problem of giving an alcoholic a drink, even if he demands it. On a larger scale, it is equally unethical to "just give people what they demand" if it is something that is clearly going to debase the quality of their lives—drugs, sleaze, violence, amorality, and gossip.

Is this an endorsement of censorship? Of course not. The drug problem in this country clearly illustrates that laws are easily thwarted. The attempt to outlaw a human activity just because it is immature or harmful undermines society's respect for other, more important laws. The answer lies in a stronger ethical recognition of the need to aspire to higher standards, not cater to the most immature wishes of the masses.

It is in this area that business must recognize and define a greater sense of responsibility. One of the great issues of the day is the ongoing use of tobacco products, even though they are clearly harmful to health. Should tobacco be banned by government? Of course not. Such a law would just be a windfall gift for organized crime, and plunge us right back into the raucous Twenties. Should the government impose strict restrictions? It probably will—and they probably will be ineffective. Should the church speak out against it, and condemn smoking? It did not work with drinking, so why would it work with smoking?

What, then, can be done? The answer lies in awakening business to its ethical responsibility. Why blame just the tobacco industry for the ills of smoking, when truckers carry cigarettes to stores across the country, who willingly sell it to their customers? Business involves more than just manufacturing. It embraces distribution and marketing as well. The whole business world has an ethical responsibility to act with greater restraint for the good of society—in the issue of tobacco, in the case of alcohol, in fighting the drug wars, in eliminating organized crime, and in reforming the news media.

Once again, however, it must be remembered that business is just a form of self-expression within society. If business has an ethical responsibility to act with self-restraint, all of us who consume the goods and services of business have an even greater one. Ultimately, human ethics emerge from the mind and heart of each of us, as we learn to respond to the evocation of the life of spirit within us. We cannot just sit back and wait for business to act, unless we like being a hypocrite. We should be reluctant to cast stones at business for its ethical lapses unless we practice perfect discipline and self-restraint in our own consumption of alcohol, tobacco, cheap novels, rock and roll music, violent movies and television shows, and, of course, drugs.

Let it be remembered: the vast majority of business goods and services meet a definite need of human beings and society. We need homes to live in, clothes to wear, food for the table, books to read, and so on. Ninety percent of all industry is focused in meeting these needs. But as business refines its ability to deliver these goods and services, new businesses spring up to meet less peripheral needs. Billions of dollars are spent every year on cosmetics, candy and chewing gum, comic books, trashy novels, and of course recordings of the relentless noise which now passes as music.

There is nothing wrong or immoral about spending billions on cosmetics or chewing gum, but the question does arise: is it the best use of these funds? Should some of it be diverted to more noble uses—for instance, promoting the development of the mind and creativity? It is not reasonable to expect government to curb these markets; it is not even reasonable to expect business to do so. But if consumers shifted even ten percent of the money they waste yearly on candy, gum, and popular music to the purchase of books and materials that would enrich their thinking skills, business would soon follow their lead.

The easiest choice to make lies in our selection of entertainment. In spite of the constant reiteration of the apologists that sleazy movies are only made because the public wants them, it needs to be remembered that the most popular movies of all time tend to be ones that show good people doing good things. The *Star Wars* trilogy is an excellent example. Many of the most violent movies ever made, by contrast, have done poorly at the box office. Each of us has the ultimate power over business: the way we choose to spend our money. If we demand ethical maturity in business, it will respond—and quickly.

Of course, the choice of product or service is not the only ethical issue confronting business. Many businesses have been tarnished by the widespread practice of shady marketing and sales methods. The banking, insurance, and investment industries are constantly taken to task for unscrupulous practices. Homeowners and auto owners must be constantly on guard against unethical repairmen. In some cases, the unethical procedures actually cross the line, and the unwary consumer ends up dealing with criminals, not business people. It is not just enough for consumers to recall the adage "buyer beware." It behooves the entire business community to reward strong ethics and encourage it among its ranks. Only when the business community takes steps to eliminate fraud and malpractice will the faith of the average person be restored in the basic honesty and integrity of business as a whole.

Another persistent problem in the business community is the tendency to focus on short-term issues and opportunities, frequently to the exclusion of any long-term impact. As a result, business people sometimes become abnormally absorbed in immediate profitability, current stock prices, and keeping investors continuously happy with performance.

None of these is an insignificant concern, to be sure. But if viewed only in the framework of this quarter and the next, they can distort the total picture the business person must deal with. Effective executives must have some idea of where the business ought to be in five years, ten years—even twenty years—while considering the decisions that must be made affecting this year's growth. They should not only ponder where they want to be, but also how they can get there. What is the future for their industry? What innovations are approaching around the next corner of time? How can they best meet these needs? What level of manpower will be required? Is it possible to work with the union to be ready for the challenge ahead?

Time and again in business, short-term thinking has led to costly mistakes. In one case, a large Fortune 500 company bought a series of small companies just for the sake of diversification. Two years later, it started selling them off—usually at a loss—because it decided to focus more intently on its core business. This kind of haphazard decision making could be avoided by looking occasionally at the larger picture.

In other cases, short-term thinking leads to impatience. If a new project fails to demonstrate profitability within a year or two, funding for it may well be terminated—just before a major breakthrough would have turned around its lack of success.

Of course, the larger picture is not just defined by time. Business enterprises have a soul or inner spirit just as individuals and nations do. The vast majority of managers and stockholders are unaware of this inner dimension to businesses, but it is nonetheless quite real. It has a will and a purpose—and will be served.

Managers and executives do not have to hire either gurus or mystics to become aware of this inner spirit to their business. The link can be made quite simply, by spending time recognizing the larger purpose their enterprise serves. If we open a store selling tires and shock absorbers, for instance, we are a small part of the automotive industry. This industry is part of the larger transportation industry, which serves the need of humanity for mobility. Mobility, therefore, is the inner essence of our work—the purpose our business activities serve. By reflecting on the nature and meaning of mobility and how it has enriched the human experience, we begin to connect automatically with the inner essence of our business. This attunement, in turn, allows this inner spiritual essence to guide and direct our thinking and understanding.

An even broader perspective can be cultivated by realizing that our tiny shop exists not only within the transportation industry but within the vast scope of all commercial enterprise. As such, its purpose is to become an active expression of providence on earth, feeding, clothing, and caring for the needs of humanity, while expanding its dominion on earth. This type of periodic reflection helps link us in powerful ways to the energies of productivity and abundance—for our own benefit as well as the well-being of society.

While a tough-minded pragmatist may scoff at any such connection between business and spirit, it is genuine nonetheless. In fact, the value of making this connection is supported by one of the commonly-accepted maxims of good business sense: if you want to be a success, then go work for a successful person. The successful person will serve as a magnet for powerful opportunities. If we can seize upon these opportunities, they may open the door for rapid success. In much the same way, if we can sense even a sliver of the noble, cosmic purpose underlying our humble shop, then we will in essence be "working for a successful person." In this case, the successful person is the universe itself! By consulting with it from time to time, and letting it guide our thinking, it becomes our mentor and guide. It can also become our protector—just as a successful vice-president might protect a junior manager.

Perhaps the most challenging problem faced by business today, however, is one that is not of its own making. It is a problem that has been imposed on business by governments, unions, and anti-business crusaders such as radical environmentalists. The great engine of business is slowly but inexorably being crippled by excessive taxation, government regulations, and restrictive labor practices.

There is no question that business has at times harmed both society and the environment with its policies and practices. But it has also demonstrated a tremendous measure of responsiveness in correcting these errors and repairing the damages. Keep in mind that we entered the Industrial Age only one hundred and fifty years ago. Early on, abuses of workers, customers, and the environment were commonplace. But business responded to these challenges. Today, it is a leader in improving race relations, eliminating sexual discrimination, and cleaning up the environment. In fact, business has exhibited far more maturity and adaptability than has government, the unions, or the environmental terrorists.

Nonetheless, the proven track record of business in co-operating with the reasonable demands of society has not stopped government, the unions, and special interest groups from pushing for more and more restrictions on business. Naturally, these groups claim to have pure and pious intentions, and point to their many triumphs over the ogre of big business—a snail darter saved here, a dangerous toy banned elsewhere. But these boasts sound like a hollow gong when compared with the towering accomplishments of the business world that they condemn—the daily feeding, clothing, and housing of billions of people, the rapid advancement in our standard of living, the developments of modern technology, and much more.

The prospect that overly zealous regulations will eventually destroy the war horse of business is genuine. Already, the rewards for innovation and new development have been crippled repeatedly by taxation, lawsuits, and regulations. Businesses must hire large staffs to take care of government paperwork which is irrelevant to the work they perform. This burden greatly increases overhead, which in turn results in significantly higher prices for everything we buy.

The two most frightening aspects of this hyper-regulation, however, are more subtle. The sheer number of regulations inhibits many creative, productive people from becoming entrepreneurs, simply because they do not want the hassle. As a result, society never benefits from the new products or services that they have to offer. The second point is potentially even more disturbing: the accountability of business, which is one of the linchpins of commerce, is being undermined by a cabal of government agencies, unions, and political activists who insist on playing that role, even though they have no right to. As a result, there is a danger that business will lose sight of its accountability to the public and become nothing but a slave to meanspirited, exploitative bureaucrats and activists.

In the rush to protect the many from the abuses of a few, we have become a society in which the many are now harassing the few. In the end, it is society that suffers the most.

Can this problem be solved? Of course it can. But the solution lies in trusting and respecting the enormous power of business to serve society. When we put our trust in government, the unions, and political activists, we are giving away more than our vote.

We are selling our future.

THE CURRENT WORK OF BUSINESS

In understanding the role of the divine workshop of business in serving the Plan of the Hierarchy, it is useful to remember that the vast scope of commerce embraces more than just the activities of offices, factories, and retail outlets. It involves the whole domain of planning and organizing that leads to the production of goods and services. In this regard, even aspects of our personal life need to be viewed in the context of commerce. Before we go to the store to make a major purchase, we engage in a process of defining our needs, making choices, and deciding how to pay for them. In this way, we participate in the workshop of commerce. In deciding how to make our living—even if we choose to stay at home and raise a family—we are also formulating plans for investing our time, talent, and energy. We are engaging in commerce in the fullest sense of the word. Indeed, the word "economy" originally meant "how one spends household monies." The whole global economy built by commerce is actually nothing more than a vast extension of the household labors of earning, saving, and spending money.

We therefore all participate in the divine workshop of business, and need to take the role we play in it seriously. A large part of our work, in this regard, is to understand clearly how the Hierarchy is trying to use business and commerce to advance its plans on earth. There are a number of important projects that are already well under way:

1. Business is being used to expose the consequences of unbridled greed and economic exploitation. The Hierarchy has been waging this ancient battle against greed and selfishness for many centuries, and will undoubtedly continue to do battle for ages to come. However, it is important to understand precisely what the problem is. There is absolutely nothing wrong with wealth per se. Great wealth may merely be a legitimate expression of the abundance of divine providence. The problem lies instead with the unfair expropriation of wealth—in other words, amassing wealth without earning it honestly, by cheating others of their share in it. A government that taxes the rich in order to "redistribute the wealth" may be just as guilty of exploitation, therefore, as a business that reaps an undeserved windfall after a natural disaster. A union that extorts dues from everyone working in a factory, whether they belong to the union or not, is just as culpable of greed as the bank that forecloses on farms during an extended drought.

Unfortunately, this distinction has been deliberately muddled by generations of demagogues who are possessed by a fervor of anti-elitism and the envy of wealth. These people consider any concentration of wealth to be obscene. They also overdose on their own self-serving vision of entitlement—that they deserve to be paid a week's worth of wages for a day's worth of work. It is, of course, all a Big Lie—but one we have heard so many times we can easily become inured to it, and accept it as true. It decidedly is not.

The unions arose by claiming that they would solve this problem. Instead, they simply exchanged one form of exploitation for another. Government, too, has asserted the right to solve this problem—but government, too, has failed to do anything but empower a new class of people to become greedy. The solution lies in embracing two basic virtues. The first is a deep respect for the need for collaboration in any worthwhile and complex enterprise. In other words, business needs its labor force, and the labor force needs business. They should view each other as partners with a common goal, not as adversaries getting in the way of progress.

The second virtue is a willingness to reward each other for their contribution to the welfare of the whole. When businesses today complain about the rate of turnover, they are ignoring the obvious solution to turnover: reward employees according to their value. Conversely, when employees gripe about the way they are treated by the company, they are forgetting the risks taken by the stockholders in providing the capital to run the company. Employees also need to remember to fulfill their end of the old equation, honest work for an honest wage.

It may be unrealistic to expect either management or labor to embrace these virtues entirely, but any movement in the right direction represents a major victory for the influence of the Hierarchy. By the same token, the tendency of the public to listen to the propaganda of anti-business demagogues represents a step backward.

One of the major influences that has caused numerous backward steps over the last two hundred years has been the insidious perversion of the principle of equality. Instead of equality of opportunity, which business provides, certain demagogues take delight in promoting equality of treatment—equality of wages and opportunities, with uniform results. These are the voices that insist upper management should be paid the same wages as ordinary workers. They are also the same voices that encourage government to tax wealth to such a degree that there would be no incentive to start one's own business. These propagandists never hesitate to label business people as "immoral," but in fact their arguments are not only immoral but also destructive, for they would reduce the working population to an insect society where everyone has equal status in the hive. This would stifle individuality and creativity and reduce humanity to an infantile state.

If productivity and innovation are virtues—and they are—then they need to be rewarded as such. To insist that a kitchen assistant who chops celery and carrots should make the same wage as a master chef is inherently dishonest because the work they perform is not the same. The only way humanity can learn about values is through the trial and error process of judging the worth of things, activities, and services. We might hire a professional lawn service to mow our lawn and trim the hedges for thirty-five dollars whereas we would only pay a neighbor kid five dollars for the same service. Is this dishonest? Is it exploitative? Of course not. The professional has expensive machinery, a crew, and overhead such as insurance to pay. He can mow the lawn in twenty minutes and be off to the next job. The neighbor kid may well do the best he can, but he does not have the experience or resources to compete with the professional. He offers less, and is paid less. Yet he still receives fair compensation for what he can provide.

It should be abundantly clear that society benefits far more from an Andrew Carnegie or a Lee Iacocca than from someone toiling in their factories. Society must therefore be willing to reward such leadership appropriately, or it becomes an exploiter itself. The inevitable consequence of maximum productivity is the accumulation of great wealth. The law of compensation guarantees it. A society that recognizes this principle and extols anyone who earns great wealth through productivity, genius, or efficiency is a healthy society. A society that promotes class divisiveness or the envy of the rich and creative, however, is an ailing society in danger of losing its basis for abundance.

In business as well as every other human venture, society needs a healthy blend of balance and common sense. While no one should be motivated by greed or selfishness, it is equally true that the universe supports creativity, efficiency, skill, talent, genius, enlightened leadership, and productivity. If government insists on involving itself in business—a bad idea but an ever-growing reality—then it should consider programs to encourage greater individuality, risk-taking, and investment, instead of the volumes upon volumes of regulations that limit and restrict the opportunities of business to succeed. Above all, it should strive to return to the day when wealth and success were not instantly adjudged to be crimes, and in fact were achievements worthy of honor.

2. Business teaches greater cooperation. At first, all of the power of a business was concentrated at the very top. As a result, policies were cast in lead and were exceedingly slow to change. Throughout the last one hundred and fifty years, however, businesses that clung to that antiquated model have been passed by time after time. They were not responsive enough to the needs of their customers to anticipate changes in their business. As a result, they were left at the gate while competitors roared ahead. Ford Motor Company lost its leadership position in car sales because Henry Ford insisted that all cars be painted black. When General Motors introduced a choice of colors, it quickly displaced Ford in the driver's seat. Even though Ford soon mended its ways, it could never recover the market it had lost.

While power and authority does flow from the uppermost levels of a business downward, the operative word is definitely "flow." If authority is not delegated and entrusted to the proper employees, they are unable to perform their work effectively. Moreover, they are unable to provide the feedback from customers that is so vital to a company's well-being. In fact, in many instances today, it is more efficient to let the supervisor or even the employee on the spot make a decision that will keep a customer or client well-satisfied.

Such delegation of authority has become possible because today's workers are more knowledgeable and competent than their grandfathers may have been. And it makes sense: some of the greatest innovations in technology have developed out of suggestions from the foremen and laborers on the production line. Product design and utility almost always improves when input from sales specialists is solicited prior to the design stage. In addition, the worker begins to take greater pride in his or her overall contribution to the company.

The drive behind this subtle change is not just to introduce a new model for management seminars. From the viewpoint of the Hierarchy, this shift in management makes it more responsive to customer need. It is leading toward an eventual integration of the purposes of those who offer services with the requirements of those who pay for and receive them.

Once this responsiveness is learned in business and commerce, it is the plan of the Hierarchy to introduce it into government, as the antidote for bloated bureaucracies. Most of government is comprised of elitists who sit in their offices, puffed up with bizarre economic theories and radical ideologies, totally disconnected from workaday realities. If their performance were judged on the basis of how effectively they serve the needs of the citizens, most would lose their jobs and be forced to find honest work. Eventually, however, the law of compensation will expose their lack of usefulness, as the push for cooperation reveals their stubbornness and selfishness.

3. Business teaches basic life skills. It is expected that youth will learn about ideas and thinking from attending school and college. But just as we cannot learn to swim from a textbook, it is not possible to learn many basic life skills without jumping into the stream of experience. Business provides both an incentive and the reward for learning these lessons. After all, if we cannot control our anger or our impatience, we will probably suffer when it comes time for a promotion. There is no teacher as powerful and thorough as Professor Experience. For most people, it is the business world that provides these lessons.

Part of these lessons are the basic skills and knowledge needed to perform the task at hand; part of them may be areas of competence that were not effectively learned in school. But in addition to these types of learning, there is an extensive set of lessons in living that must be mastered by anyone hoping to do well in commerce:

1. Decision making. When governments make decisions, they are usually heavily influenced by ideology, special

interests, self-interest, and a host of prejudices and grudges. It is not uncommon for local communities to experience cost overruns of millions of dollars on projects coordinated by politicians or bureaucrats.

Such colossal losses are rare in business, because business is held accountable. As such, managers on the way to leadership learn how to make good decisions—and how to cut their losses when disaster is imminent. Those who let personal grudges or preconceptions color their thinking find themselves looking for a new line of work.

In education today, decisions are made on how others will feel about it. Hurt feelings are to be avoided at all costs. In business, decisions are made on the basis of what will work.

2. Conflict resolution. One of the Hierarchy's most important projects for ages has been the effort to decrease the adversarial relationships among all human groups. Divisiveness of all kinds has long been a huge problem in every facet of society. The most obvious example of this divisiveness is the constant warfare that has characterized human history. But it is not just war that perpetuates these ancient cleavages. Religions strive against one another, classes compete with one another, races perpetuate deep seated animosities toward one another, and the list goes on. Today, division is fostered even among the sexes. Even in our "civilized society," we stupidly perpetuate divisiveness in the way we discuss issues—we debate from one side or the other, instead of trying to define a common ground that everyone can agree on. As a result, the fight goes on—over special privileges, income, protection, or just high moral ground. Nowhere is this more poignantly illustrated than in the "debate" over abortion, where "pro life" collides with "pro choice," spawning violence and terror instead of agreement and reconciliation. In this case as well as every other one, each intransigent side is stained with blood.

This adversarial style is deadly because it polarizes issues into good versus bad. The middle ground, where balance and solutions are usually to be found, is rejected—and condemned—by both sides. Worse, the opposition is soon demonized, rendering any attempt at bridging the gap impossible. Intellectual war has been declared, and the only acceptable solution is to fight until only one side is left standing, no matter what the cost to society—or the combatants. This is an approach to human problems that should have been discarded with the Stone Age. It defiles the potential for intelligence and goodwill of the spiritual dimension of our being.

Business, however, is the one bright shining light in this sordid mess of conflict. Business people soon learn to negotiate with customers, competitors, and even the government. When problems arise in the workplace, they must be solved and left behind. Government agencies can—and do—stall and discuss and posture for years without actually solving any issue or problem. Psychologists try to solve problems by studying the origin of a problem, assessing blame, and then excusing the victim. Theologians do a sophisticated two-step, urging their followers to increase their stamina and faith so that they can "stay the course." Most of these efforts only create an illusion of trying to solve the problem; we might as well try fighting dragons with fairy tales.

But business is replete with incentives to solve problems and disincentives to allow them to linger. As a result, business people are better equipped than most everyone else to see the Big Picture about real problems. They learn to recognize a) all of the important factors that have contributed to the problem; b) all of the factors and forces that might contribute to its solution; c) the real issues underlying the superficial symptoms; and d) what and who need to make sacrifices in order to generate an effective solution. Business people do not waste time trying to posture or stall; they tackle the problem head on and work to eliminate it. They use the skills of analysis, mediation, and negotiation to cut the toughest problems down to size.

3. Intellectual creativity. As the work load of the average employee has shifted progressively more to the realm of ideas than physical strength or prowess, businesses have quietly assumed a major role in helping talented people to learn to think more clearly, effectively, and creatively. Unlike other institutions, business cannot rely on old standards and vested traditions—it must innovate and discover new ways of meeting market needs. It therefore has a strong incentive to teach its people how to "think outside of the box" of known practices.

Business does not teach employees how to paint or compose music, of course—the kind of activities normally associated with creativity. It teaches them how to envision the possibility of computers while everyone else is still using quill pens. This kind of creativity embraces four steps: a) discovery, b) validation, c) interpretation, and d) application. The discovery of Scotch tape was somewhat accidental; the researchers at 3-M were working on a different project altogether. The first prototype of Scotch tape was actually a failed attempt to achieve much different results. But one of the researchers happened to observe that the "failure" kept sticking to everything. He was able to set aside his original expectations and see the potential of a piece of tape that stuck to everything. In this way, he transformed an apparent failure into evidence of great potential. The result was Scotch tape—plus an excellent example of intellectual creativity.

Business is also proving that creativity can be taught. It has been a pioneer in presenting techniques for stimulating creative thought to businesses. One of these techniques, for example, encourages people to find seeds of creative thought in just about every circumstance of life. The inspiration for streamlining the design of a cable of hundreds of wires, for example, might come while preparing a spaghetti dinner.

As many others have said before, the great Creative Intelligence that made the world is present throughout everything visible. We simply need to teach our eyes to see it.

This is not to suggest that business is rapidly becoming a visionary think tank. As always, business insists on practical results. This orientation is very useful in the development of creative skills. Many creative people get excellent ideas, but either fail to perceive their true meaning or let preconceived notions limit their understanding of the underlying potential. As a result, they leave out vital facts and arrive at inadequate solutions. Psychologists and politicians who assume, for example, that poverty is the cause of crime seem incapable of comprehending that discipline, values, and personal habits might also be important factors. In business, however, ideology and pet theories are generally overlooked in favor of getting a problem solved. The pragmatic approach of business to common sense solutions helps liberate the creative process from prejudice and sentimentality.

Business also gives us the ultimate test of all creative work—it demonstrates with pure objectivity whether or not our idea meets a public need. Many writers, artists, and musicians create primarily for themselves. It is just an added bonus if others also appreciate their work. Such self-absorbed attitudes are impossible in business, however. Creative talents must be focused on producing something the public can use constructively. In this way, creativity becomes a strong bridge between the realms of potentiality and the world of practicality.

4. The skills of maturity—teamwork, motivation, coping with stress, and self-discipline. The business world is also an excellent classroom for learning basic skills of human maturity. At first, it would seem that this should be more the realm of psychology. But psychologists have too often abdicated the role of teaching psychological health in favor of treating psychological abnormality. Yet business people, especially managers and supervisors, need skills in motivating people, tapping their strengths, and fostering cooperation. They also frequently need to learn to deal with the stresses that attend

their work—deadlines, competition, and government interferences. These are practical problems that must be dealt with in practical ways—not by running experiments on white rats. To meet these needs, businesses are providing educational opportunities to help their employees and managers learn basic human maturity.

The involvement of business in encouraging self-discipline and good work habits has been a part of the commercial world ever since the first laborer was hired. Little has changed in this regard, except that the value of self-discipline has lately come under attack in many parts of society outside of the business community. Psychologists worry that the self-disciplined individual is repressed and neurotic. Educators prize good feelings and a strong self-esteem as far more important than self-restraint. Government penalizes hard workers and transfers their wages, through the medium of taxes, to people who do not work at all. These aberrations of the value of self-discipline will eventually pass, but it is business that continues to protect and nurture these virtues, while the rest of society decries them.

5. The work ethic. It is almost trite to state that business is built on the work ethic, and yet it is true. But "work ethic" has become a phrase that people repeat glibly without thinking. It literally means that the role of work is of great value in our life. We derive not only our income from our work, but a sense of purpose and meaning as well. Being employed in a useful vocation gives us a sense of fulfillment that cannot be found in any other dimension. As a result of the work ethic, we respect others who achieve success through hard work—and we respect ourself for the labor we perform. We may even go so far as to love our work and cherish the company that employs us, a dangerous concept in these "sophisticated" times.

The fact that a strong work ethic is viewed suspiciously by some segments of society only underscores how important the work of the divine workshop of business is. The work ethic on which America was built is rapidly losing ground to the "welfare ethic"—a counterfeit ethos which proclaims that it is government's role to insure that all of its citizens are content. Somewhere along the line, we have forgotten that the pursuit of happiness involves hard work. We are slowly being brainwashed into believing that government can actually guarantee it.

One might argue that these same lessons—conflict resolution, creativity, maturity, and all the rest—can be learned in government jobs or educational positions. But this is not true. Anyone who has ever bought a stamp in any big city post office knows the deadening impact of bureaucracy on competence and initiative. Anyone who has ever taken classes from a tenured but brain-dead professor likewise knows that colleges seldom inspire brilliance or accountability.

4. Business makes philanthropy possible. One of the reasons why certain individuals are permitted to amass overwhelming fortunes, while others are not, is because they have demonstrated the generosity and wisdom required to be an effective steward of this great abundance. Andrew Carnegie was the prototype of the successful industrialist who could accumulate an amazing amount of wealth in a short span of time, then devote the rest of his life to reinvesting it in philanthropic ventures which enriched human life around the world. Carnegie also wrote extensively on the subject, encouraging others blessed with wealth to follow his lead.

It should be obvious that philanthropy is not possible unless the economic structure of society allows individuals to amass huge fortunes. If all monies were equally distributed, as some people promote, no one would have enough resources to accomplish anything significant. In all likelihood, there would be no library within biking distance—and no opera house, symphony, playhouse, food kitchens, or shelters, either. Business provides the opportunity for philanthropy to enrich our lives.

But what is amazing is the contagiousness of the generosity that inspires philanthropy! The example of wealthy industrialists like Carnegie, Ford, and Rockefeller inspires small business owners to take on the jobless and train them to be effective employees. It motivates them to mentor local students who need help in learning basic skills of discipline and maturity. It encourages them to take active roles in sponsoring and helping local charities.

Some people, of course, think that it is better to leave such programs for government. But government is not motivated by generosity in funding these programs—it is motivated by partisan ideology. As a result, only those programs which embody the ideology of the moment will be funded. Other, perhaps even more worthwhile, programs will be left on the drawing board.

Business does not respond to ideology or partisanship. It responds to the spirit of generosity and the genuine needs of the community. In addition, business does not invest money in projects just for the sake of seeming to care. It invests money to produce results. It is therefore a much better administrator of these projects than government.

These are just a few examples of the way in which the Hierarchy is presently using the divine workshop of business to promote reforms and new directions in human civilization. It may be surprising to some, but business actually has a better record of responding to its spiritual direction than most other key institutions in society. There is much more that can be done, of course, but business does far more than its fair share in bringing light into the dark corners of the world.

SUPPORTING THE PLAN FOR BUSINESS

It is not necessary to become an entrepreneur in order to participate in and support the spiritual Plan for business. Since business and commerce exist within the context of society as a whole, there is a valuable role for us to play, even if we are a teacher, a farmer, an artist, a healer, or a scientist. Moreover, since we are all consumers of commerce, it becomes something of an obligation to play an enlightened role in supporting the divine Plan for business—if we are a true spiritual person.

Our first obligation is to assist in healing the poisoned attitudes and beliefs that have crept into humanity's thinking about the nature and purpose of business. It is not necessary to pretend that business people are perfect or saints on earth, for they are not. It is just necessary to understand that most of them are not criminals, polluters, or exploiters, either, and point out the fallacy of this belief to others.

A good place to start in changing attitudes would be the erroneous notion that wealth is inherently bad. This distorted notion is especially prevalent among spiritual aspirants, who have a tendency to try to prove their devotion to spirit by rejecting everything of the earth, including money! They will even misquote the Bible, claiming that "money is the root of all evil." The actual passage reads: "The love of money is the root of all evil." It is greed and selfishness, in other words, that traps us in the worlds of form, not generosity and the right use of abundance.

Some misguided aspirants go so far as to create what can best be described as a "poverty consciousness," in which they make poverty a badge of "spirituality." Nothing could be further from the truth. It is abundance, not poverty, that is a spiritual ideal. It is reckless, perhaps even evil, to assume that anyone with wealth or property has acquired it by illegal means or at the expense of others.

It is time to clean out all of these ridiculous concepts about wealth and business, just as Hercules cleansed the Augean stables. We need to look beyond our prejudices and narrowmindedness and begin to respect business people for their remarkable accomplishments—for providing jobs for billions of people, for providing goods and services that make our lives healthier and more comfortable, and for creating an economy that lets everyone who wishes to work to prosper and flourish.   We need to see business people as agents of divine Providence on earth, even if they occasionally do not live up to that ideal.

Part of this cleansing process means recognizing how much our values have been debased in modern times. "Profit" has become a word of scorn. By contrast, handouts—or entitlements, as they are now called—are viewed as the embodiment of compassion. Working in a soup kitchen is almost universally regarded as noble, but working in a business is considered to be crass and demeaning, even if we are putting bread on the table for our family, educating our children, donating to charities, and supporting the unquenchable thirst of our government for taxes. Some people in society even consider the pressure to get and maintain a job to be cruel and demeaning!

Above all, we need to begin to appreciate that our commercial enterprises, large and small, are the great engine that generates wealth and power for the whole of society. If America is the richest country in history, then credit for this accomplishment needs to be given to business. Government did not create it.   Our universities did not create it. Social reformers did not create it—they only know how to spend it.   It is business that created this great wealth—and it is business that sustains it.

It is highly arrogant for the intellectual elite to presume that they know best how to spend money that they did not generate! Just as parents know a whole lot more about raising their children than the neighbors do, or the social workers downtown, or local politicians, so also the people who generate great wealth—the business people of the world—know a whole lot more about spending money and preserving wealth than anyone else.

If we have been guilty of condemning business in the past,

we need to mend our ways. Instead of taking cheap shots at an institution we clearly do not understand, we should learn to celebrate its vast achievements. We should rejoice in its wealth, its productivity, and its genius.

Unfortunately, anti-business attitudes are so ingrained in mass consciousness that it will take more than an occasional conversion to sanity to reverse their full impact. In spite of the failure of Marxist economies in recent years, there are still many college professors who continue to preach communist doctrines of economics and history. There are still strong forces in government who would impose a centrally-controlled, socialist economy on this country, destroying the work of business in the process. The evidence of the unworkability of these theories surrounds us on every side, and yet these voices persist. Obviously, they will continue to persist until individual citizens decide to end the bathetic cycle that debases our ideals of freedom, hard work, and free enterprise.

In addition to changing our attitudes, we can also support the spiritual work of business by learning about and acquiring as many of the spiritual values of this institution as we can. These include such archetypal qualities as efficiency, initiative, productivity, pragmatism, service, cooperation, innovativeness, responsibility, discipline, thoroughness, and effectiveness. It also includes learning to think and value the mind as a legitimate instrument for work.

It is not necessary to become a perfect example of any of these qualities—the average business certainly is not. But as we seek to invest some of these qualities in our self-expression, we are silently supporting the larger, spiritual Plan that is manifesting through the divine workshop of business. We are attuning ourself to spiritual purpose, and this helps attune us to the actual work of commerce.

Perhaps the most significant way we can support the divine Plan for business, however, is to try to live life as though we were ourself a thriving business. This exercise begins by viewing ourself as the CEO (chief executive officer) of our lifestyle. Each day, then, we approach the duties, activities, and challenges of life as though we were a business striving for maximum productivity—and profit, of course. Instead of battling with our spouse, we try to negotiate a harmonious agreement. Instead of berating our kids, we delegate authority to them and encourage them to take on responsibility. Instead of viewing problems as disasters, we regard them as opportunities for advancement and achievement.

This simple exercise may seem like a lot of work, but is not. It helps us become aware that we have a measure of personal authority and wealth—talent, time, and energy—to invest in life. If we invest it in ways that will bring a profitable return, we will be happy and fulfilled. On the other hand, if we invest it in picking fights, dodging responsibilities, or trying to get an advantage, we will shortly make a mess of our life.

The practice of this exercise does not lead to a life of self-absorption or selfishness. It leads to a deeper understanding of our role as a child of God, endowed with a powerful potential for wisdom, talent, goodwill, joy, and courage. These spiritual qualities are not only our birthright, but are also unlimited resources we are meant to invest in our daily activities. We can squander them, as government so often squanders funds. We can hide them under a rock, where they will lose their value to us. Or we can invest them wisely in the people and events of our daily life.

If we can learn these lessons from the enlightened example of business, then society can learn them, too. Slowly, it will transform itself into a much more responsible, peaceful, and productive organism. Society will achieve the glory intended for it.

And the work of the divine workshop of business will be fulfilled.

The Divine
Workshop of Government

THE SOUL OF A NATION

Fiorello la Guardia, the colorful mayor of New York City, once observed that there is no Democratic or Republican way of collecting the trash. In this pithy remark, he captured the fact that politics transcends the partisanship of our political parties, even though we usually cannot see beyond our own beliefs and special interests. Just so, government transcends the agencies, laws, courts, legislatures, and services that we typically associate with it. Whether we are talking about city hall, the governor's mansion, or Washington, these are just symbols for the totality of government. The true government of any nation also includes its conscience, purpose, design, and character. Collectively, these intangible elements are the true source of any govenment's authority.

Part of these intangible elements of government are embedded in the traditions, constitution, and mythos of any nation. But in addition to these long-established attributes, there is also a living, spiritual element which is constantly involved in guiding and directing the physical agencies of government. This spiritual portion is a living core of powerful values and ideals—the soul of a nation.

Just as each human personality has a soul, with its own goals and design, so also do nations. Unfortunately, the parallel does not cease here, for just as human personalities often ignore or thwart the intent of their soul, the same is true with nations. When such disharmony occurs between the soul and the personality, either in the individual or the nation, many problems arise in physical life—problems that do not go away until the personality, or public will, accepts the authority and guidance of the soul.

Our formal government is intended to be a custodian or agent for the spiritual will of the national soul. In effect, government becomes the "personality" of the indwelling spirit. The more responsive the government is to the soul, the more accurately it will express its purposes and plans without distortion or dilution.

Figuratively, it can also be said that any nation has a heart and a mind. The heart of the nation is meant to express goodwill and nurture the growth of the people. The mind of the nation is meant to demonstrate the core character traits and special talents which are the destiny of the nation. Government, therefore, is meant to act in such a way that it reveals the true essence and power of the national heart, mind, and soul.

No such maturity can be expected from a government, of course, until it comes of age. Just as with individuals, governments can be young and immature. We do not expect five-year-olds to display much wisdom. We do not demand much courage or compassion from ten-year-olds. We expect adult behavior only from adult people. In much the same way, it would be impossible for an immature government to express the full wisdom, goodwill, and spiritual will of its national soul.

It is for this reason why so many nations behave like spoiled children or neurotic adolescents, despite the fact that none of this behavior is compatible with the character of the soul. Occasionally, a nation may even behave in psychotic ways for a short period of time. On rare occasions, countries may even seem to try to commit suicide—or at least die a violent death.

Fortunately, nations—like individuals—can be healed, and even reborn. This healing occurs when, directly or indirectly, new life enters a nation from its soul. As with humans, the soul of a nation is a great resource for healing, renewal, and reform. It usually requires a crisis, however, to rouse the people of a nation to a level of concern where they invoke this healing or rebirth. As the people meet the crisis, and overcome it, the new life of spirit is integrated into the nation's laws, traditions, and psyche. The nation thereby grows, just as individuals do.

As we become aware that the great work of a nation is a macrocosm of the impulse to grow which characterizes our individual lives, we can see the value of understanding more about our national spirit, its purpose, and its character. What is the innate temperament of the soul of our nation? What are its special gifts? What are the major national lessons we are learning? What is the best way to solve the problems posed by these lessons?

As might be expected, the national purpose will vary slightly from country to country, just as it varies among individuals. To be sure, all governments must perform a certain core of duties—enforcing law and order, promoting education, building roads, and defense. But all nations also have a deeper purpose which reflects their unique part of the divine Plan for spiritualizing our culture and civilization.

Great Britain, for instance, has responded to its spiritual plan by demonstrating the right use of authority, a fair system of law and justice, and an enlightened governmental paternalism to the world. Being an older and more mature nation, it used the vehicle of the British Empire to bring these principles to less developed countries throughout the world. Naturally, these lessons were not always perfectly embodied, and abuses did occur. But without these influences, tribalism, despotism, and arrogant oligarchies would still be ruling many of these countries. The truth of this fact has been abundantly proven, as Britain withdrew its authority from these countries in the twentieth century, only to have all too many of them revert back to tribal and despotic ways. It is clear that the influence of the British Empire was inspired and benevolent while it lasted.

The United States, by contrast, has its own set of purposes and goals, even though it was nurtured into self-government by England. The United States has been given the assignment of demonstrating that government can serve as an agent of goodwill and unity, by promoting domestic harmony and co-operation out of diverse elements, people, and cultures, while preserving an environment of maximum personal freedom and independence. Like the work of Great Britain, this is no small task.

The full complexity of this assignment becomes apparent only when we compare it to a similar task—parents trying to raise their children in an atmosphere of love but without spoiling or indulging them. They want their children to be-come independent adults who can think for themselves and pursue their own interests, and yet the parents do not want to repudiate their own interests and beliefs in so doing. An even more difficult task would be to encourage their children to act with courage and self-initiative, even while giving them the full measure of support and helpfulness that a child requires. Reconciling these possible extremes becomes a difficult chal-lenge to most parents.

On a national level, the divine work for the government of the United States is even more complex and confusing. Its goals have not yet been met, but we are struggling to respond properly, even though we are still at the stage of a young adult. Our country has been populated by peoples from every part of the world. Somehow, we have managed to integrate almost all of these diverse peoples into a single whole called "America." To be sure, there are still smoldering animosities and unresolved prejudices that continue to this day, but no other country in history has been able to absorb so many cultures and synthe-size them into a strong, successful population. This synthesis has not been imposed by an iron-fisted tyrant, however; it is the result of the willingness of generation after generation of immigrants to be assimilated into a new destiny.

The nature of the soul is reflected in the character or temperament of the country. This character is embodied in the myths, traditions, and inspired writings of the nation. In the case of the United States, the main elements of temperament are self-reliance, independence, generosity, and charity toward all. Some aspects of this national character are paradoxical. We cherish tolerance and personal freedom, and yet we are very serious about morality. We talk about the American dream of success one moment, and cheer for the underdog the next. We view self-sufficiency and responsibility as major virtues, but likewise honor charity and cooperation.

The Declaration of Independence andConstitution state the goals and ideals of the United States quite clearly. In Europe, the authority of government was supposedly derived directly from God, who invested it in the reigning monarch. What a contrast the Constitution of the United States is, as it begins: "We the people...." This was to be a government ordained by the people, serving the people. As such, the Constitution also featured a Bill of Rights, specifically guaranteeing a variety of important rights to the citizens. It codifies the principle that unless the citizens specifically grant power to a government, it cannot presume it. Although this right has at times been abridged by overly-zealous officials, it has largely served the country well.

It is not hard to see that these original writings were inspired documents spelling out significant portions of the spiritual design for the emerging nation. They have led to a nation which insures the freedom of each citizen to become whatever spirit has designed him or her to be. This freedom is to be protected and not hindered, either by state or by religion. Moreover, all citizens are equal—an extended family, in a way. There are differences among us, to be sure, but we are expected to tolerate one another and help each other become strong, independent, and self-sufficient.

Each nation in the world has its own soul. Each national

soul has unique purposes and intents. It is a mistake when Americans try to imitate government systems in Sweden or Japan or Russia or the Sudan. It is equally misguided for other countries to try to imitate America. It is one thing to admire our freedom and aspire to similar liberties; it is quite another to try to impose the American culture or system onto their national traditions. They need to listen to and respond to the soul of their own country, not ours. After all, "cooperation" has a much different cultural meaning in Japan than it does in America. Each nation has its own course to follow—its own spiritual destiny.

Not all nations are designed to be democracies, either. Some national spirits promote very close supervision of its citizens—others do not. Some are best served by a powerful central government, while others deliberately encourage authority to be spread out into states and communities.

Each form has its weaknesses and strengths. Sometimes the very same characteristic leads to both weaknesses and strengths. In the United States, for example, one of our great strengths is that the government protects the freedoms of the citizens. This in turn has led to one of the weaknesses of the system, because not all citizens are equally willing to shoulder the responsibility to take care of themselves. They then put pressure on the government to think for them, make decisions for them, protect them from all dangers real and imagined, and even feed, house, and heal them! Some elements of the nation want to meet these "needs" of the people, whereas others see such involvement as the death knell of freedom. Through it all, we are learning that rights do come with responsibilities, and this in turn leads to a rapid acceleration of the development of our human and spiritual potential. It also leads to a certain amount of divisiveness, as the people who have not yet learned the relationship between rights and responsibilities become envious of the achievements of those that have.

There is no perfect form of government. The best we

can hope for is a government that adequately embodies its spiritual design and meets the legitimate needs of the people during its tenure. In order to appreciate this concept fully, however, we need to recognize the possibility that at times the seeming shortcomings of government might represent a valid spiritual purpose. It is reasonable to assume, for example, that slavery was allowed to exist as part of the spiritual plan during the first seventy-five years of the republic so that it could be repudiated definitively. It is just as reasonable to see that Watergate served a valuable role in re-energizing our national values and ethics, even though it was a painful chapter in history. Just as good parents may refuse to help their children with their homework, because they know their children must master these lessons and learn to think for themselves, the weaknesses and problems of any governmental system may be highlighted for the express purpose of inciting reform. Such crises are, in fact, a clear sign of greater spiritual influence and guidance from the national soul.

What, then, is the work of government, from the perspective of its national spirit? It is to generate a climate of lawfulness which inspires its citizens to tap the full potential of the nation's destiny or design. Fostering such a climate is not an easy achievement for any government. It requires enlightened leadership at the top and the inspired education of the citizenry. The best leader would be one who regularly articulates the plans and purposes of the national spirit, either consciously or unconsciously, and conveys that vision to each and every citizen.

In the United States, this ideal would require the leaders of all branches of government to make the preservation of freedom their most urgent priority. Freedom, in other words, would have to become something more than the topic of a speech at Labor Day picnics. It would have to become the controlling value or principle of the acts and policies of our leaders. The people, in response, would need to make personal responsibility their most urgent priority—to do for themselves what they have lazily expected government to do for them until now.

There would still be special protection and help for the less fortunate, but the goal would not be just to maintain these people, but rather help them learn what it means to become a responsible citizen themselves. Only then will they be ready to accept their full heritage in the American Dream.

It is the spirit of each nation which sets the standards by which that country can achieve greatness. Together, these national spirits work to promote the growth of humanity as a whole. It behooves each nation to learn to become responsive to this inner spirit, for only then will it be able to play its destined part in the divine workshop of government. Only then can we as individuals begin to glimpse the larger meanings of the idea of "citizenship."

KEEPING THE MONSTER HAPPY

The primary, overriding problem in government today is that it is too big, too intrusive, and too expensive. One hundred years ago, governments throughout the world were still relatively small and limited in their ability to interfere in the lives of their citizens. Today, as a result of the growth of bureaucracies and technological advances, government has become like the proverbial eight hundred pound gorilla. It goes where it wants to go and does whatever it wants to do. Often, it is well-behaved and well-received. But sometimes it is intrusive, intimidating, and destructive. It complicates life instead of improving it. It may even create trouble in the name of relieving problems.

In fact, government has become so strong and pervasive that it has become the equivalent of a pagan religion for a large number of people—the fountainhead from which great material and legal blessings flow. This growth in government has transformed politicians and bureaucrats into a kind of entrenched priesthood, with the halls of Congress becoming "the mother church." Unfortunately, the sacrificial offerings being conducted on the altar of democracy usually end up being the freedoms of the people.

Even the election process has become something like old-time tent revivals, with frenzied evangelists stirring up the faithful to "believe" in the personal savior of government and fear the demons of the other party.

How has this idolatry crept into government? The explanation consists of one word: "entitlements." Almost everyone who gets a check from the government, be it a paycheck, a research grant, money to run public broadcasting, unemployment, welfare, or social security, has come to believe in and depend upon the demigod Ittaxem. The word "entitlements" conveys the reassuring notion that government is only giving out what we deserve anyway, but let there be no question about it—all of these people have a hand in government's back pocket. How can they possibly vote objectively, when their vote is effectively bought with every check they receive?

Unfortunately, this pagan idolatry enjoys widespread support from groups who would have decried it vigorously in earlier times. The most prominent example of this support is the media. When America was founded, it was the newspapers that roused public sentiment against the injustices of the British Crown. Today, the media seems ready to barter its last shred of integrity in order to support the divine right of government to be mammoth. They, in turn, have been joined by academics who are behaving as poorly as the monks of the Middle Ages, who dutifully supported the pope no matter how corrupt he was. Both of these groups uniformly support the belief that government is the one great benevolent power that can fix all problems and lift us out of confusion, misery, and suffering. All we have to do is pay more and more taxes, to keep the monster happy, so that it can hire more and more bureaucrats, invent more and more regulations, and find new ways to intrude into our lives.

Out of this abdication of traditional roles, a second major problem of government has arisen. It is surrounded by a climate of emotional frenzy and intellectual hysteria. The immense power and wealth that has been focused in government drives all kinds of otherwise sane people stark raving mad. They are drawn to the outer edges of government like moths to a flame, lusting for their share of the bounty. As a result, they lose any ability they may have had to view issues impartially or even consider the possibility that big government might be a threat. They read 1984 as teenagers, of course, but have long since forgotten its chilling message.

There is no doubt that governments throughout the world have done many good things and can do far more. They are ideally constituted to initiate reforms and solve the many problems arising as people and communities interact. But utopian schemes did not work when tried one hundred years ago by religious fanatics, and they do not work today when embraced by scholars and government officials. The so-called "Great Society" is now on the verge of producing the "Bankrupt Society"—even in the midst of rapid economic growth. The problem does not lie in the good intentions of the people who sponsor these programs, but in a more subtle issue. Government programs inexorably attract abuse and corruption. The larger the scheme for reforming society, the more vulnerable it is to abuse. But it is never government that foots the bill. It just demands higher taxes.

Government needs to learn to limit itself to activities it can do well: law enforcement, public health, building roads, trash collection, defense, and so on. When it tries to branch out and become a source of benevolent help for its citizens, it inevitably fails, simply because these kinds of programs are so easily corrupted. A large part of every dollar spent on Medicare ends up in the pockets of corrupt suppliers and billers. A large part of every federal dollar spent on education ends up being used to promote partisan social issues instead of teaching children.

The worst aspect of this problem is the underlying belief that government is a pagan idol from whom all blessings, rights, and privileges are derived. At their very best, governments are never more than an agent for supervising the interaction of individuals and groups throughout the nation, as they strive to live up to the ideals of the national spirit. Power is meant to flow through the government to its citizens, to be used by each as he or she sees fit. No government has the right to hold onto that power or use it to tyrannize or control its people.

Just so, no government is the source of any of its wealth, power, or legitimacy. Governments are meant to be a custodian of a nation's resources, a regent who serves the people as quietly and as inconspicuously as possible. The old adage about children would be more appropriately applied to governments: they should be seen but not heard. We should know them only by their achievements, never by their intrusiveness in our lives.

Experience teaches us that it is deceptively easy to spend or give away someone else's power or money. Unless the money or power is our own, there is no real incentive to practice either efficiency or accountability. Governments are not immune to this principle. Therefore, it is very important to find a way to limit the power and money they can usurp for their insatiable appetites.

The third major problem facing many governments, especially democracies, is the direct result of the freedoms they guarantee. The United States in particular is suffering from this problem. While the government can guarantee the protection of specific rights, it is not able to guarantee that citizens will act with a corresponding sense of responsibility and maturity! The principle involved is very simple. Every right and privilege in life comes with a corresponding responsibility to exercise that right maturely. The right of free speech, for example, does not allow us to destroy another person's reputation with lies and misinformation. We have a responsibility to speak accurately, if not wisely. We also have a responsibility to remain silent whenever speaking would cause injury. We have a limited right to bear arms, but we also have the responsibility not to kill other people.

All too many people respond to freedom in silly ways. They exercise their right to smoke and drink themselves to death, instead of exercising their responsibility to practice temperance. They pursue the right to squander money, instead of fulfilling their duty to care for their families. They wallow in the "right" to be lazy and unproductive, then demand to be taken care of by the state.

It is easy enough to spell out what government must do to protect and ensure our rights. It is much harder to legislate responsibility. Any attempt to pass a law that all citizens must work for a living, for instance, would be hooted down as an intrusion on their "right" to do nothing—a right that does not actually exist. It would also lead many to think that they have a right to a job if they want one, even if they have no talents or skills to offer!

As a result, most of the efforts to legislate responsibility have been punitive. If a spouse fails to provide child support as agreed to in a divorce decree, he or she can be forced to pay. Yet disincentives of this nature do not usually encourage these people to become more mature; they usually just drive them to go underground and drop out of conventional society. Again, experience teaches us that dogs and people respond better to rewards than to punishment. And so, it is normal to expect people to be more interested in pursuing their freedoms than in fulfilling their responsibilities, even though they are part of the same package.

Throughout the ages, in fact, freedom has all too often been interpreted as freedom from most obligations, rather than the freedom to become a better and more productive person. Liberty has often been wrongly interpreted as license to do as we please. Rights and privileges have been taken for granted, as a gift without obligations—like the air we breathe. Responsibility, on the other hand, has usually been viewed as an onerous burden, not the key to growth and new opportunity.

These three problems—the size of government, the idolatry of government, and the promotion of freedom without responsibility—have caused in turn a host of additional problems for modern governments. A few of the most troublesome include:

1. The increasing tendency of citizens to prefer dependence on government to self-determination and self-sufficiency. We have become a nation of spoiled children, waiting for our national nanny to feed us, protect us, and heal us when we ail. It is unrealistic to expect politicians to refuse to respond to the cry for greater assistance. This dependency, therefore, is not a problem of the machinery of government as much as it is the addiction of special interest groups to their monthly fix from Washington. It has created the monster of "entitlement mentality."

It must be remembered that this concept of entitlement was totally foreign to the thinking of the Founding Fathers. They tried to serve the spiritual purpose of creating an environment in which each citizen would be free to develop his or her self-expression to the fullest degree. It never occurred to them that government would end up in the business of crippling the drive for self-sufficiency and creativity by handing out money!

Still, this is exactly what has happened. More and more people every year believe that government is responsible for providing them with a good life. Unfortunately, this attitude reduces citizens to insect-like status, and it reduces our culture to the lowest common denominator. The best and noblest elements of society are sacrificed in order to support the weak and the indigent. Aspirations, goals, ideals, and achievement are scorned, because they embarrass those who do not have them. In the process, a new kind of tyranny is born—a tyranny of the masses. The vitality and creativity of the productive members of the nation are sucked dry to support the nonproductive and the uncreative.

Government was never designed to be the protector of the poor and the nonproductive from the majority. It was designed to govern all people and give all people an equal opportunity at success. When any class of people becomes dependent upon government, it upsets this basic principle.

How then are we supposed to care for the poor and the disadvantaged? Obviously, the answer lies in finding a solution that expresses the underlying spiritual goals of our nation. The government can be involved to some degree—for instance, by granting tax relief to the poor—but it should take a back seat and encourage other segments of society to step in and initiate more constructive programs. Business has indicated a willingness to do so; many charities are already deeply involved. Education has a role to play, as do the churches. Government should restrain itself to leading and encouraging; for the most part, it should stay away from doing. The word "do" should be a verb used by the individual, not the government.

A good prototype for this kind of help is the type of assistance many families extend to elderly parents who are unable to live alone but cannot afford live-in help. These people need and deserve much loving care. But they ought not to become the centerpiece of the family's life, nor the sole reason for the family's existence. They are important, but not the most important—or even a top priority.

Governmental programs to help the disadvantaged should embody this same model. The assistance offered should in most cases be temporary, until the disadvantage can be overcome. The assistance should likewise be given in such a way that the recipient is rewarded for progress in becoming self-reliant.

2. The resurgence of tribalism instead of a national culture. One of the major efforts of the Hierarchy one hundred years ago was to put together small states into larger nations with a common culture and values. Unfortunately, in the last twenty-five years, the advances made have been largely undone, as several large nations have been "Balkanized" or split into many smaller nations, often along the lines of ancient tribal divisions. Even the United States has not been exempt from this trend, as the reappearance of ethnic priorities and multiculturalism has undone many of the gains of the "melting pot." In the process, nationalistic pride and aggressiveness have been resurrected.

In this country, much of the damage has been done in the push to end all discrimination. It is true that there has been a great deal of discrimination against many racial and religious groups throughout the history of America. It is likewise true that discrimination is a major issue that must be solved. The only question is: will the solution to this problem destroy something even more vital to the nation?

If the effort to protect one group from prejudice leads to the codification of uniform rules and standards, fairly and consistently enforced, then discrimination will rapidly become a ghost of the past. On the other hand, if the effort to solve the problem results in granting special privileges to victims of prior discrimination, the vicious cycle of discrimination will be perpetuated.

Unfortunately, government tends to choose the latter method over the former. The impact on society has been to stir up new levels of competition and hostility among the races—in other words, renewed tribalism. Instead of a common set of rules for all Americans, we now have separate sets of rules for blacks, whites, Hispanics, men, and women. Victims of discrimination are given special consideration in hiring, contracts, admission to college, and standards of behavior. Prior acts of discrimination are "cured" by opposite acts of discrimination today. Yet common sense tells us this will not work. More injustice is never a cure for injustice. New dirt is never a cure for old dirt!

Concurrently, an effort has been made to promote pride and dignity among peoples who have suffered past discrimination. There is a solid psychological basis for this approach: those who have been unfairly led to feel inferior will benefit from praise and support. But "black pride" is too often a code word for the hatred of white people. Feminist pride almost always involves a slam against men.

In these ways, the movements of multiculturalism and diversity, although begun with good intentions, are actually serving to create new schisms in our society. Each group, armed with moral superiority and new laws, is competing for a finite number of jobs, contracts, and promotions in society. Every time someone wins, another human being loses. In this way, the very essence of freedom is being perverted. Freedom of opportunity now means only "freedom for the dispossessed"—not freedom for everyone. Equal opportunity actually means legally enforced unequal opportunity. This is a major break from the guidance and inspiration of the spirit of America. It is also a step which ensnares government as a willing conspirator to perpetuate prejudice. The damage being done to society in the name of progress is enormous. It is a legacy that future generations will not be happy to inherit.

3. The growing arrogance of government agencies and bureaucrats. Armed with the mystique of governmental omnipotence and the unthinking belief that government is the great provider, strange changes are occurring in our bureaucracies. There is a growing attitude that government owns all the rights and suffers the citizens to exercise them. There is likewise an apparent belief that government owns all the wealth and income, and it merely allows us to keep a small portion of it for our private use.

Even worse, government bureaucracies seem determined to bypass the will of elected representatives and courts whenever possible, substituting their regulations for due process of law. They claim the right to harass, confiscate, imprison, and control the lives and freedom of citizens—all because of their assumed "mandate" to protect the public interest. They picture themselves as the appointed guardians of everything from the environment to public safety and morality.

Governments, of course, do have the right to control the actions of citizens in instances described by law. The police have a right and a duty to stop speeding or drunk drivers. But all too often, agencies of government presume authority they do not have. They begin to believe that the power to govern emanates from their office. It does not; the power to govern emerges from the people.

This is no small point: there is a vast difference between a democracy that serves its citizens and a tyranny that exploits its citizens. All too often, our government has become the latter—especially in its uncontrolled bureaucracies.

For freedom to work, the agents of government must act with responsibility, too—not just the citizens.

4. Apathy and cynicism among the citizenry. When government promises everything and delivers very little, the people are quickly disenchanted. Government agencies are frequently nonresponsive to the legitimate requests of the public. Even something as simple as renewing license plates is often turned into a day-long nightmare of waiting and red tape when handled by government. Politicians seem to be more concerned about protecting their own interests than in serving the interests of their constituents. Voters have watched as special interest groups and radical elements have hijacked key government programs and agencies, leaving the vast majority to support the very narrow agenda of the few.

When efforts are made to call attention to these failings, the bureaucrats and government officials close ranks to protect their domain. They treat the citizens raising the protest as the enemy. As a result, any real dialogue becomes impossible. Debate is reduced to shouting and name-calling. The citizenry is thus forced either to take sides or just ignore the process.

It is perfectly reasonable for the average citizen to become apathetic or cynical in this political milieu. There is no quick fix for this cancer in government, but there is a cure. It was demonstrated centuries ago. It is called citizen action—the determination of the citizens to keep themselves informed and active in supervising government policy, elected officials, bureaucrats, the media, and the courts. It is not an easy task, but an indispensable one, if our democracy is going to continue to function.

Is it possible to reform the government? Of course it is. All that we have to do is remember that the Constitution begins, "We the people." Just as we sat by and let the government grow huge, we can now take action to demand that the government begin to downsize, not by radically cutting out services but by redefining what government should and should not do. We need first of all to clarify our sense of national purpose, common values, and standards. The tyranny of the weak and unproductive must be exposed and rejected. Handouts and entitlements must be replaced by genuine charity and helpfulness.

Based on this review, we must then begin to redefine policies. It should be the primary role of government to help everyone have a chance to succeed, but governed by the same rules and standards. The government expression of compassion must be expanded from compassion for the conspicuously needy, and redefined as compassion for everyone alike—including the rich, the successful, and the talented. They must have the same rights as everyone else, or no one has any freedom at all. They must have the same opportunities as everyone else, or no one can expect fair treatment.

Finally, the government must once again be made accountable to its citizens. It is glib to say that it is accountable—that every election makes it so. It may be true that elected officials are accountable, but the vast reaches of government agencies and bureaucracy are not. We must give government incentives to eliminate waste, improve the quality of services, and respect the need to stay out of our lives whenever possible.

Is this vision too utopian? No, it is merely consistent with the spirit of America and the larger, spiritual design for good government. It would herald a return to the original meaning and value of freedom—not freedom from hardship, but freedom to be self-sufficient, self-initiating, and, yes, self-governing.

INITIATING REFORMS

In a young society, the work of government is often quite basic: holding the people more or less in line, for their own good. In a democracy, however, such an attitude in government would be insulting to the people. The work of government shifts to a higher level: to initiate reforms that will inspire the people to become more responsive to the spiritual ideals of the soul of the nation.

America was one of the first countries to build the process of reform into the very structure of government. Every election gives us the opportunity to send the government in new directions, if the voting public so chooses. Every election therefore is an opportunity to discuss key issues of government in the open, and modify policy. Every election is a window for reform.

Most of these reforms do not arise by accident. In many instances, the awareness of the public of a scandal, a conflict of interest, a controversy, or an ethical lapse has been carefully inspired by the spirit of the nation—not to annoy us with troublesome problems, but to urge us to pay attention to our national life. If we look beyond the issues and think of them in terms of the emerging spiritual ideals of enlightened individuality, productivity, innovation, intelligent charity, and harmony, then it should not be too difficult to understand how the spirit of America is guiding us—or what it wants us to do.

Some of the principal reforms occurring within our government, as well as many other governments, at the present time include:

1. A push for more accountability from politicians, bureaucrats, and other government leaders. Over the last forty years, a "golden triangle" has been formed among the intellectual elite in government, academia, and the media which threatens to distort and limit public information and discussion on key issues. Dissenting voices are simply ignored or not taken seriously. Since the press is a central part of this unconscious conspiracy, it has become very effective in muting public outcries for change.

As the media establishment loses the stranglehold on the dissemination of information that it has enjoyed since the Fifties, the opportunity will arise to smash this clandestine cabal. This process can be accelerated as more and more intelligent people decide to stop believing anything they read or hear in mass media. They need to learn to go outside the system to acquire their knowledge of what is truly happening in government. When this occurs in sufficient numbers, the triangle can be snapped.

Even though government officials mostly resent the intrusion of public watchdogs, the skeptical eye is the solution to the current lack of accountability in government. We must once again learn to take pride in blowing the whistle on waste and abuse, at every level of government. We must act as the public did in one state, when it was learned that the government was using taxpayer money to combat infertility in welfare mothers. The governor was forced to eliminate the program.

In another case, the government wasted more than a billion dollars in the early Nineties on nuclear testing, even though there was a moratorium on such tests! Not one nuclear device was tested during this period—all the money was spent on maintaining buildings and employees on a standby mode, in case tests would resume.

Finally, in many states it has become nearly impossible to fire incompetent teachers. It takes two to three years and roughly a quarter of a million dollars to plod through all the hearings and reviews required to discharge just one incompetent teacher. Yet all of this expense is included in the cost of educating a child.

When will this lack of accountability stop? The answer has been proven repeatedly: when the public demands it. As always, reform begins with ourselves, as we revisit our priorities and duties as a citizen.

2. A campaign to reform entitlements. Entitlements are an economic time bomb that threatens the economic viability of the whole system. Those receiving entitlements now form a highly vocal and visible constituency, and it will not be easy to balance their demands against the needs of all citizens. The solutions to the problem are well-known and have been thoroughly outlined; they simply have not been implemented. If this trend continues, it will inflame an already heated class war to riotous levels. If history is a guide, however, the problem will have to reach crisis proportions before any constructive steps will be taken. In other words, this is a reform that we will purchase dearly, probably with bloodshed.

In addition to reforming the actual entitlements, it is even more important to puncture the "entitlement mentality," the self-serving philosophy that we are not responsible for ourselves—government is. It will not be easy to dislodge this attitude. First, many politicians have no qualms or shame about pandering to this destructive belief. Second, the current psychological climate has made heroes out of victims of all stripes. It has therefore become difficult to criticize the lifestyle or values of others, let alone suggest the need that they assume more responsibility for themselves.

The reform of this mentality will require a massive effort to educate the public about the facts of life, inside and outside of government. Obviously, such a campaign will draw instant criticism from almost all politicians, bureaucrats, and the beneficiaries of the entitlement programs. It will therefore have to be conducted from outside of government—and outside the normal channels of the press and professional educational circles.

A key part of this educational effort will be a continual effort to expose the easily demonstrated fact that governments provide less service, of poorer quality and at a higher cost, than private enterprise. This fact has already been demonstrated in the field of education, where even underfinanced parochial schools regularly outperform the results of nearby public schools, for a fraction of the cost per student. It is also regularly demonstrated in the construction of facilities. It is almost axiomatic that a new courthouse anywhere in this country will take twenty years to build, with a cost overrun of at least $100 million. A new headquarters for a large company, however, can be built in less than a year—and under budget.

The evidence that government ought to get out of the business of providing services that business can provide at a much lower cost is mountainous. It is just a matter of time before the recipients of government largesse wake up to the fact that they are being cheated and abused by their dependency on government, instead of helped.

3. An effort to make our government more civil and responsive. The public could benefit immensely by a new climate of tolerance and patience. At the moment, it seems as if government wants to remove every possible grievance or insult from every public place. There are rules about what we can and cannot say at work. There are laws that describe what we can and cannot do in raising children. There are laws as to when and where we can smoke or drink. There are even laws forbidding us from celebrating religious holidays on public property.

Political correctness is rapidly corroding our cultural life and manners. There are always self-righteous people willing to draw up rules of conduct and apply them to everyone else. We need to tell these people in no uncertain terms to get out of our hair. We need fewer rules and regulations and more civility. We need fewer laws and lawsuits, and more good manners. We need to learn to treat one another with respect. Unless this issue is faced and corrected soon, there will be a wholesale escalation of petty people seeking outrageous compensations for their own irritability and intolerance. As usual, however, it is likely that true reform will not occur until this trend reaches a crisis level.

In the meantime, there is no reason why intelligent people cannot start putting the emphasis on the right issues. Instead of whining about every little imperfection in life, we should devote more of our time talking about what is right and good about life. We should praise and celebrate the advancements of health care and technology and science that expand our worlds and let us live longer. The little wrongs that irritate us so much will seem even smaller if we balance them with a healthy expression of gratefulness and appreciation.

In this regard, for example, it would make much more sense to thank a veteran of World War II for his sacrifices and those of his fallen comrades, than to spend our time complaining about the Pentagon or the Department of De-

fense. It would make far more sense to rejoice in the glories
of nature than to constantly complain about the disappearing
rain forest and blame it on the usual whipping boys in business and commerce. And it would make far more sense to
be thankful for the advances of health care than to complain
about medical malpractice. Mistakes will always be made by
human beings, but the biggest mistake of all is to obsess about
imperfection. A person who is always assessing blame and
never expressing gratitude is condemning himself or herself
to the life of a malcontent.

Let us be realistic. The constant threat of a malpractice
suit does not inspire any doctor to want to perform surgery,
let alone attract youngsters to study hard and become doctors
themselves. An occasional expression of public gratitude for
a job well done would be a far more powerful inducement.
If we fail to practice good manners, we may well succeed only
in driving competent doctors out of practice.

If we are adults, there should be no need to protect ourselves from every inconvenience and insult. The notion that
we should turn to government for this protection takes a bad
idea and makes it tyrannical.

**4. A continued effort to promote the general wel-
fare of the people.** Two hundred years ago, "welfare" was
a word that referred to the well-being of the whole populace.
Today, it has been corrupted to refer only to the well-being
of the most needy elements of society. Government needs
to "reinvent" welfare once again, so it includes more than
just caring for the poor and disadvantaged. It must define
an ideal of citizen self-sufficiency, and tailor all of its welfare
programs to helping every citizen achieve it. Naturally, the
poor and disadvantaged will receive the most help, but the
goal will be to motivate everyone to realize the American
Dream.

It might be helpful if the government viewed this task
as if it were an adult trying to help handicapped children.

Is the adult a caretaker—or a teacher? The easy path is to do whatever the children cannot do by themselves—feed them, clothe them, and help them walk. Such caretaking addresses the immediate needs of the children, but soon becomes expensive—and restrictive. The children never develop skills of their own; instead, they become dependent upon the caretaker. The more challenging path is to teach the handicapped children how to care for themselves. It requires enormous patience and repetition, but in the long run, it rescues the humanity and productivity of the children.

Almost all people are handicapped in some way; it is by overcoming our limitations that we grow. If we are fortunate, we receive the help we need to recognize these handicaps and conquer them. For the most desperately poor members of our society, it is right and proper for government to provide this help, so long as it is directed at helping promote the true welfare of the individual, not just give him or her temporary comfort. Temporary comfort has a way of extending into generations of dependency.

Such a reform will require a truly determined effort by government, because the crusade to "protect the rights" of the poor and disadvantaged has become a lucrative industry—an industry that is far more interested in maintaining its power base than in solving the problems of poverty. In this regard, it may be helpful to learn a lesson from countries that have far more serious problems of poverty. In India, for example, there is a strict rule that charity must go to correcting the actual social problem, not just relieving the symptoms of it.

5. An effort to establish a stronger sense of identity for all Americans. Much effort has been given to end discrimination in this country, but too much of the effort has been one-sided, thereby creating new divisions and perpetuating the problem into the twenty-first century. In addition, ethnic and racial divisiveness has actually increased in the past few decades, bringing on a new round of culture wars.

Until now, the effort of government to solve these problems has been heavily tinged with guilt, shame, and remorse. Our current generation has been held accountable for the alleged sins of earlier generations. Heavy penalties in employment, college opportunity, and government contracts have been assessed for just being a man or a Caucasian. Even worse, the whole country has been plunged into a crusade to revamp our high school and college curricula to meet the needs of diversity. This campaign threatens to weaken substantially the core of our value system as a nation.

Mature people learn how to cope with unfairness and suffering. It is never pleasant, but the best solution is to put it behind us and do everything we can to make sure the future is more promising. If we let ourselves be trapped in self-pity and endless recriminations, we will trap ourselves in the past.

Society must do the same. Minorities have unquestionably suffered from unfair discrimination for much of the history of the United States. But what the crusaders forget is that many Europeans came to this country because they were the victims of persecution and discrimination in their home lands. To some degree, every new wave of immigrants suffered from sharp discrimination and rejection, until they integrated themselves into society, by setting the past behind them.

The cry of discrimination is a demand that someone else solve our problems for us. For genuine change to occur, minority groups must see themselves as the primary agents for change. They must set the past aside and integrate themselves into mainstream America. The keys to producing this kind of change are right motivation, true cooperation, right objectives, and a proper identity. The present motivation of redressing earlier wrongs must give way to a healthier, more positive motive—to play a significant role as citizens of America. True cooperation will only be attained when the old grudges and charges of racism are dropped and replaced by friendship and helpfulness. To this must be added the right objective:

a determination to demonstrate that the contributions of a particular segment of society to the overall welfare can make the rest of us forget the earlier stridency of its demands. The key to identity lies in becoming an American, not a victim.

This last point is of great importance. So long as any group of people derives its primary identity from being a victim, it will be impossible to integrate fully into society. America has never been made up of victims—it was built by achievers. Just so, America was not built by Scots or Brits or the French or the Polish. It was built by Americans—by people of many ethnic backgrounds who gave up their former identity and acquired a new one. As long as blacks are taught to be Africans first and Americans second, they will never break the cycle of discrimination. In like fashion, as long as feminists think of themselves as women first and Americans second, they will perpetuate the very problems they complain about.

These ideas are consistent with the realities of conflict resolution. As long as warring parties battle over their differences, they will never solve their problems. Resolution begins when each party begins to see that they share common values and goals with their opponents. The ability to agree that everyone is entitled to success in the American Dream, for example, is a good starting point in ending discrimination. It establishes a common bond of respect that in turn nurtures harmony.

When the army was forced to deal with the problems of racial disharmony, it adopted all the standard programs of sensitivity training. In their experience, however, this type of training only made the problems worse. The training focused on the problems of discrimination, not the solutions. It highlighted grievances and invoked guilt and humiliation. As a result, it exacerbated the very problem it hoped to solve. So the army went back to its basic instincts. It treated everyone as a soldier first, rather than as a black, a Hispanic, or a white. They taught the soldiers that they all needed to take care of each other and some day might have to trust every one of their comrades with their lives. This gave the soldiers a motivation to make friends with everyone in their unit and treat them as they would treat themselves.

Government does not need to pass more laws to enforce an end to discrimination. It needs, instead, to pursue a stronger sense of common identity among all Americans. It needs to try something it has seldom attempted—to govern by leadership instead of by law. If government is unwilling to lead in this way, then it will fall to the enlightened people in society to demonstrate that it can be done. This, after all, is a major part of self-sufficiency—not to look to government to solve a problem that would be better off solved without its interference. If enough people of goodwill recognize that the problems of racial and gender discord can be solved through the consistent expression of cooperation and respect, and not the continual airing of grievances, we will be well on our way to achieving a new level of national harmony.

6. Ending international terrorism. Terrorism has been a problem throughout the history of nations. In recent years, however, technological advances have given terrorists far more sophisticated weapons than they ever used before—poison gases, nuclear bombs, and germ warfare. As a result, terrorism poses a potentially enormous threat to the civilized world.

Until recently, America was immune to the threat of terrorism, but cracks have begun to show in its armor. There is therefore an increasing need to link with other world powers to confront and solve the problem of world terrorism. Obviously, typical measures of defense, such as the army, are of little value in protecting against this threat. Inevitably, the full solution will depend upon the willing cooperation of the public at large.

7. A gradual transition toward a global economy, culture, and government. A major part of the destined Plan for all nations during the coming centuries is to move toward a closer global alliance. The common market in Europe is a model for this alliance, which will arise to develop more uniform economic standards and practices. The United Nations may participate in this transition, but will not be the foundation for it.

Most intelligent people would agree that such a transition is inevitable and desirable. At the emotional level, however, there will be great resistance. The struggle of Northern Ireland, or to a lesser degree, Wales or Scotland, in remaining an integral part of Great Britain, highlights the strong tug of ancient loyalties and traditions that bind a people together. Such people will see any international alliance as a threat to their identity and independence. They will resist surrendering their self-determination to a huge central bureaucracy of the intellectual elite.

Some of these fears are grounded in long histories of treachery and broken treaties. As always, it is the human factor which compromises the enormous potential of the ideal. But the potential for healing the divisions of humanity and learning to act as a united whole outweigh the concerns of each segment.

Part of the work of each national government, therefore, will be to lay the groundwork for a more or less smooth transition to these new alliances. Those countries that bitterly resist it will suffer and delay—but not stop—the slow work of evolutionary change in global government.

SUPPORTING GOOD GOVERNMENT

On the eve of ratifying the Constitution, Benjamin Franklin was asked what kind of system the new government would be. "A republic, sir," he replied, "if we can keep it." In this statement, he conveyed the wisdom that a democracy can be successful only as long as the citizens stay informed about and take responsibility for the actions of their government. There are actually four sets of checks and balances in our system: the executive branch, the Congress, the courts—and the people. If government has become corrupt and its bureaucracies have become indifferent, it is only because the people have not sufficiently stayed involved in their government.

For this reason, the very first way to increase our enlightened support for the work of government is to become a better informed and more concerned citizen. We need to stay abreast of what is happening at all levels of government—and not just by listening to the carefully packaged news on television, either. We need to read newsletters, listen to radio talk shows, and seek out other independent sources of information, so that we can be fully informed about the real stories behind the misleading headlines.

It is fatal to let special interest groups and the intellectual elite tell us how to think, even if we admire or support them. Government controls tremendous power and wealth. If even one citizen stops thinking—or never begins—then the door opens for uncontrolled abuse of that power and wealth. Awareness of what government is doing—and failing to do—is the most powerful weapon we have.

As part of this effort, we need to redefine our role as citizens. Many people assume their role is to vote and pay taxes; indeed, many eligible voters do not even do this much. The rest of their involvement with government is a passive one, as a consumer of governmental services—police and fire protection, roads, schools, and the like. In some cases, the extent of their involvement is to "cash in" on the governmental pie, by making sure they get their fair share of pork, legally or not.

If we intend to support good government, we must break the habit of being a consumer and do what is necessary to become a contributor. We need to shun the easy temptation of selling our soul to Washington in exchange for a few benefits or privileges. No matter how we rationalize it, being a consumer without also being a contributor harms us more than it strengthens us. It also harms the nation instead of strengthening it.

We also need to take our role as a watchdog more seriously. Loud-mouthed victims have succeeded in hijacking
whole government agencies and using them for their special
interests in recent decades. The rest of us need to speak
just as loudly in demanding fair and honest treatment of all
citizens, not just the special interest groups.

Being a good watchdog does not mean adopting the tactics
of the special interest groups—the tactics of the hysterical
troublemakers and mischief mongers. It simply means letting
our voice be heard above the din of the madding crowd—and
in specific, letting it be heard by the politicians and bureaucrats
who have the power to make relevant decisions and policy.
The silent majority must stop being silent and become the
assertive majority.

To be effective as a watchdog, we must start asking tough
questions. When the school board proposes a tax increase
for education—for the children, of course—we must ask:
exactly how will this help the children? Why does educating
children require a larger percentage of the tax dollar today
than it did forty years ago? When a new government building
costs millions of dollars more than projected, we need to ask
tough questions. Why were contracts let without conventional
bidding? Who paid off whom? Why are taxpayers being
asked to cover the deficit?

It is not enough, however, just to become a critic. If we
truly support good government, then we should demonstrate
our commitment by cultivating the ideals and lifestyle of a
mature citizen. We should strive to act with the civility, integrity,
tolerance, personal responsibility, work ethic, and creativity
of the spirit of America. In addition, we should quietly but
consistently expect and demand the same from others. Those
who are lazy and irresponsible are not contributing anything
worthwhile to the nation. If help is offered, but they refuse
to accept it, then they must be held accountable. This is
not a question of being intolerant. It is an issue of protect-

ing the integrity of our democratic system of government.

Above all, we best support good government by becoming self-governing—by trying to live our life as though we were an agent of the soul of the nation and an enlightened citizen of the world. As we make personal decisions, therefore, we should consider their impact on the nation and the world around us. If we are tempted to make a deal that is not in the best interest of our community, we should master the temptation. If we are encouraged by others to join a protest that would undermine the basic principles of the Spirit of America, we should just say no.

To the degree that we are selfish and self-absorbed, we make a lousy citizen. To be a responsible citizen, we must learn to give up our selfish ways and forget our special interests. Good citizens are not lobbyists pushing a one-sided agenda. They are members of a community or nation, seeking to do whatever is best for the collective whole. Good citizens are never divisive; they reach out with tolerance and goodwill and try to draw even those who have opposing views into a consensus that leads to progress.

In fact, a good citizen is not just an American first and an individual second. That would be a step in the right direction for many people, to be sure, but there is another, larger step to take. In this country, a good citizen is a spiritual being first, an American second, and a productive individual third. We are all citizens of the world and children of God, as well as Americans. We must therefore be governed by spiritual laws as well as human laws, and strive to fulfill our divine design as well as live up to the destiny of our nation.

In this sense, the full work and promise of the divine workshop of government is a duty for each of us, a way in which each of us can make an important contribution to the advancement of humanity and the emergence of the life of spirit on earth.

The Divine Workshop
of the Healing Arts
and Sciences

OUR DESIGN FOR WHOLENESS

When we are ill, nothing is more urgent than the need to get well. Yet when we are well, there is nothing we take for granted more than good health. As a result, both individually and in society, few of us have attained much understanding of the true dynamics of health. Even health professionals tend to have scant appreciation for the underlying nature of wellness. They are thoroughly versed in their specialized approach to physical health, of course, but they usually lack any real perception of the spiritual principles and goals of health.

The physical, mundane role of health is to satisfy the needs and desires of the body to feel good and be comfortable in all of our physical activites. The inner, spiritual role of health, by contrast, deals with the liberation of the life force and the fulfillment of the design of our spiritual essence, the soul. These two approaches to health are often radically at odds with each other—and, in fact, seldom intersect.

For this reason, it is difficult for most people to grasp the full implications of the spiritual work of the healing profession. Our focus of attention is personal and subjective. If we are sick, we want to get well. If we feel fine, we want to "live life fully"—which all too often includes abusing the body with smoking, drinking, immature emotions, bungee jumping, and other unhealthy activities. Furthermore, we approach health in a very expedient way. If we are sick, we want a pill that will make us well—not a lecture about the esoteric dimensions of disease. We also tend to be impatient. If we are sick, we do not want to wait for the Federal Drug Administration to approve some new treatment. We want health now.

Spirit, on the other hand, has different objectives. If we have cancer, the soul may be far more interested in letting us learn how our resentments have "eaten away" at us than in preventing our death. In fact, it might be quite determined to use death to build up a strong awareness of the need to exercise better control over our wayward emotions. It may use a timely accident to force us to pause and reflect on the direction of our life, and begin to act in healthier and more mature ways in the future.

Health, however, is the one institution of human civilization that few people ignore entirely. We can ignore art, and still live comfortably. We can tune out the games of politicians and still lead a full, enriched life. We can even recover from an inadequate education, as virtually every child today will have to do. But sooner or later, we will pay attention to and need health care services. At that moment, health will be of paramount importance to us.

This characteristic of modern health means that the divine workshop of the healing arts and sciences is affected far more than any other institution by the average person. Artists notoriously ignore the average tastes of mass consciousness. Scientists follow their own interests, isolated in their laboratories. Government may seem to be responsive to the people, but it is actually controlled by bureaucracy, special interests, and politicians. The standards of health may be dictated by professionals, but the professionals in turn must be responsive to the patients who come to them.

The patient actually has enormous power. There is not just one branch of the healing arts; there is in fact a vast spectrum of possibilities, ranging from the traditional practice of medicine to faith healing, herbalism, and physical manipulations. Some of these specialties claim to treat all maladies of the body and mind; others are more modest and restrict themselves to a narrow field of competence. No one form of treatment has demonstrated the ability to heal all maladies in all people at all times. Each contains some ability to treat illness and restore health under the right circumstances. It is up to the patient to determine which one.

The irony of this situation is that the patient is the least likely person to recognize the psychological and spiritual elements of healing, or even care much about them. For this reason, the odds are extremely high that most patients will select a form of treatment which will address only the physical symptoms of their problems. The underlying causes, which are likely to reappear later on, are often totally ignored.

In fact, it is only within the last one hundred years that the psychological aspects of illness have drawn any attention at all. Even today, most health professionals and the public pay little heed to the impact of the emotions on physical health, let alone the influence of spiritual forces and designs. As a result, the art and science of healing remains a very one-sided, one-dimensional activity. Most people view it strictly as the repair of the physical body whenever it breaks down. For this reason, the goal of healing almost always is to prolong life and keep the physical body as comfortable and symptom free as possible—from the point of view of the personality.

The mission of the divine workshop of healing, on the other hand, is quite different. Its primary goal is to bring human beings, whether or not they are "ill," into greater harmony with their soul and the laws of health. The focus of this work, therefore, is to facilitate the life and plans of the soul, not just relieve symptoms and restore function. In treating depression, for instance, the objective is to liberate the joy of the soul to overpower despair, not just attack the causes of personal disappointment—or mask the problem chemically. In handling a case of acute bacterial infection, the inner work of healing strives to augment the life force and healing mechanism of the body, not just fight the infection.

In simplest terms, the spiritual work of the healing arts and sciences is to stimulate the healing powers and design of the soul for wholeness—wholeness of body, mind, and spirit. This principle applies to every living organism, from microbes to races and nations. To translate this into a common sense approach to healing, we can state that a "body" is healthy if the whole personality honors the purpose and qualities of the soul as it acts. A person who acts with gracefulness, wisdom, and integrity, therefore, would be a healthy person, even if they suffered occasional aches and pains. But a person who leads a self-absorbed, superficial life will be unhealthy, even if he or she seems to be physically fit. The seeds of illness are already at work at unseen levels creating mischief, because the person is not expressing the qualities and vitality of the soul in daily life.

To make sense of this spiritual aspect of healing, we must understand that the physical body and the personality are vehicles the soul uses for its self-expression. They are designed to be agents of the wisdom, love, joy, power, talents, and plans of the soul. Whenever they fail to live up to this design—which is fairly common—the door is opened for the breeding of unhealthy conditions.

It would be helpful if most health professionals could embrace a basic understanding of this concept. It will be a long time, however, before the average person comprehends it. For most people, it is so absurdly esoteric that it is virtually meaningless.

Still, it would be helpful for health care specialists and their patients both to understand certain key principles:

1. We all have an inner, spiritual life. It is an integral part of life.

2. This inner life can be a guide and healing resource.

3. Health is a lot more than just "not being sick."

4. The way to health lies in working with our inner vitality and our spiritual design for wholeness, and observing the laws of health.

5. Regardless of the methods they use, health care professionals ought to be guided by these principles as they treat patients.

The idea of an inner, spiritual life is not a new one to many people, but their beliefs seldom match reality. Unable to comprehend the abstract nature of spirit, all too many people impose a materialistic definition on their concept of the soul. For example, they assume that the soul is only the accumulation of all of our life experiences on earth. They insist that mind and character are just the result of electrical and chemical functions in the brain. They even go so far, in some cases, as insisting that consciousness is the result of brain activity, and that our character is just a byproduct of our interactions with others and our physical experiences.

Such notions are even more bizarre, of course, than the ancient tales of knights in shining armor defeating fire-breathing dragons. We can believe anything we want, but it does not alter reality. The life of the body and personality are extensions of the soul, not the other way around. Thought begins with the mind and is registered in the brain, thereby producing electrical and chemical changes. The seeds of our character and talent emanate from our spiritual purpose and design. The soul is a benevolent influence upon every facet of our earthly experience. It is the primary source of health and well-being for our personal system, and all efforts to heal and restore should begin with it—and strive to serve it.

Indeed, this inner life ought to be regarded as the true owner and "designated driver" of the body and personality. It is the soul's design that is meant to be in charge of our thinking, attitudes, and behavior—not our personal cravings, desires, or urges. If it is, then we will enjoy good health most of the time.

The idea that health is more than just the absence of symptoms is beginning to be recognized in health circles, but it, too, is still being approached in materialistic, not spiritual, terms. The wellness of the physical body is still used as the primary barometer of health. The maturity of the emotions is ignored, so long as we "feel good" about ourself. The content of our mind is largely discounted. Our ethics, values, and lifestyle are rarely considered. Such superficiality will not suffice. Spiritual health needs to be seen as a dynamic daily expression of the inner virtues and spiritual forces of the soul—not just a state of comfort, peace, and intellectual contentment. Health occurs as the body and personality harmoniously express our inner purpose and spiritual design for wholeness.

When we understand this, then we have laid the groundwork for activating the healing process. Healing occurs as we integrate the vitality and design of spirit into our thoughts, emotions, and physical activities. This work of healing requires a lot more from us than just believing that we are being healed—or eating all the "right" foods and exercising a bit. It demands a wholesale revision of the structure of our personality and lifestyle, so that our beliefs, sense of identity, values, goals, and habits are all stamped with the presence of spirit. Building this structure of healthiness or wholeness in our character enables us to receive and honor the actual living presence of spirit. It is also the one sure thing that will guarantee good health.

Every health care professional has tapped some part of the total health picture. But almost none of them has taken the clue that has been given them and used it to search out and find the whole tapestry. As a result, their success can only be partial at best—until they come to respect the basic principles of spiritual health laid out here. When they begin using these principles to teach their patients the basic facts of good health, then their success ratio will improve dramatically—not so much in relieving symptoms, perhaps, but most definitely in terms of promoting health.

To simplify, it could be said that the work of healing is:

• To learn and demonstrate the laws of life, the laws of right human relations, and the laws of health and healing.

• To make soul contact in our own life, demonstrate the right relationship between the soul and the personality, and reveal the right relationship between the mind and the body.

It may not be realistic to expect every health care professional to demonstrate full soul contact, of course. But at the very least, every sincere health professional has the duty to understand that health emanates from the soul, not from medicines or herbs or adjustments. Health professionals also need to understand that every human body responds to divine law. Their primary function, therefore, should be to restore a proper balance between the patient and the wholeness of the soul. In this regard, they should see themselves as agents of the life of spirit.

In today's world, a major part of this restoration will involve healing imbalances in the emotions. The vast majority of diseases can be tied to the fact that patients carry with them a wide assortment of grudges, disappointments, frustrations, and resentments. Until these conditions are cleansed and replaced with goodwill, gentleness, patience, cooperation, and helpfulness, the effectiveness of other healing protocols will be limited.

Can all of this be done with anything less than the power of the soul? No. Mere belief in the right ideas is a starting point, but not the full achievement. For the healing arts and sciences to reach their full power and attainment, it will be necessary for health care professionals to recognize that their efforts will work best when they are able to tap the healing power of spirit. They must do more than relieve symptoms— they must help reconnect the patient to his or her own inner source of wholeness. They must be living proof themselves, in their own lives, of the dynamics of spiritual wholeness.

It will take eons to achieve this goal—but it is the goal of the divine workshop of the healing arts and sciences. It is, moreover, the true work of humanity—to learn to transform ourselves so that we become proper agents of spirit on earth.

PROBLEMS IN PROMOTING HEALTH

The divine workshop of the healing arts and sciences has registered unusual growth in the last few decades, but there are still many core problems left to be resolved, as old ways of thinking clash with new insights and methodologies. As with every other institution, most of these problems are unredeemed pockets of immaturity that affect all human beings, and society—not just health professionals. These are the "seven unhealthy sins" of ignorance, egotism, inertia, prejudice, jealousy, irresponsibility, and selfishness. Even with the rapid changes in understanding and treatment, most health professionals continue to adapt far too slowly to the true needs of the their patients—and the direction of the inner self.

Beyond this, however, there are nine key problems that keep the health care system from realizing its full spiritual potential at the present moment. Many of these problems have been with us for centuries, and most of them will continue to limit the effectiveness of our healing efforts for millenia to come. Nevertheless, they need to be confronted and resolved. The nine basic problems are:

1. Humanity's definition of health is inadequate. Basic maturity of emotions and mind is rarely recognized or honored, while childish acts of "spontaneity" and "the lack of inhibitions" are widely cherished as signs of exuberant well-being. If anything, maturity is viewed suspiciously, as a sign of old age—and hence, decay. "Feeling good" is often held up as a sign of health, while anything that feels bad to us is automatically rejected. As a result, our definition of health is reduced to the level of emotional reactions. The plans and designs of the soul are eclipsed.

In actual fact, what feels good is often very bad. People smoke tobacco and drink alcohol, after all, because they make them feel good. They intellectually know these acts are undermining their physical health, but they do not care. Feeling good today is worth the risk of cancer or other disease thirty years from now. Just so, a moment's petulant outburst of irritability or anger usually feels good to us—but it leads to the corruption of our nervous system and eventual decay of our self-control.

On the other hand, actions that make us feel bad today often are quite healthy to us in the long run. Listening to our conscience, admitting mistakes, asking forgiveness, granting forgiveness to others, swallowing our pride, giving up destructive habits, making sacrifices for our children or marriage, and many other such acts may be painful for a moment or two, but they help attune us to the source of health within us, our spiritual design for wholeness. Instead of postponing the pain of the moment and carrying it with us for years, so that it can wreak havoc in our system, we dispel the pain and free ourself of its curse.

Our sloppy definition of health also leads to the common tendency to place great emphasis on the well-being of the physical body and ignore our psychological health, as though psychological elements are unimportant unless they represent a major neurosis or psychosis. It is commonplace for people with a stunning measure of prejudice, hostility, anxiety, pessimism, parasitism, or arrogance to be viewed by health professionals as "healthy" and "normal"—just because their physical systems have not yet broken down. Yet someone who carries an excessive amount of hostility is just as much a candidate for a heart attack as someone who ingests too much cholesterol. A pessimistic or fearful person is just as likely to develop problems with their immune system as someone in the conventional "high risk" categories. To dismiss these immature attributes as "just a part of human nature" is tantamount to believing that dirt, rats, and mosquitoes are a normal part of the human household, and pose no health hazard.

At its extreme, this ignorant definition of health establishes death as the ultimate opponent to be defeated, whereas death is often a part of the healing activities of spirit. The ultimate opponent of health is estrangement from spirit, not death. Our present preoccupation with prolonging life at any cost often interferes with the true work of healing—to make the personality more aware of the true source of its design for health and vitality.

This improper definition of health is deeply embedded in our health traditions, and fiercely protected by the egos of millions of people. There are more health professionals today who defend anger as essential to protecting ourself against threats than ones who advocate the development of goodwill, tolerance, and forgiveness. There are likewise more who justify anxiety and pessimism than ones who encourage self-control and optimism. Until the basic standards and values of health and wholeness are revised, not much genuine progress will be possible.

2. The health delivery system is focused on combatting disease rather than building health. Most people do not even recognize that there is a difference between the two.

The worst example of this orientation toward disease is the common obsession of psychologists in linking the distress of earlier events with the problems of the adult personality. In this way, many people have been convinced that the defining events of their lives have been their darkest hours of pain and suffering. But reviewing past trauma does not necessarily heal present confusion. It may well just strengthen the sense of pain and anguish, making the patient more vulnerable than before. Misery, like anything else, tends to increase when exercised.

Such patients desperately need to learn that their confusion and stress are caused by a deficit of spirit in their character—an absence of wisdom, joy, compassion, or strength. A greater measure of joy or peace would have let them triumph over the earlier problems, and it would have let them manage their current hardships as well. They are far from helpless, but they are healthless. They lack the wholeness of a more mature person.

Other examples of this problem abound. It is now popular to insist that being overweight or lethargic is not a sign of ill health, so long as the condition does not "bother us." Just so, as long as we can accept our anger or anxiety as "normal," we are encouraged to pretend that we are healthy.

The unfortunate corollary of overlooking the warning signs of yet-unmanifested disease is the routine tendency to ignore mature qualities and insights as sources of healing. If a person has trouble trusting and cooperating with specific individuals, his ability to trust some people is generally ignored. If another person constantly expects the worst to happen, his capacity to be optimistic in other ways goes unharnessed. If yet a third individual has trouble procrastinating, his or her achievements in the past are deemed irrelevant. In point of fact, these partial expressions of maturity can be powerful healing resources that can act as a seed of future health and renewal. It is the work of the health professional to identify these seeds of latent maturity and encourage their development.

The problem of a disease-oriented health delivery system is summed up in the fact that the act of diagnosis is the process of detecting illness, not health. Health professionals usually are not trained to detect health. Often, by the time diagnosis detects the presence of a disease, it is too late to treat it without taking drastic measures. Yet even these measures do not promote true health—they simply stave off even worse developments.

There is a growing number of health professionals who claim to build health, yet focus only on physical regimens and a few superficial methods to calm the emotions and make them feel good. Most of these programs focus almost entirely on diet and exercise. Yet only a diet of healthy, nutritious ideas and wholesome emotional qualities can truly produce health—and such a diet is virtually unknown. In fact, many of the people who fastidiously dote on the purity of their diet and exercise are quite content to consume psychological garbage and exercise their emotions with criticism, gossip, and self-pity.

To others, the extent of "building health" is the daily repetition of affirmations or visualizations. While these may be steps in the right direction, they are only baby steps. Adults need to move toward genuine contact with spirit. Placing a bumper sticker on our car that says "Visualize World Peace" is nothing more than a joke if we then drive like a hot-headed maniac.

Of course, even if the health profession understood this principle and reformed the system so that it promoted the building of health, there would still remain the monumental project of retraining the general public to actually pursue maturity. So far, very few health consumers have shown any interest in making such changes.

3. Health consumers are dangerously passive. With a few wonderful exceptions, the average consumer of health services wants someone else or something else to do the healing for them. By demand, the health care provider is forced to prescribe the magic words or herbs or pills or diet that instantly make the patient well. The patient wants to be able to sit back and have health reappear without any effort on his or her part.

Many health care providers, unfortunately, are happy to play this role. They revel in the image of being a modern shaman who magically cures the patient without any thought, work, or sacrifice.

The twin evils of laziness and egotism preserve this distortion of the healing process. Yet there are two other underlying factors as well. Very often, patients are unwilling to accept greater responsibility for their own health; they want to shift this onerous duty to the health care provider. Then, if anything goes wrong, they can sue. In addition, even if a patient does want to contribute to the healing process, he often does not know what to do—beyond hoping that a higher power will help. This latter problem could be easily solved if health care providers took the time to teach patients the simple steps and precepts that will enable them to contribute to the healing process.

4. Public attitudes toward health and healing are saturated with dense materialism. Simply put, most people would sooner believe in the power of pills and surgery—or herbs and diet—to cure them than they would believe in spirit. This does not mean that they do not believe in God; it just means that they do not want to view spirit as a primary source of healing. They want to perpetuate their neat division of life into things of the physical plane and things of spirit. In this cosmology, the things of spirit can be deferred until later. Until then, they have license to be practical, down to earth—in other words, materialistic.

Most people, for instance, react with something between reluctance and annoyance when asked to consider the psychological problems behind their chronic physical illnesses. Unfortunately for them, there is a definite relationship. Chronic pessimism and criticism play havoc with our body. Whatever irritates our emotions soon begins to irritate our organs—especially in the stomach region and the bowels. Patterns of stubbornness, rigid thinking, and judgmentalism often lead to stiff muscles, rigid joints, and a cranky colon. Anxiety and hysteria produce conditions of emotional indigestion, which lead swiftly to conditions of physical indigestion. If we have a block in our creative self-expression, we may also develop congestion in our lungs or lumps in the breast. If we feel lonely and unloved, we may eventually become congested in the pelvic region. In other words, habitual emotional moods do have a definite impact on our physical well-being.

When such conditions arise, most patients try to fix them in a purely materialistic way—by popping a pill or by trying to avoid some outer factor that they believe is related to their illness. They might try to find relief from allergies, for example, by moving to a climate which is less allergenic. These steps may ease the symptoms of their problem, but they do nothing to cure the underlying roots of the illness—because they continue to carry with them their habits of irritability, anger, righteousness, and intolerance.

If the suggestion is made that there may be deeper roots to their ill health, the common responses are denial, rationalization, and projection. They deny that they have contributed to their problem; they are just a victim of modern living, their doctor, or some other evil. They further rationalize their immature emotionalism as justified and normal. In other words, they claim to need their anger, fear, distrust, grief, or hostility in order to deal with the impossible situations of their life. They may also project their own immature attitudes on to everyone else and then assume that it is always the other person who is behaving badly. In these ways, they manage to avoid confronting the shallowness of their own approach to living.

The persistent reliance on these defense mechanisms may actually sabotage any effort being made by the soul to promote health. As hard as it may be to understand, the mind-body connection is already working for chronic complainers of headache or constipation; the act of complaining literally creates new headaches and more constipation. It would be a simple step for these people to activate the same mind-body connection to heal their distress, but they are usually too involved in their irritability to understand. They would have to accept their responsibility for wrong thinking and wrong attitudes, and then change them. Unfortunately, the vast majority of such people find it easier to continue blaming others and life for their problems, and so little changes. The creative potential of the mind and spirit to build health is ignored, and a major opportunity is lost.

There is one variation on this problem of materialism. There are cases when the healing power of spirit is accepted, especially by the religiously disposed, but with the expectation that spirit will do all the work. The personal need to change thinking, attitudes, habits, and lifestyle to more completely embody the life of spirit is never seriously considered. Unless the distress is overwhelming, most people are unwilling to sacrifice the comfort of long-standing habits and attitudes, even when they are clearly destructive or irrational.

5. The average human personality is not integrated. The process of linking physical health to the healing resources of spirit requires two steps of integration: the integration of our thoughts, emotions, and strength into a cohesive personality, and then the integration of our talented and skilled personality with the spiritual design of the soul. Needless to say, few people have made very much progress in achieving or completing this integration. And yet, the lack of integration makes a person highly vulnerable to any disease that threatens.

Wherever the integration of a personality is weak, its psychology will be marked by ambivalence, confusion, and division. Extensive conflict will estrange the mature and immature elements of character. The individual will often fail to live up to ideals and values. Common sense will often be overruled by fear, anxiety, or pessimism. In some, the conflict tosses them back and forth, like shuttlecocks, between the need for independence and the craving for security and comfort.

If these divisions are allowed to persist through an entire adult life, the damage which is done to the health mechanism is severe. The healing mechanism of the personality needs to be integrated in order to collect and employ the healing resources of spirit. Any interior conflict or schism will seriously undermine our capacity to restore lost health.

One type of person who suffers from a lack of integration is the individual who, in spite of being intelligent, frequently does stupid things that sabotage his well-being. He fails to act when he has a great opportunity, or petulantly ends a relationship with someone who is very important to him. Such a person lacks the ability to harness his personal will to coordinate his values and goals, so that he may use this strength to control his desires or urges. A person who loves his or her spouse and yet has an affair anyway is a sterling example of someone who is not using the personal will to control behavior.

Unfortunately, many people have been told that the use of the will to control their feelings and urges is very bad—it suppresses their emotions. Of course, it is this advice that is very bad. In the effort to avoid suppressing our feelings, we end up suppressing our maturity, fulfillment, competence, and growth in character!

There is no pill or diet for reducing the divisiveness that accompanies the lack of integration. Yet this is one of the most common factors leading to disease in our modern world. Unless this lack of integration is treated as the real problem, whenever it occurs, whatever treatment is tried will ultimately fail. At times of greatest stress, the most immature elements of the personality—usually our unhealed anger or fear—will take over and behave in very self-destructive ways. This same vulnerability and lack of stability will also restrict contact with our spiritual nature, thereby insuring repetition after repetition of the cycle of disease.

6. Health professionals need to reduce the stigma of mental illness. Psychological illnesses have always been a part of life, and they are rapidly becoming more prevalent. This increase is the natural result of the added complexities of our modern lifestyle combined with the fact that the average person is becoming more sensitive to both physical and psychological stimuli. If an individual is not sufficiently integrated with his or her spiritual core, too much stimulation can lead to a breakdown in self-control. Unfortunately, too many people continue to associate such breakdown with shame and guilt, and this makes it hard for them to avail themselves of the many treatments modern psychology offers. Family and friends who might be able to urge treatment before a total breakdown occurs are still apt to deny the warning signs, and wait until it is too late.

The answer to this problem must be a realistic one. It does no good to simply redefine serious mental illness as a normal aberration that everyone else must tolerate. Illness is illness and must be treated as such. Instead, the answer must involve increasing the public's understanding of psychological disease and promoting a more loving, tolerant atmosphere in which it is treated. It is care these people need, not shame and guilt.

7. The health profession must reduce its fascination with the use of high-tech gadgetry for diagnosis and treatment. A cold is still a cold, whether it is diagnosed with a tongue depresser or a machine that costs hundreds of thousands of dollars. Many of the technological advances of health care have been valuable, useful additions to the treatment of medicine. But in too many cases, health care professionals are letting machines supplant their own trained observation and skill, to the disservice of the health care consumer. High technology does not automatically lead to superior diagnoses and treatments. Its use should be limited to those functions in which it is truly needed.

The health care profession needs to remember that no machine can help the patient become more attuned to the life of spirit. Technology has its place, but we must always remember that healing is an art as well as a science.

8. We must cure our morbid fascination with

death.   The fear of death is an age-old phenomenon.   It will not go away easily.   However, the tendency of health professionals and grieving families to prolong life at all costs is absurd, counterproductive, and totally inconsistent with the life of spirit.

The healing profession makes two mistakes in this regard. First, it believes that death is always a defeat of the healing process.   Second, it believes that death is the cessation of all existence.   Both of these assumptions are grossly wrong. The mission of the health profession is to improve and sustain the quality of life so that the spiritual self can express itself through the personality productively.   Mere existence as a vegetable is of no use to the soul; the soul requires a capacity to express its qualities and powers through its personality in some meaningful way.   This does not mean that the soul requires the personality of a saint—but there must be some ability to pursue the activities of human living.   Prolonging a life that has no ability to act in any meaningful way actually interferes with the purpose of the indwelling soul—and this is as true for an infant as it is for a ninety-year-old in a coma.

Death of the physical body is not the cessation of anything except the physical form.   It is often, in fact, the ultimate relief for chronic pain or persistent discomfort—and therefore a blessing.   Health professionals need to come to terms with death and accept it as a natural, even wonderful transition into a different phase of human existence and experience. Physical death is but a doorway we all must pass through. There is no reason to fear it or delay it at all costs.

9. Health care providers are far too competitive and uncooperative.   Humans take pride in their knowledge, skills, and accomplishments.   This pride is natural and desirable—in moderation.   But when health professionals condemn the work of other health care providers, without even understanding the value or worth of their contribution, pride becomes arrogance.

Each branch of the healing profession makes an important contribution to our understanding of health. It is tempting to accuse other health professionals of fraud and deception, but the potential for fraud exists in all branches of healing. Nonetheless, it is common for allopathic physicians to mistrust and criticize chiropractors and homeopaths, even while chiropracters and homeopaths spread mistrust of medicine. People who work with Chinese herbs distrust those working with Western herbs. Massage therapists try to stick needles into acupuncturists, and acupuncturists sometimes return the favor.

This is unseemly behavior. Ultimately, the charges and accusations serve to confuse only the health care consumer, who is trying to find relief for his or her problems. It is not uncommon for a patient to need the simultaneous help of several of these modalities in order to get well. If one professional is bad-mouthing the work of another, it gravely complicates the healing process for the patient. It is an unnecessary abuse of the role of healing.

These are severe problems, but as always, they only affect the delivery of health care in the physical realm. They do not interfere with the ongoing influence of spirit in the divine workshop of the healing arts and science. The problems delay the development of more effective treatments, and prolong the existence of disease on earth, but they do not upset the overall mission of the spiritual life.

THE WORK OF HEALING

To the average health professional, it would seem that the work of the healing arts and sciences is basically the discovery of new ways to cure disease and improve health. This narrow view, however, misses most of the real inspiration which is occurring today. The underlying purpose of this divine workshop is to help all of humanity better understand its roots in consciousness—and the ability of consciousness to control and transform mental, emotional, and physical matter. Illness is a sign that the ability of consciousness to control matter is not yet perfect. The true experimental work of the divine workshop of healing, therefore, lies in the area of tapping the mysteries of consciousness and applying them successfully to form.

In the West, the healing arts and sciences began as a search for the treatment of disease. More recently, the value of disease prevention was enunciated, and public health measures were implemented to improve sanitation, the quality of drinking water, better methods of food storage, pasteurization of milk, the practice of antisepsis in surgery and child birth, vaccinations, and much more.

The healing arts and sciences now stand at the beginning of the third great stage of this evolutionary process: creating or building health. This new approach has been labeled "health maintenance" or "wellness creation." The patient is weaned from the old belief that life and disease are just "things that happen to us" in favor of a more active philosophy—that each of us can and should play the central role in controlling our various environments. We are meant to create health, maintain our well-being, and grow in character and skill. It is our responsibility to forge a close tie with the inner self, so that it can help us create and sustain good health.

Currently, most of the work of introducing this concept is focused on educating people to adopt correct lifestyle practices. Usually, this effort is directed mostly at physical aspects of the lifestyle, instead of the emotional, mental, and spiritual—because it is hard for the average person to comprehend anything more profound. There is, however, a strong effort being made by the Hierarchy to encourage personal growth in character, virtues, responsibility, the healthy use of the emotions, and the skilled use of the mind. In addition, there is a very quiet but intense effort to teach more and more people to turn to spirit as the primary resource for creating and building health.

To aid in this development, a number of new—to the Western public—healing methods and disciplines are being emphasized by the Hierarchy. Some of these systems are being imported from the East and rapidly integrated into Western science. Two of the most important are acupuncture and Ayurvedic medicine. Each of these systems come with a full, complex philosophy of the nature of health in mind and body already developed. The technical part of acupuncture works by manipulating the energies of the subtle or etheric nervous system. The technical facet of Ayurvedic medicine involves herbs, diet, eliminations, and lifestyle practices.

Care must be taken in absorbing these systems, lest the eager Western mind assimilate only the specialized concrete practices and ignore the philosophical insights that accompany them. The great value of these systems is that they already feature a cohesive holistic philosophy which is far more inclusive than the mechanical approach of Western medicine. They stress that our personal health does not exist in isolation from what we think or do or how we respond to our environment. On the contrary, our health is directly influenced by what we think and how we relate to our work, family, spirit, friends, enemies, problems, environment, and destiny. Our health is also affected for better or worse by what we eat, what we read, our basic mood, and the nature of our leisure activities.

This holistic approach to healing is very much needed in the West today. The Western equivalent of these systems has always existed, but has largely been ignored. The Eastern version is more readily available at present and, because it seems more fascinating, it is also more appealing to the average student.

The Hierarchy is also busy introducing various types of "energy medicine" which treat the magnetic grid of the etheric body instead of direct action upon the dense physical body. This etheric body is not well recognized by science at this time, of course, but it is the energy field which is treated by acupuncture, homeopathy, deep massage, spinal manipulations, and the use of magnetism, electrical treatments, light, and sound. As change is produced in the etheric body, it leads to a corresponding improvement in the health of the physical body—sometimes quite rapidly.

The art of healing with these many forms of energy medicine is often more advanced than the science. The ability to produce healing results tends to outstrip our scientific ability to explain exactly why it works. The Western mind will have to learn to work with the pragmatic principle that "if it works, don't discount it" in order to integrate these advances in our standard practices. This may occasionally require unusual flexibility, however, because the Western mind tends to be horrified at accepting any process before understanding it. This skepticism greeted the discoveries of Pasteur, just as it now greets the advances of energy medicine. We need to understand that these energy medicines do indeed work, and often they work exceedingly well—sometimes much better than accepted western treatments.

Oddly, one of the easiest ways to test and prove the efficacy of these energy medicines will be to study the unhealthy impact of "bad energy"—the subtle toxicity of noise, bad popular music, noxious odors, toxic miasmas such as "sick building syndrome," and strong electrical fields in our environment.

Yet another project under the supervision of the Hierarchy is the rapid growth of research into the genetic causes of health and illness. At the moment, most of this research is focused on using genetic information to forestall or prevent the emergence of illnesses. In other words, if a doctor can predict vulnerability to a serious disease based on the genetic makeup of the patient, that individual might be able to prevent or postpone the onset of the illness by making changes in key lifestyle choices and practices. Eventually, however, this research will also lead to new methods of direct treatment—

for example, providing genetic material that would enable an injured or diseased body to repair itself and produce whatever had been deficient or missing on its own.

Likewise, the Hierarchy is supporting a major drive to understand and master the operation of the human immune mechanism. The immune mechanism is part of the frontline defense system maintaining wellness as well as fighting disease. The hidden benefit of investigating the immune system is that it will lead to valuable insights into the mind-body connection. The old paradigm presupposed that consciousness was generated as minute changes occurred in our biochemistry and electrical state, thus changing emotions and thoughts. Now, this excessively simplistic and upside-down theory is being questioned and modified. Research has led to the discovery that our state of consciousness—our mood, focus of attention, expectation, and alertness—can initiate powerful and pervasive changes in the immune mechanism. In other words, far from being an epiphenomenon of the body, consciousness has the proven ability to control the most sublime systems of the physical form. Science has proven the existence of one of the many verifiable pathways between the mind and the body.

In addition, this research into the immune system also reveals that the human body and mind already function in a holistic way. Each part of the body rapidly communicates with all other parts of the body. Thus, if we are sad, angry, or anxious, the subtle effects of these moods are broadcast to every part of the body, producing a depressing or irritating effect on the entire system. On the other hand, if we are touched by the healing power or joy of spirit, a similar broadcast occurs, but with the opposite effect. It restores and rejuvenates the body and produces a bouyant effect on our health.

The philosophical and psychological implications of these scientific discoveries are revolutionary. Health care professionals are just beginning to translate these ideas into new approaches that can then be used by health consumers to support healing and the creation of health.

There have also been some remarkable developments in research into the nature of the aging process. It is being discovered and verified that it is not the process of growing older that leads to decay and illness. Instead, the culprits are the loss of active interest in living plus fixed, inflexible concepts about the future. It is being proven that the ability to adapt, the capacity to let go of the past, the value of having a meaningful purpose in living, a positive outlook on the future, a sense of worth, and similar attitudes are very powerful forces in retarding the ill effects of aging. In this way, the virtues of cultivating an enlightened approach to the work of building health are being studied and verified by science.

All of these projects contribute to the primary work of the Hierarchy in the divine workshop of healing—to promote a growing interest in taking individual responsibility to make contact with and harness our inner, spiritual potential.

There are three key principles to the work of cooperating with our own inner healing potential:

1. We are all endowed with unlimited healing resources.
2. There is a hidden message in all major illnesses.
3. The skillful use of the mind can link us with our healing resources. We can then learn to direct them consciously into the body and personality, healing illness and injury—even before they occur!

None of these concepts is new, but humanity is finally reaching a stage where more people can understand and work with them. The most important development is the rapidly expanding awareness that major chronic illness or disability include symbolic messages about changes we need to make. The correct interpretation of this message often leads to profound psychological insights about the need to revise our self-image, cultivate a healthier sense of purpose, and begin expressing more maturity in our character. In many cases, these insights are indispensable to the cure of chronic conditions.

These developments imply that the step forward in the odyssey of healing is to educate people in the art of self-healing. The groundwork for this education is already being laid, but so far most of it has been too simplistic and passive to produce profound improvements.

Finally, the Hierarchy is trying to focus humanity's attention on the polluted ideas and emotions of mass consciousness as a source of disease. Hordes of fanatics (a disease in and of itself) are eager to tell us about the pollution of our physical environment, but hardly a voice is being raised to call attention to the far more deadly and insidious pollution of the ideas and feelings of mass consciousness. One of the biggest polluters, of course, is the entertainment industry, with its obsession with violence, horror, criminality, incivility, stupidity, and self-absorption. Television talk shows, which thrive on reducing complex issues to two combative extremes, cripple our capacity to grasp the subtleties of life. The adversarial nature of political debate pollutes our national consciousness and ability to reconcile conflicts. The hardball tactics of lawyers defending obviously guilty criminals obscures our appreciation of justice. Psycho-babbling pop psychologists pollute our ability to discern right from wrong and practice personal responsibility. The champions of political correctness—aside from inhibiting fair and honest discussion of issues—poison our ability to act with tolerance and accountability. Every day, a huge amount of emotional and intellectual garbage is dumped into mass consciousness through all media. It is repeated and spread in offices, classrooms, and beauty parlors as though it were "no big deal." In truth, it is every bit as harmful as raw sewage in drinking water.

This pollution is not just a hazard to our emotional and mental well-being. Such toxins as world-wide pessimism and fear can have a direct, corrupting influence on physical health. Until now, its impact on human well-being has been largely ignored by the healing arts and sciences. It therefore remains a problem waiting for a solution.

COOPERATING WITH THE PLAN FOR HEALTH

The work of supporting the emerging plan for the healing arts and science demands more active involvement than just supporting cancer research or taking our daily dose of vitamins! We must stand ready to give up our passive role as a health consumer and embrace the challenge of creating our own internal mechanism of healing—the mind-body connection that links us to the soul.

This reform in attitude begins with common sense changes in our lifestyle—practicing sensible moderation in what we eat and how much we exercise, while eliminating unhealthy habits such as smoking and consuming too much alcohol. But it involves far more. We must be willing to accept primary responsibility for becoming and staying healthy. We should see health as a process that begins long before we are exposed to illness, and sets in motion desirable patterns that greatly reduce the likelihood of ever contracting serious disease.

This responsibility cannot just be a set of glibly-mouthed words. It must come alive in what we do and how we live. We must educate ourself about the nature of health for the body and the mind. We must learn to integrate the personality. We need to acquire useful techniques for creating health.

In addition, we must learn about the laws of life and what it means to cooperate with them. We must comprehend the law of consequences, and understand that our actions produce real and appropriate reactions. We need to grasp the law of increase, and understand that if we exercise our anger, it will balloon out of control. On the other hand, if we exercise our thankfulness, our reasons for being grateful will increase.

We also need to understand fully the meaning of the old axiom, "As above, so below." One simple expression of this law can be seen in the tendency of unresolved conflict and frustration to produce new rounds of irritation and strife. If we do not care for the illness and stress that accompany these problems, we need to clean out the patterns of emotional immaturity that are producing them.

For many people, the work of creating health will require the adoption of new practices. For some, these new regimens will begin with adopting a right mental and emotional diet—consuming large amounts of spiritually-based thoughts and feelings—and some emotional fasting—refraining from anger, fear, self-pity, and guilt.

In addition, many people urgently need to learn specific techniques for managing adversity, loss, insult, regrets, and old resentments and fears. Almost everyone will need to learn to make genuine, not imaginary, contact with their spiritual self. They can then use this far greater power in their daily meditations to flush out old remants of anger, fear, sadness, and insecurity.

It is not enough to believe that we have a soul—we must establish direct contact with it. We must embrace it as the true owner and driver of the vehicle of the body and personality. Once we make true contact with spirit—which may take years of intense work—all of our other efforts will become far more productive, from relaxation to habit control to emotional enrichment and beyond. We will also be able to summon the support of the soul in revealing to us its innate design and plan for a healthy mind, emotions, and body. We can call on the soul for guidance to make sense of our problems, for goodwill to help us heal anger, for joy to help us overcome despair, for courage to help us heal fear, and for peace to help us heal frustration.

None of this can happen without a massive redefinition of our priorities. Contacting the life of spirit and integrating it into our health and life is not as simple as picking out a new suit of clothes to wear. It involves a wholesale reorientation of our values and priorities. We must be ready to sacrifice personal wants and preferences to make room for the plan and the will of the soul.

In practice, this is somewhat akin to the kind of effort an alcoholic has to make it order to reform himself. He has to make staying sober his top priority and sacrifice every other whim and want to the pursuit of this goal. In other words, we must be driven by the purpose and direction of the soul, not by the pursuit of money, sex, power, or fun. We must likewise downgrade the importance of always being in control, always having to be the center of attention, always feeling comfortable, and always being safe.

None of these activities need be completely abandoned—just permanently and genuinely relegated to a subordinate status in favor of the purpose and direction of the soul. Mere belief in its power and authority is not enough; neither is the act of "surrendering" to its authority. It is amazing how many people have surrendered to the Lord, only to continue behaving in the same immature ways as before.

The sure sign that we are making progress in this re-orientation to the healing power and presence of spirit is a growing capacity to collaborate with spirit in expressing our inner spiritual qualities and direction. Our character becomes "sweetened" as we learn to respond to the travails of life with new patience, deeper understanding, and a much more profound level of benevolence. Our emotions become less reactive and personally focused, and we become more active in pursuing the creative challenges of life.

We should not wait for others to begin making this level of contact or for others to show us how. We do not need to wait for any group or nation to vote on the proposition. We dare not wait for our health professional to tell us to do this or we will die. Instead, we can begin right where we are and take action based on what we already know. Then, we add to that knowledge and understanding every day.

At the very least, we should make it a daily habit to assess and review what is good and bad in our lifestyle, thinking, and attitudes. A second important step is to make a daily attunement to the soul and its qualities. This can be as simple as dwelling on the value of the many qualities of the soul—joy, peace, harmony, strength, goodwill, compassion, wisdom, integrity, dignity, and beauty, to list a few. The third step is to create a healthy lifestyle that puts the intent of our spiritual self above the urges and wishes of the personality.

As we learn to take care of ourself in this way, we can begin to encourage others—perhaps even health professionals—to join us in the cultivation of health. First the few and then the many is always the way spirit enters earth.

Above all, we need to reject the growing trend to shift responsibility for health care onto huge and impersonal bureaucracies. This movement emphasizes the politics and economics of health care far more than health itself. Politicians love to talk about how much they will help us receive health care. Some of their ideas have value, but we must always remember that health begins with ourself. Government can neither promise nor deliver good health, because ultimately each of us is the controlling factor in how healthy we are. We cannot delegate this responsibility to any one else, be it a health professional or a paternalistic govenment.

Healing is an inside job—and only we can do it. The healing arts and sciences stand ready to deliver the technical assistance we need, if we reach the point where we cannot provide for ourself. But we are the one who controls our health in the first place.

The healing power of the soul has always been a part of our life. If it has been obscured, it has been eclipsed only by our own blindness and ignorance. The soul wants us to be healthy. The Hierarchy wants us to discover the life of spirit within us. These are also the objectives of the divine workshop of the healing arts and sciences.

Life is designed to make us whole. It is our duty to do so.

The Divine
Workshop of Religion

WITH ONE VOICE

Deep within each of us is a spark of divine life that continually nurtures and impels us to grow in awareness, explore our environment, and develop our skills. Not all of us are religious, by any means, but almost every one of us is spiritual at this deep, unconscious level. We are drawn to work in government to learn to express divine justice and authority; we are attracted to the arts to learn to express beauty and harmony. We pursue a career in education to serve the light of wisdom; we join the world of commerce in order to help enrich and expand the abundance of life. In most cases, we are unaware of the spiritual impulses that guide us, but they are active deep within us. In much the same way, each institution of society makes its unique contribution to advancing the plan of God on earth, even though the evidence is often hard to see.

It is all the more disappointing, therefore, that the one institution that has been plainly assigned the task of revealing God and helping us establish a proper relationship with divine life has become bureaucratic, materialistic, and almost wholly lacking in any revelation or expression of spirit. Has religion given us God? Has religion taught us how to tap spirit for comfort, guidance, and joy? Only rarely. Most of the time, it has waged crusades against one another that make political wars seem like playground activities. It has openly engaged in jealousy, dogmatism, competitiveness, and aggression. It has never flinched from using fear, condemnation, guilt, and shame to manipulate its believers. It has exhibited levels of bigotry and intolerance that have made the worst elements of racial prejudice seem tame. Throughout the world, religion has become a force of exclusion—the direct opposite of the inclusive power of spirit.

No matter how badly religion has fallen short of its noble mission on earth, however, the divine essence of its inner teachings and activities is still noble and actively influencing humanity. The inner church remains open to all who develop the eyes to see and the ears to hear. The inner church—the divine workshop of religion—is still at work, as always, striving to inform us about the facts of God, the nature of God, our relation with God, and how to live a godly life. It contributes to the well-being and advancement of humanity. It just does not use organized religion as a primary or even an important vehicle for its work.

Efforts are underway, of course, to reform this tragic situation, so that religions become linked once again to their spiritual essence. Implementing the needed reforms will not be easy, however, for the problems of religion are deeply entrenched. The church has all but lost sight of its true purpose on earth, and seems to have little interest in regaining what is missing.

The mission that religions are meant to perform is to act as a source for spiritual leadership on earth. This work is comprised of five key elements:

• Leading group worship.
• Teaching about the nature of God and our relationship with God.
• Providing counseling and healing.
• Acting as an agent of healing and charity in the community.
• Serving as the conscience of the community.

It might be argued that many churches and temples provide all of these services. The real question, however, is: do they touch and reveal the presence of spirit in the process? The answer is usually no. Some charismatic churches touch a strong emotional fervor—but not spirit. Most churches and temples try to invoke the compassion and strength of

God—but fail to establish the necessary wavelength that makes invocation possible.

The proof of this absence of spirit in the halls of worship is obvious. If a preacher condemns the wretchedness of humanity from the pulpit, it should be obvious that there is no contact with spirit at the altar. When a mosque is filled with envy and hatred for the enemies of Islam, it should be obvious that even praying five times a day will not make contact with spirit. Spirit is not interested in our religious rituals; it responds to our spiritual practices—our expressions of goodwill and helpfulness, our charity and service, our cooperation and tolerance, and our wisdom.

Let us therefore examine the five key elements of the mission of religion on earth, but from the point of view of revealing the potent life of spirit on earth—not just talking about it.

Leading group worship. Any individual can pray to and worship the Creator. It is not necessary to be in church or temple to worship God—it should be an integral part of our daily life. The reason for attending a church worship service is to magnify the power of the individual. As a group of like-minded people gather, the massed devotion and invocation can create a far more powerful experience of the divine than is usually possible individually. When this worship is led by a member of the clergy who is skilled in the science of invocation, then heaven can come to earth in a most powerful way.

The united effort in proper worship is very much like singing in a chorus. Each member in the chorus has just one voice, but the combined voices, when properly led and singing the same song, can produce an unparalleled result. In worship, the idea is to pray and sing with just one voice—not the voice of the pastor or rabbi, but the unified voice of the congregation.

As an extra measure of divine forces is summoned in group worship, it becomes easier for individuals to make their own contact with the light and love of spirit. It is not uncommon in such worship for individuals to sense inwardly a closeness to the Creator and a buoyancy of spirit—a level of attunement they are unable to achieve alone. At such moments, the life of spirit has an opportunity to enrich and heal the body and the personality in ways that may have been previously closed.

The conscious personality may not even be aware of these inner experiences, for spirit enters our awareness at very deep levels. But if a new measure of spirit does seep in, it will eventually become obvious, as we begin approaching the trials of life with new patience and serenity, with more joy and self-respect, and with less resentment and fear. Or, we may find that our conscience has been plucked—or there may suddenly be a new sense of gratitude for all of our blessings.

The liturgy and scriptures of every major religion have been carefully designed to induce this type of group experience. Unfortunately, few churches train their clergy to be able to lead such a service effectively. If the minister or rabbi or priest has no effective contact with the life of spirit—which is usually the case—how can the congregation as a whole make a meaningful connection?

Indeed, many religions have actually closed off the likelihood of this kind of experience of spirit. Instead of encouraging each member to make contact with the life of spirit within, and thereby be better prepared to make a good contact during group worship, too many churches and temples have actively discouraged such individual effort and exploration. They have told their followers that the church is their only avenue to God! This message imposes barriers between the individual and spirit, instead of removing them.

2. Teaching about the nature of God and our relationship with God. There are three major sources of information about the life of spirit available to us. The first would be the scriptures of any major religion. The second is what religions have taught us, based on their own dogma and theology. The third would be our own life experiences and intuitive impressions about spirit, either in group worship or in our own meditations. The first source is a wealth of inspiration and revelation. The third can be as well, providing we are contacting spirit and not just the idealized level of our feelings. But the second is a morass of misinformation which should be approached only with great caution. The problem with theology is that it usually does not describe the life of spirit as it is; instead, it describes the life of spirit as theologians would like it to be.

One teaching common to all religions throughout the ages is that God is the creator of heaven and earth. In other words, God is the creator of both invisible designs and laws of spirit as well as the visible forms animated by these forces.

Different religions, however, have stressed different aspects of the nature of God. The Jews emphasize the fact of divine order and God as the supreme lawgiver, Who created everything and set it in motion in accordance with divine laws and immutable principles. The Buddha emphasized the nature of divine wisdom, the cause of suffering, and the way to find release from it. The Christ revealed divine love and the need to demonstrate this love in right human relationships and spiritual service.

All of these teachings flower on the same tree and are useful to every one of us, whether we were born in the East or the West, and whether we are Jew, Moslem, Hindu, Buddhist, or Christian. Why then are so many religious leaders so competitive—and so eager to condemn other religions? Such people have succumbed to the pettiness of their own religious dogma.

All of these religions also emphasize that each of us has a relationship with God. God is not just the Creator of all life and the giver of all laws, but is also a vital part of our livingness wherever we go and whatever we experience—even though we may continually fail to recognize this Presence within us.

This truth is a difficult one for many people to accept, largely because so many religions demand that their followers believe in dogma without evidence or understanding. The irrationality of such a leap of faith offends the intelligence of many good people, and rightly so. It is not the mission of religion to ask us to believe anything irrational. The work of religion is to convince us that our relationship with God is real and valuable.

In elementary school, we learn addition and substraction. We do not have a clue that the advanced applications of these basic principles will be geometry, algebra, trigonometry, and calculus—or that we possess the talent to learn such abstruse subjects. Nonetheless, we do; it just lies hidden in the recesses of our youthful personality.

Just so, we have a divine nature within us, and there is a strong linkage between this divine nature and our personality. We may not be consciously aware of this linkage yet, but it is there. The life of spirit embraces the personality throughout its life, saturating it with the vitality, love, and wisdom it needs to fulfill its design. The very fact that we are alive is evidence of this connection.

Older brothers and sisters can confirm the reality of algebra and geometry to a doubting child. In the same way, the spiritual leaders and saints of every religion throughout the ages stand together as testimony of our individual connection with God—and the enormous potential of the spiritual resources within us. Only an ignorant person would dismiss such testimony without conducting a thorough investigation of the evidence they have left behind.

This evidence is what the churches and temples should be teaching us. It is sad that most religions are more interested in their dogma than in celebrating these truths. A Catholic priest should be just as excited to share the evidence of a Yogananda with his parish as he would be in talking about Saint Francis. A Jew should be just as proud to point to Padre Pio or Mother Teresa as evidence of the God within us as he or she would be in talking about David or Moses.

To this failing is added a second: little or nothing is done by today's religions to translate this profound truth into a coherent methodology for enlightening our character and lifestyle. The power of understanding the fact of the life of spirit within us is that it enables us to contact and harness the treasures of divine life. A major part of the work of religions is to teach us the details and process of improving our relationship with God. While this teaching may legitimately be based on believing in God, mere belief is not enough. A gardener cannot produce results just by believing that he will enjoy a full harvest at the end of the season. He must roll up his sleeves and plants seeds, cultivate them, and protect them from the ravages of the environment and predators. Those religions who teach their followers to believe and then stop there are cheating their followers of the joy, beauty, wisdom, and healing of the full religious experience. They are giving them a hollow shell instead of a cornucopia of abundance.

Faith in a benevolent God is just a starting point. As scriptures say, we must add understanding to our faith, and then add the ability to express the qualities of spirit to our understanding. In this regard, it is also the work of religion to help people move beyond mere belief and learn the tools of living a spiritual life. These tools include prayer, meditation, contemplation, confession, invocation, dedication, and right activity. As we master each of these tools of spirit (see Volume III of this series), we are able to bring the presence of God within us into our daily lives as the expression of new wisdom, love, joy, courage, self-control, and perseverance.

These lessons complement the value of group worship— they do not replace it. The failure to teach these methods of personal enlightenment stands as an indictment of modern religion.

Providing counseling and healing. In earlier times, before the advent of psychology and scientific medicine, the pastoral work of counseling and healing was a far more important duty for religion. It is still important, but today it is oriented more toward helping confused people find their moral compass. The minister, priest, or rabbi guides people to clarify or revise their spiritual values as they apply to the major issues of their lives.

This work provides a unique opportunity. If churches began to fulfill their duty to teach people to build a proper relationship with God, it would inspire many people to begin examining their lives in new and courageous ways. This self-examination has a tendency to dredge up unredeemed conflicts and vulnerabilities. Since these issues are rising in pursuit of greater spiritual health, it may not be helpful to go to an average psychologist for assistance in sorting out the resulting paradoxes and confusion. A skilled member of the clergy would be in a much better position to help—presuming that he or she has already gone through the same process of self-examination and has achieved a measure of enlightenment.

At present, of course, pastoral counseling tends to be little more than just platitudes and the offering of a brief prayer. While even this can be reassuring, it tends to produce few genuine improvements. The real work of counseling should be to help people learn to interact with the love and guidance of spirit to transform the quality of their lives.

While the role of psychological counseling might be defined as helping the confused and the broken to regain health, the role of pastoral counseling ought to be to enable the healthy spiritual aspirant to put the life of spirit to work in daily activities.

Acting as an agent of healing and charity in the community. Divisiveness is one of the universal problems in our communities and nations today. Religious leaders are meant to serve their communities by acting together to heal these divisions, and the distrust that results from them. These leaders should be known for their wisdom, patience, and skill in bringing people together to reason—not to condemn, accuse, or oppose. Because religion is supposed to be knowledgeable about the principles of right human relationships, they should be able to inspire their communities and nations to implement them.

In the same vein, religious leaders have long been trusted to provide charity for the needy members of humanity. Over the centuries, millions have benefited from the food, clothing, and shelter provided by organized religion. This is a proper and inspired role for religion to play, since humanitarian service is a key way to demonstrate the spiritual dimension of right human relationships. Religion needs to continue in this service—not with the motive of converting the heathen, but rather with the purpose of setting an inspired example.

Providing a conscience for the community. As the institution chosen by the Hierarchy to embody and teach the laws of life and the principles of right living, religion is the best equipped to provide ethical leadership.

Historically, the effort to play this role has been undermined by the fanaticism and righteousness of religious zeal. As the great defense attorney Clarence Darrow once said, "Religious people usually know right from wrong; they just don't find much that is right." The religious enthusiasm for condemning what is wrong or sinful has often silenced any effort to celebrate what is right. This imbalance has rightly offended many thoughtful people, and has caused religion to lose credibility as a voice of conscience. Such excesses as the Inquisition and other examples of religious persecution have not helped, either.

In spite of these serious failings, the spiritual design for religion still includes the potential to provide a moral foundation for our secular activities and choices. It is important for every individual to learn the basic lessons of morality and ethics—and it is even more important for government, business, and the rest of society. To regain credibility, however, religion will first have to put its own house in order.

As flawed as modern religion is, it still serves much of its spiritual design. There is a great need for its services, intelligently delivered. This need is confirmed by the consistent support for religion by the vast majority of humanity, in every nation of the world. Even though Russia was formally atheistic for seventy years, the religious spark was kept alive by the people. The vast majority of people know the value and worth of the life of spirit, and look to religion to supply it. This is a truth that will never die, no matter how corrupt religion might become. It is a necessary part of human life. It serves an irreplaceable role.

We should not be content with less than the best.

THE PROBLEMS OF RELIGION

It has been said that the words of the Bible were written in ink, but the word of God can be written only in the heart. In other words, the work of the divine workshop of religion may have been corrupted by dogma and polluted by impure motives, but it flourishes throughout the world in the hearts and minds of people who refuse to lose sight of its true message and work. Time after time, in every epoch and nation, these true spiritual people have risen up and demanded that religion reform itself and return to its true inspiration and base—the life of spirit. John the Baptist and the Christ were two such people. So were the Buddha and St. Francis. The writings of Joan Grant indicate that similar reforms were required as long ago as the ancient dynasties of Egypt.

Once again, we live in a time when it is clear that religion has lost its way—and needs to be reminded of its true spiritual compass. It will take massive reforms to put religion back on the proper track of serving humanity. But no matter how far the church strays, it is important to remember always that there are thousands of good people around the world who are serving faithfully the divine mission of religion, inside or outside of the formal institution. Albert Schweitzer was one, Mother Teresa another. Padre Pio was a third. These people, and many more like them, are the guarantee that religion will rebound from its current ineptness and once again become a powerful force in helping humanity know and serve God.

Where religion has reduced our relationship to God to an empty ritual, the loss to humanity is enormous. Where religion has traded in its spiritual authority for the dead carcass of theology, a covenant of silly rules, and a set of superstitions, the damage to humanity is incalculable. The arrogance of the clergy and the tendency of religion to exclude all but true believers from the grace of God is scandalous. And the modern effort to sell God as a "feel-good" version of Barney who expects little or nothing from us but wants to be our friend is absurd. In many cases, it is just as well that most churches have become little more than centers for polite social gatherings; it limits the damage that is done.

Both the clergy and their followers share the blame for many of these problems. The clergy have often failed in their task to understand God and present divine life to us in intelligent, sensible ways. But the public has also played its part in cheapening religion, by being reluctant to leave behind their earthbound attitudes or make the sacrifices of habit and priority that are needed in order to pursue a spiritual life. Their main interest in religion is as a source of comfort, and so they have turned religion into something tranquilizing.

We still hear talk about love in church, but we see few living demonstrations of tolerance or goodwill, either in thought or deed. We are told that we must know God, but are then told that God can be known by us only through the church—preferably through formal worship and ritual.

None of this has gone unobserved in the Hierarchy, which is hard at work planning and instituting reforms for the worst of these problems, as it has in ages past. Some of the major problems, and the reforms that will cure them, include:

1. Bureaucratic overload. Every institution eventually has to battle the deadening effects of a growing bureaucratic structure that serves itself instead of the group's purpose or members. In the West, there is a good deal more Churchianity than Christianity. The problem is even worse in other cultures, other religions. The clergy often completely strangle the spiritual life of a community. In the process, they presume authority that they do not have. Individual thought and creativity are suppressed. The attempts of intelligent people to reject dogma are condemned. It is claimed that the grace of God can be found only through "proper religious observances."

The problem of bureaucratic overload is that it is like the neutron bomb—it kills all signs of life but leaves the buildings standing. The church or temple becomes an empty symbol, but is in effect far more of a barrier than a bridge to spirit.

The solution to this problem lies in decentralizing the power and authority of the clergy, scuttling lingering notions of absolute power or wisdom being invested in any human leader of a religion. The best minister, priest, or rabbi is one who responds directly to the Hierarchy—not to a bishop or pope or imam or lama.

2. The worship of dogma and tradition instead of God. Like an old person, whose joints have become stiff and whose arteries are sclerotic, religion seems to suffer the ravages of old age. Because humanity and society are growing organisms, there is a tendency for religious teachings and rites to become rigid and narrow. In this way, a great revelation for one generation may become a confining platitude for a subsequent one. Our interpretation of the principles of right human relationships may become narrow and cramped. The theological concepts that challenged us in the fourth century may now serve only to burden us with guilt and shame.

When a business no longer operates profitably, it closes its doors. When a government becomes too abusive, its citizens rebel. But this natural process of renewal and innovation is missing from religion. The most youthful of the "modern" religions is a millenia and a half old. Some may be as old as ten thousand years. As a result, their followers are trapped in the shells of ancient rituals, instead of being encouraged to act with charity and compassion. They are expected to obey rules designed for a pastoral, nomadic life, rather than taught to be tolerant and inclusive toward their fellow human beings.

Most of these religions are stone dead. They deserve to be buried and replaced by new ideas that link us more effectively to God. If this seems like a startling statement to make, the magnitude of the problem demands it. It must be remembered that if any religion fails to reveal to its followers the path to God within them, one of the major purposes for its existence has been extinguished.

Whenever we must look somewhere other than a religion to find God, that religion has ceased to serve a valuable function. It should be left to decay on the compost heap of Zoroastrianism and other wornout faiths.

3. The arrogance of the clergy. The proper role of the clergy in any religion is to facilitate the attunement of people to their inner spiritual resources and design for wholeness. This duty is fulfilled by leading group worship, invoking divine blessings, consecrating people, places, and activities, and teaching the good news about our divine possibilities. The clergy is supposed to celebrate the presence of God, not their own collective egos. There are many excellent people serving in the clergy of all major religions today. Unfortunately, there are not enough of them.

In all too many cases, the clergy impose manmade rules on their followers, instead of helping them understand the laws of God. Even worse, they browbeat and intimidate their followers by threatening to withhold blessings and privileges unless they prove themselves to be "true believers." In some cases, it is accepted without question that unless a person is baptized or confirmed, they will spend eternity in hell.

No member of the clergy has this kind of power! Those who claim it are arrogant, bigoted, and a plague on their followers. We should never forget that religion is made for people, not the other way around. People are not and never have been the plaything of an arrogant clergy or theological thugs. The authority of the life of spirit is the Light and Love of the Creator. Any arrogation of this power by a human leader is a false presumption of authority. The fact that almost every religion condones this arrogation of authority—and even glorifies it—demonstrates how corrupt some religions have become.

4. Enslaving people. Humanity was made in the image of God. We were endowed with spiritual strengths and talents. The mission of religion is to celebrate this divinity within us and show us how to harness it. In this way, religion can liberate people from the bonds of suffering, ignorance, superstition, fear, and despair. It can teach us to view God as an eternal companion and friend.

Unfortunately, this is usually not the message religion delivers. Too often, the message ends up being just the reverse: that while God is wonderful, people are pathetic wretches who must believe that if they pray hard enough and believe strongly enough, God will have pity on them and grant them eternal life—even though they do not deserve it.

This bizarre notion enslaves people instead of liberating them. A slave is a person who has no rights or privileges, cannot question the authority of the master, and cannot make any choices or decisions about his or her life. The slave can only obey and work. If all we can do is believe and obey God, then we, too, are a slave. The statement that we were created in God's image is just a hoax. In other words, we end up having to rely on faith alone to rescue us from a mess we did not create.

But, as scripture says, faith without the good works which implement it is worthless. It would be like believing in food without eating any, or believing in swimming but drowning because we believe that God will swim for us! Genuine faith is an important attitude that can link us to our divine possibilities, but it does little more than open the door into the rich dimensions of spirit. We still need to walk through the door and learn what we can do with these great spiritual treasures. We still have to translate these spiritual energies into daily expressions of tolerance, goodwill, strength, wisdom, joy, and peace. If we ignore our potential for active collaboration with spirit, we severely restrict our independence and ability to serve.

In the last several thousand years, many human beings have reached the threshold of liberation. They have developed competent minds and a reasonable amount of curiosity. They need to be taught methods of effective prayer, meditation, and other tools of spirit so that they can cross the threshold and learn to make conscious contact with spirit. Religion, unfortunately, has failed to keep pace with these developments. Too often, they still treat people like the slaves they were ten thousand years ago.

It is time for a massive round of updating.

5. Sin-centered rather than God-centered religions. One of the most serious weaknesses in modern healing is its focus on illness rather than wellness. Just so, one of the worst problems with religion today is its common focus on sin and evil, rather than God and spirit. Every Sunday morning, pulpits across the fruited plain resound with the gong-like sounds of preachers condemning sinfulness.

Those who deliver such sermons defend them on the

grounds that they must hate evil. But they are not just rejecting evil; they are becoming drunk on their condemnations. They forget that Jesus told us: "Do not resist evil, but overcome it with good." This statement means that hate and anger are inappropriate responses to evil and sin. Evil and error can only be redeemed by the goodwill and tolerance of the life of spirit.

We do not need religion to reveal to us the nature of humanity's problems. We hear about them every night on the news. The work of religion is to reveal what we are lacking when these problems arise—the love or wisdom or strength or joy or peace of God. In addition, religion is meant to show us how to make contact with these spiritual forces and use them skillfully to resolve our failings and flaws.

One of the hallmarks of demagogues is the penchant to wax righteous in finding faults in others—or humanity as a whole. Not content just to point out the error in some action, they feel compelled to heap guilt, fear, and loathing on the victims of their wrath. Many a weak ego has become an instant lion of power just by condemning "bad people."

Religion has its share of demagogues, as does every institution, although the majority gravitate into politics. In the jaundiced eyes of the demagogue, Satan gets far more attention than God. Everything bad—and the vast majority of the good as well—is attributed to the work of the "evil one." People are warned to expect the devil to tempt them at almost any time—and to be constantly on guard for his mischief.

Devil mongering represents another ploy to enslave the faithful, this time by binding them in the chains of fear, doubt, alienation, and despair. God and divine help are portrayed as aloof and almost inaccessible, to be earned only by a lifetime of pious, servile belief. The devil, on the other hand, is constantly at believers' ears, waiting to whisper sinful ideas and plant them in their minds.

Such an emphasis rapidly turns the worship service into the adulation of the devil, rather than the adoration of God. As the fever pitch of fear and self-loathing grows stronger, the congregation becomes obsessed with sin. Their lives become controlled by sin. It becomes impossible for any of them to register any facet of the inner life of spirit or its qualities. They would be far better off just to stay home.

6. Denial of the subtle life. Part of the genuine work of the divine workshop of religion is to help people become aware of the more subtle, nonearthly dimensions of life. Our divine nature is real, yet invisible and intangible. Our thoughts and feelings are real, too, yet likewise invisible and intangible. So also are the energies of spirit that we contact when we make connection with the soul.

To understand this point, we can think of consciousness as having three levels or degrees. The first is our ordinary awareness, which informs us about the physical plane. This is our awareness of the gross or material aspects of life. It is like the form of a rose. The second level is more subtle, and deals with our emotions and thoughts. It is more like the perfume of the rose. The third level is the most sublime, and is the level of spirit and God's abstract qualities. It would be like the magical impact of beholding the beauty and perfume of the rose.

In order to make conscious contact with spirit, we must be able to work not only at subtle levels (thoughts and feelings), but at sublime levels—the joy, peace, harmony, benevolence, and wisdom of God's life. Yet religion treats these subtle and sublime levels as though they do not exist. Efforts to investigate them are either ignored or condemned.

The failure to teach these truths about life exposes the in-consistencies of modern religion. We are expected to believe in life after death, because Christ died for us, but if we dare communicate with friends and family who have died, we are viciously attacked and ridiculed—even though the so-called dead are actually quite alive. Likewise, we are supposed to cultivate our relationship with God, but are simultaneously discouraged from practicing any of the many techniques that would help us improve this relationship!

Every saint and religious leader throughout history has demonstrated the reality of the subtle and sublime realms of life. They have called us to follow their lead in exploring these dimensions. It is only the petty-minded clerics, who have no understanding of spirit to begin with, that treat the subtle and the sublime with such disdain. These elements of life are important to us—and important to our spiritual growth. If they are obviously the part of every saint and prophet the earth has known, it would behoove us to explore and master them as well. Otherwise, we will continue to be the slave of ignorance, trapped in the material world.

7. The growing phenomenon of "religion lite." Perhaps as a reaction to righteous fundamentalism, a new form of religion has recently appeared—a religion without sin, guilt, or any obligation except to feel good. The goal of this religion is neither salvation nor redemption—just feeling good about ourself and life. Just as the shallowness of pop psychology has watered down the profession as a whole, so also the appearance of religion lite is threatening to dilute the power of religion. In the feel good world of religion lite, no one sins or is ever wrong—we just make alternate choices. The only real sins would be to feel bad, repress our feelings, or hurt the feelings of another. Truth becomes as adaptable as stew—anything we want is acceptable.

In religion lite, God is a servant who will gladly and dutifully fulfill our wishes and desires. In return, absolutely nothing is expected of us—certainly not effort or service. Unfortunately, what feels good is usually good for nothing. Religion lite is not faith—it is just wishful thinking. The god of these true believers has no more substance or power in our lives than Tinker Bell.

The spiritual life is one of work and meaningful sacrifice. It requires an honest effort to recognize our shortcomings—not flippant rationalizations and self-serving congratulations. Religion lite is just a wading pool for those who are not quite ready to take the plunge.

In spite of all these problems, there is still good news. The institution of religion has made remarkable though limited progress in the last one hundred years. The evils that dominated Western religion during the Middle Ages have been laid to rest. Even the terrible emptiness of materialism during the nineteenth century has been largely overcome. The service religion performs in the world helps balance its failings and excesses.

For this, religion ought to thank its faithful following, who have continually relit the torch upon the hill, even when the formal church has let it expire. Through their efforts, the light still shines—and has spread into every corner of the world.

THE DIVINE PLAN FOR RELIGION

The potential for evolution and change is just as great in the divine workshop of religion as it is in any other institution of society. In fact, the need for reform is even greater in religion. But the leaders of religion are not especially responsive to change and reform. New ideas tend to be rejected faster than a fundamentalist can shout, "Praise the Lord!" Religious leaders believe that God spoke two thousands years ago, then retired into silence. To their minds, they own the exclusive rights to what God said. And they are not about to change with the times.

In many ways, this steadfastness is admirable. The great revelations of the Christ, the Buddha, Moses, and Mohammed are meant to be safeguarded and perpetuated. They are not meant to disappear. Thanks to modern printing and scholarship, this is not likely to happen. The Bible is the bestselling book in the history of the world, and it is not apt to be displaced by Stephen King any time soon.

It is not the world scriptures that are in need of reform, however. Their message of good news is eternal, and the principles they reveal are as fresh and as relevant today as two thousand years ago. What needs to be reformed is organized religion, its theology, and its methods of delivering the message.

The revelation of spirit and the nature of God is not a special event that occurs only sporadically. It is a continuous happening here on earth. In every generation and region of the earth, there are always great teachers present, opening the door for those who are ready to make connection with the divine life. Not all of them specialize in the work of religion—they can be found laboring in every one of the divine workshops. But their revelations of the nature of spirit are just as important and as appropriate for their times as the sermons of a great religious personage.

Sadly, most religious leaders ignore the significance of these revelations. For them, a new translation of scripture is far more exciting than a scientific discovery that proves the reality of the soul!

A second fact that most religious leaders overlook is that our human nature and culture are evolving. We are not the same people we were ten thousand years ago, or even one thousand years ago. We change and grow. Not everyone grows, of course—the skeptics and cynics have been stuck in the ruts of their disbelief for eons, just as the theologians and clerics have been stuck in their militant beliefs. But the rest of the human family is alive and well, and has moved ahead on the path of destiny. Eventually, even the cynics and true believers will catch on and catch up as well.

One of the clearest signs of growth has been in the mental and intellectual capacities of the human race. In the few hundred years since the Renaissance, there has been a tremendous burst of creative activity and expansion of our understanding of the nature of life, the universe, and ourselves. The human race as a whole is far better educated than even one hundred years ago. We care for one another and protect each other in ways that were undreamed of before this century began. Our capacity for tolerance has likewise expanded rapidly.

All of this growth has occurred in spite of—and in part because of—the recent world wars and lesser conflicts. As terrible as it is, war can also produce benevolent results. It can force vast numbers of people to give up old beliefs and habits that trap them in endless cycles of suffering. It can force us to rebuild cities and civilization. It can forge new alliances throughout the world and lift the spirit of cooperation to a new plateau. It can even cause the peoples of the world to unite as one voice to ask God for deliverance from the scourge of war. That very invocation, which was made during the last world war, was the heartfelt plea of the religious people of the world. It went unnoticed by their religious leaders, however.

Today, millions of people stand ready to learn new truths about God and to receive new insights. They are ready for new insight into who they are and what needs to be changed in society. They are looking to religious authorities throughout the world for guidance, but so far the religious authorities have failed to provide it. Soon, they will turn elsewhere.

Unless religion responds to this readiness of its followers, it is in danger of becoming irrelevant. Our spiritual nature and obligations will never be irrelevant, but if the people who are ready for the next level of contact with spirit fail to get a response from religion, they will turn their backs on it and search elsewhere. They will plunge themselves into whichever activity—business, the healing arts and sciences, education, the arts, or science—seems most likely to provide the answers they seek.

The Hierarchy, however, stands ready as always to help

religion to grow. To some degree, this growth is already occurring—not in religion as of yet, but in other disciplines. Psychology has taken over the job of counseling. Physicians and psychologists are providing new answers about death and dying. Hospitals and clinics are beginning to experiment with spiritual healing. Informal education is picking up the need for instruction in spiritual truths and methods.

The evidence of change surrounds religion on all fronts, and yet the resistance continues. None of these new developments is being taught in seminaries. Organized religion still sees most of these activities as something of an oddity. When asked why they do not modify their curriculum to include these new disciplines, the answer tends to be: "Our people are not ready for these changes."

In spite of this resistance, the Hierarchy is marching forward with its plans for reforming the divine workshop of religion. If it cannot work through the established clergy, then It will simply bypass it, and find receptive channels among doctors, psychologists, counselors, and teachers. If organized religion ends up irrelevant, it will be only because it turned down the chance to initiate these reforms itself.

This new work is of two kinds. The first part involves the integration of new ideas and beliefs into our understanding of the spiritual life. The second outlines a new role for the clergy as religious leaders.

Actually, none of the new ideas being integrated into religious thinking is especially new. They have been a part of human thinking since long before the advent of recorded history. But on the whole they are new to Western thought. Some of them are being imported from Eastern traditions and revised and updated to fit our current and future needs. Others are being reintroduced to the West in ways that make more sense than before. These "new" ideas and principles include:

• **The law of cause and effect.** The Christ articulated this principle when He stated: "As you sow, so shall you reap." In other words, every action we take—even in our mind or heart—produces a reaction of like kind. The harm we do to others—no matter how innocently rationalized—will come back to haunt us. The liberties we take with the rights and property of others will influence the way others respect our rights and property. At the other end of the scale, if we act in productive, helpful ways, we will receive help when it is needed.

This principle does not interfere with our free will. We all have the right to be an obnoxious boor, if we so choose. Nothing can stop us. But we do not have the right to choose the consequences of these actions. We will be unable to stop the onslaught of obnoxious, boorish people who descend upon us. This is how the law of cause and effect works. No measure of fantasy, wishes, or tears of regret will be able to undo the inevitable consequences of our actions. Once an action is set in motion, it cannot be recalled. It can be mitigated, by taking steps to make amends, but it cannot be stopped.

The reason the Hierarchy is emphasizing this law at this time is not just to help us clean up our immaturity, although this certainly is a major benefit. The law of cause and effect also happens to be a major key to accelerating the work of growth and creativity in all areas of life. If we wish to build greater health, this law can be used to show us the steps to take to achieve that goal. If we want to generate wealth, this law can help us sense and seize the opportunities that will lead us there. If we want to improve relationships, the law of cause and effect is the perfect blueprint for mastering respect and kindness.

Naturally, the application of this law to our life also helps us accelerate our spiritual growth. If the life of spirit is characterized by the qualities of compassion, generosity, wisdom, joy, strength, and peace, then the shortest route to integration with spirit would be mastering the expression of these great qualities in our relationships, work, and ser-vice. The more we work with these spiritual essences, the more we learn to cause good things to happen in our life.

• **The law of rebirth.** The mere mention of this principle tends to send shock waves throughout the Western world. And yet, the majority of people on the planet are quite familiar and comfortable with this doctrine. In any event, introducing it more completely—and intelligently—into Western thinking is a major priority with the Hierarchy.

Part of the adverse reaction to the idea of rebirth lies in the fact that the definition of this process has been poorly described. In some cases, it is confused with transmigration. In other cases, it becomes an excuse for unbridled fantasy. It is natural for intelligent people to shy away from such distortions. But it is also important for intelligent people to seek out a proper understanding of rebirth, because it is a fundamental law of life. It also happens to be of great importance in understanding the nature of spirit and the human psychology.

The current obsession, for instance, with childhood trauma and neglect as the major cause for neuroses is terribly mistaken. The cause of a patient's deep distrust or alienation is probably not related to parental abuse at all, even if it did occur; it is far more likely to be unresolved issues of distrust and alienation carried over from earlier lives. The choice of parents in this life was just the inevitable consequence of the law of cause and effect.

The attempt to heal adult problems based on childhood problems almost always results in an incomplete recovery—or no recovery at all. But when the core problem from a series of lives is treated, frequently the patient seems to recover almost miraculously.

• **New methods for working with the life of spirit.** For several millenia, the most common methods of teaching people to make contact with spirit have been passive in nature, based on surrendering the personal will to the guidance and love of divine authority. For most people, this was the only way they could learn to detach from their intense focus in the life of the personality. Unfortunately, once this detachment occurred and contact was made with spirit, the personality was often too weak and unmotivated to be of much use to spirit.

Today, many people who are ready to enter more fully into contact with spirit are blessed with a far more developed mentality than people in earlier times. It is not necessary to render them passive; in fact, it would defeat the very progress in thinking and understanding that they have made! As a result, the old methods are outdated and need to be discarded.

Discarding them, however, will not be easy. Many religious authorities declare with great confidence that the life of spirit is virtually unknowable and that we should not even bother making the attempt; we should just "get ourself out of the way and obey." This is a medieval concept. It was demeaning to the human spirit then, and is downright insulting to our potential today. Our need is to become more actively responsive to God's will and guidance. This connection is best made by activating the best within us—not by turning ourself over to God so that God can act through us. If God must put us to sleep in order to use us, what contribution are we making? Why would God bother?

Fortunately, many good people reject the notion of surrender, and find ways to make active contact with the life of spirit without the benefit or aid of clergy. The now-famous twelve step program developed to help alcoholics recover is an excellent example of an initiative that has helped thousands of men and women attune themselves to their divine possibilities.

Other areas that require the acceptance of "new" methods of contacting spirit would include:

Prayer.

Meditation.

The science of invocation and evocation.

• **A revision of teachings on death and dying.** The example of the life of Christ should have liberated us from the threat of death. Sadly, our fear of dying is so deeply entrenched that even two thousand years later, many people have not gotten the message—including almost everyone connected with religion.

Indeed, throughout much of history, reglious teachings about death have been used primarily to terrorize and subdue, rather than to enlighten and comfort. The threat of demonic torture in hell is still with us, alive and well in the hearts of fundamentalists. This false teaching needs to be repudiated by religion, and never again sanctioned. Far from being a sanctuary of comfort, the church has become an incubator of fear.

This is totally unnecessary. The last things we need to associate with the act of dying are fear, guilt, and confusion. Yet this is what has happened: religion has hopelessly confused the doctrine of salvation and redemption with the issue of survival after death. These two issues need to be detached from each other. The survival of the personality has nothing whatever to do with our religious beliefs or practices. Everyone survives death. The work of religion is to help us become aware of the life of spirit and teach us how to build a strong relationship with it. This focus is not affected by death or the dying process.

The great purpose of religion, in other words, is not to "save us from the evil one," but to rescue us from ignorance and superstition—including exactly this type of nonsense. If we harness the light and love of spirit to become a better person—a person of goodwill, responsibility, discipline, and charity—then we are doing all that is possible to insure a good life, a peaceful death, and a productive existence thereafter.

We need not fear death. It is just a transition into a new phase of experience. In many cases, in fact, it relieves us from suffering. It most certainly does not impose upon us new suffering—there are no demons standing by to torture us for our sins. The real demons of life are the ones in physical life who stand up in pulpits and screech at us about our wretchedness.

Death is just life without the physical body and its limitations. It affords a reunion with friends who have died before us. It enables us to pursue interests and lessons we started but could not finish in the physical world. It is a time for joy, not sorrow. It is the beginning of the next phase of our spiritual journey.

Death does not estrange us from the soul; neither does it come between us and the great love and peace of God. The soul never leaves us, God never abandons us—in death or at any other time. We may turn away from the divine life in confusion or ignorance. We may even feel lost and alone. But even if we lose our way, the soul never loses us. God never loses us. The spark of divinity within us links us inseparably to divine blessings.

This is the simple truth about salvation, as well as the simple truth about death. Our relationship with God is not a deep mystery; it is an easily verifiable truth. The church needs to see the simplicity of these ideas, and correct its teachings about these key issues.

In addition to incorporating these new and revised teachings into the work of religion, the Hierarchy is also busy defining a new role for the clergy. This revision will alter the selection, training, and work of the clergy.

At present, it is too easy for unsuitable people to enter the clergy. It is time for the church to begin looking for candidates for the clergy who already demonstrate a talent for the profession—not just a talent for preaching, but a talent for making contact with the life of spirit and translating it into constructive help for others. In other words, these should be people who are capable of practicing what they are going to preach.

The training also needs to be more comprehensive—and directed more toward practical spiritual experience than the study of the Bible and theology. The clergy needs to be taught how to make direct contact with spirit, so that when they preach, they truly do preach the word of God. They need to be taught how to summon healing energies, so that when they counsel the confused or visit the sick, they can do something more effective than just hold hands and give comfort. They need to be taught how to peer into the hearts of troubled people, as Jesus did with the woman at the well, so they can give guidance and support that will help people transform their lives.

Such training would have to begin with learning the skills of prayer, confession, meditation, and invocation. It would require a long period of study, contemplation, and self-examination. No one would be allowed to act as a cleric until he or she had demonstrated a capacity to express wisdom and virtue on a regular basis.

Religion needs enlightened leaders, not just people who can parrot scripture and exhale platitudes. It needs dedicated lay people to assist in the ministry. But the Hierarchy cannot impose reforms on religion directly. The will and wisdom to change must come from within.

SUPPORTING THE PLAN FOR RELIGION

The inner side of religion has always taught us that we are children of God and that we "take God with us" wherever we go. God always meets us at our point of need. If we fail to recognize the Creator at those times, it is only because we are unable to see through the disguise.

We need to appreciate the importance of these subjective experiences in pursuing a religious life. Religion is not something that happens to us or comes to us. It happens within us. The primary talents of religion are "the eyes to see" and "the ears to hear." These subtle and sublime skills enable us to understand the words that God has written in our heart.

One of the traps of the religious life is the tendency to want to use the force of righteousness to make changes for the better. On the surface, this desire seems laudable, but there is just one hitch. All too often, our desire for change does not include our own life. We assume that everything within ourself is all right, because we have been anointed by the life of spirit. So we project our zeal of righteousness toward others and society. We start preaching at our friends and colleagues about their need to reform and change.

The impulse to redeem is indeed a strong one in the religious life. But it needs to be directed inwardly, not outwardly. We do not support the work of religion by forcing it on others. We support religion best by making enlightened changes in ourself—in our awareness, character, and behavior. Our own inner life is the proper workshop for our personal labors. These changes should focus on:

1. Cultivating right beliefs and intentions.
2. Acquiring right understanding.
3. Observing right spiritual practices.

We cultivate right beliefs and intentions by deepening our awareness that the fullness of God's blessings and grace is always available and accessible to us. As Paul put it, "Nothing stands between you and God's love for you." This statement must be interpreted as literally and as thoroughly as possible. Ignorance, fear, despair, anger, guilt, and indifference may seem to eclipse divine light and love, but nothing can eclipse the power of God's will that these divine forces reach into our heart and mind. If there is a breach of contact, therefore, the problem is of our own making—not God's. We have become too consumed in our misunderstanding, denial, confusion, or rebellion.

The enlightened belief we need is the unwavering faith that God is a wise and benevolent Power that is always accessible to us. This Power is greater than our body and personality. It knows us. It loves our highest good. And It supports all of our efforts to embrace this highest good and express it.

The enlightened intention we need is an unwavering commitment to pursuing our spiritual design for wholeness. This intention must become the number one priority governing our thought, feeling, and action.

We cultivate right understanding by exploring our divine possibilities. Each of us has been given a rich endowment or birthright, filled with the treasures of spirit. These treasures are our own potential for expressing wisdom, love, joy, courage, gentleness, peace, endurance, and beauty in our life. We are meant to explore these treasures and convert them into talents and skills. We are meant to translate them into habits of daily living. Sometimes, we will use these treasures to repair parts of us that have become broken—our hope, our confidence, our trust, or our respect for others. Eventually, we learn to use these treasures to enrich our self-expression and charge it with divine power. In this way, we gradually come to understand the nature of divine life—and what is expected from us as we interact with it. This understanding builds a powerful bridge from earth to heaven—from our personal awareness to the very core of spirit.

These treasures are always with us. They are not given to us by some religious ceremony. No one puts God into us. God is already there! And no one can build the bridge for us. We must build it through our own hard work.

We cultivate correct spiritual practices by adding right effort to our faith and understanding. First we believe, then we understand, and finally we act. We act by setting aside time each day for conscious spiritual contact. This contact should include study, a review of the insights of the day, and a subjective attunement to our inner life.

The study should be a daily reading of scripture or other inspired text, followed by an in-depth reflection on its inner meanings. We are not just reading for literal words, but for the spiritual essence or principle the words describe.

In the review, we take stock of recent experiences and

events and try to extract their inner messages. We consider how we need to revise or update ideas or beliefs we have held in the past. In this stage, our own life becomes our "bible"—a special message from God to us. To tap the full power of these messages, we must learn to sense the "invisible presence of God revealed by all visible things."

This review should remind us of the benevolence of God, the capacity of divine life to support all worthwhile activities, and the larger purposes of our activities. It can also highlight conflicts, wrong attitudes, and self-deceptions that need to be repaired.

In the work of attunement, we use a method of prayer, meditation, or invocation to get on the same wavelength as our innermost spirit. This work is not just a time of relaxation, where we try to empty out our mind and become numb! It is a time of focused activity, as we turn our attention away from sensations, memories, and feelings, and direct it toward the love, wisdom, and power of spirit. In this way, we rise to a more sublime level of awareness—a level of awareness that transcends ordinary thought and feeling. Our goal is to make a connection with our divine resources and possibilities. As we come closer to this goal, we begin registering new degrees of insight, peace, love, joy, and courage. We become buoyant with spirit.

We are doing nothing less than moving toward the center of our being—a center of tranquillity, understanding, and power. At this center, we tap the capacity to heal ourself, make sense of life, and renew our faith. We are also better able to sense the purpose of our memories, beliefs, and urges, and integrate them more effectively into our concept of who we are. We are better able to forgive enemies, bless tragedies, and rejoice in the future, because the inclusive nature of spirit enables us to see the divine possibilities in all of these things, too.

These are the three primary steps of inwardly cooperating with the Plan for the divine workshop of religion. There is also much outer work to be done—but it may be severely restricted by the institutions to which we belong. Organized religion is notoriously reactionary. But there are always points of light in religion that are responsive to new ideas and directions. When possible, we should approach responsive leaders to suggest the discussion of new experiments and activities. Such a request could lead to the formation of a small study group, perhaps with assigned reading. In turn, this could become the basis of eventually establishing classes in personal growth or healing.

There is no reason why such activities must be conducted in a church or temple—or even be blessed by the clergy. It is still true today that "Wherever two or more are gathered in my name, there I will be." Any small but sincere group effort is able to summon the presence of God. The group eventually becomes its own church or temple or mosque.

Religion is not held together with bricks and mortar. The true church or temple consists of men and women of goodwill striving to lead a responsible life of charity and helpfulness. The true house of God is our indwelling soul. The true worship of God is our ability to express the presence of God in our daily activities. Everything else is an adjunct.

It is our responsibility to find what is holy in life—or to make it holy by sanctifying it with spiritual purpose and love. If we think and act in these terms, we can enter any house of worship and find the service to be an enriching experience. We can also begin to see that our work, our home, and our community can also be "houses of worship," informally, if we take the simple step of expressing the presence of God while in these places.

The inner work of religious activity makes sense only if it is then expressed in some meaningful way in our outer experience. We are not meant to hide our light and keep it secret, but share it with everyone, so that they can be inspired by its warmth and comfort too.

Our final destination is not instant bliss. It is more a

steady awareness that our life is unfolding within the greater life of God—and so is everyone else's. As we meet opposition, therefore, we do not have to draw back in anger, seeing our opponent as an enemy. We can reach out with cooperation and reconciliation. Whether it is accepted or rejected, we have still honored the best within us. We have demonstrated the primary effectiveness of the work of religion on earth.

Having entered into darkness, we have revealed the light within us—the light that shines forever.

Renewing Civilization

One of the most common ailments of the spiritual aspirant is despair. It is easy to look at the state of the world and be overwhelmed by the work ahead of us. It is tempting to read history and bemoan the fact that it is repeating itself all over again—and the last cycle ended in disaster. There is no question that the world is filled with conflict and corruption. But despair is not the right response to these problems. It is itself a sign of immaurity and ignorance on the part of the aspirant.

Conflict is actually fertile ground for evolutionary change. It is not necessarily an omen of our imminent descent into chaos. Those who oversee the work of civilization are able to look ahead several centuries. They have consulted the blueprints for civilization's unfoldment, and are able to see how the problems of today will lead to the maturity of tomorrow. They have grasped our noble goals and destiny. They recognize the problems at hand—but they are also aware of the solutions. In fact, they have already planted the seeds for these solutions and are busy tending them.

Despair is an option we cannot afford, if we want to play our part in assisting the work of the Hierarchy. Humanity already has more despair, pessimism, and doubt than it needs. It is exactly these negative, querulous attitudes that in turn breed resistance to change—and resistance to change is the single most significant factor in slowing down our potential to evolve. Indeed, it is our collective resistance that often forces the Hierarchy to use conflict and corruption to inaugurate needed reforms.

In personal growth, the soul generally gives us multiple opportunities to learn our lessons without pain or suffering. In most cases, however, we ignore these opportunities. So the soul must devise methods for attracting our attention. These efforts often fail as well; we are too entrenched in our comfortable ways. But the spiritual will of the soul cannot be denied. And so, the only option that remains is to upset our comfortable ways. When this occurs, of course, we scream bloody murder and wonder why the soul is treating us so roughly. We have forgotten the numerous times we turned away from spirit.

Much the same pattern occurs in society. The plan for growth in each of the divine workshops of civilization is well known—among those who have made the effort to inform themselves. Many opportunities have been set before humanity to make the necessary changes and reforms. But most of these opportunities have been ignored. This leaves the Hierarchy with only one choice: to let conditions deteriorate to the point where incompetence, scandal, and corruption become so obvious and outrageous that vast numbers of people begin to demand change. Only then will the call for reform, voiced now by the people as well as the occasional visionary, be taken seriously. The entrenched resistance is defeated, and new spiritual vitality is able to enter into the life of society.

There is much wisdom in the old saying that new wine must be poured into new wineskins. The use of old wineskins would cause the new wine to spoil. Just so, the old structures of belief and tradition must be replaced before new ideas and methods are introduced, lest they pollute or compromise our efforts to grow.

This principle is easily observed. A habitually hostile person will soon begin finding fault with wonderful new friends. The perpetual pessimist will find reasons to complain, even if he or she is being helped. The constant worrier will find something to fuss about, even if it is the lack of things to fuss about!

True evolutionary growth requires constant change. There is no valid reason for fearing change or even stress—they are signs of a healthy society. The signs of an unhealthy society, by contrast, are stagnation and stability.

In our modern times, the tempo of life has been accelerated

in every aspect of society—and not just because of the advances of technology. The pace of activity has been deliberately accelerated by the Hierarchy, as it tries to stimulate society's desire to implement reforms and adapt the structure of our major institutions. This stimulation has magnified the problems of bigotry, ignorance, selfishness, and exploitation—but not in order to make life more difficult for us. The goal is to evoke us—even provoke us, if necessary—to inaugurate some part of the divine Plan for the spiritualization of civilization. Therefore, instead of despairing and wondering why God has abandoned us, we should remain cheerful and thankful that we live in such exciting times—and can participate in the work of renewing human civilization.

We can best serve the divine Plan for humanity by looking for the signs of it in the world around us—and by keeping faith that it will succeed in the course of time. When confronted with evidence of humanity's stupidity, selfishness, and greed, we need to look beyond this evidence and sense the opportunity at hand for leading mankind to a new level of maturity. We need to remember that the power to make these changes lies within the divine possibilities for humanity—and within each one of us. By growing as diligently as we can, we contribute to the radiation of God's light on earth—and become a force for the redemption of humanity's problems.

If, on the other hand, we succumb to despair, we will begin to resent the problems confronting society, tempted to condemn the "evil doers." This approach will sour our relationship to God and inadvertently add to the cloud of darkness and gloom that feeds the very problems we deplore! We become part of the problem, rather than an agent for the solution.

The choice we make is actually more important than we may realize. It influences a good deal more than just our transitory mood. Our attitudes toward civilization are highly contagious. If we are upbeat and optimistic, we inspire others to look for solutions, too. But if we are pessimistic and grim, we will poison society with our gloom. We will become a burden to humanity, not a source of light.

In addition, we need to discover the value of appreciating the work of spirit on earth, through each institution of society. The act of appreciation is a good deal more than just passive admiration. It is an investment of respect that actually increases the value or worth of an effort or activity. A child might rebel against the strict rules set down by his parents, but later in life appreciate how important those rules were in helping him develop self-discipline. In this way, the sensible guidelines of his parents gain even more importance for him.

In this spirit, it is important for each of us to appreciate how much greater than usually supposed are the contributions of business, education, healing, or religion. Everyone who continues learning as an adult is part of the great work of education. Everyone who sincerely prays or meditates serves the grand work of religion. Everyone who participates intelligently in commerce, even as a consumer, plays a role in the work of business. Everyone who strives to understand himself or herself better is contributing to the work of the healing arts and sciences. Everyone who appreciates good art and literature becomes a supporter of the divine workshop of the arts.

By faithfully supporting the best within each of these departments of human life, we likewise help others learn to appreciate the importance of genius and excellence. At the very least, we become a more informed and intelligent spokesperson for the true inner purposes being served by these activities.

The more we understand these inner purposes, the more likely we can make a meaningful contribution of our own. We do not have to be the president of a college to enrich education, or a senator in Washington to introduce reforms into government. The central sources of power in these institutions are seldom responsible for inaugurating true reforms. New directions and ideas are more likely to spring from someone working in a garage, or a citizen introducing a campaign to reduce taxes, or parents demanding new educational policies.

Above all, we need to realize that the greatest contribution we can make to the divine Plan is to live our life with as much light and love as we can. No matter who we are or what we do, we are a center of divine influence. We may not be an executive or a manager, but we can approach everything we do with the organization, efficiency, and intelligence that are the cornerstones of the Plan for business. We may not be a rabbi or a priest, but we can approach everything we do as though we were filled with the presence of God. We may not be a professor, but we can look for and find the lessons we need to learn from the experiences of life. As we try to live life with integrity, ideals, goodwill, intelligence, and helpfulness, we automatically become an agent of light. We radiate the light of spirit through every thought, feeling, and action we take.

Every decent person can make this contribution, no matter how poor or rich he or she may be.

The work ahead of us in spiritualizing humanity is indeed monumental. It will require a long period of effort, change, and sacrifice by millions of people. It will involve more discomfort and conflict than we have yet seen. But as long as we do not succumb to the temptation to be discouraged, apathetic, or cynical, we will triumph. It is the will of God that we succeed. With God, the Hierarchy, and divine law on our side, how can we do anything less?

We cannot afford to sit back and let others do the work for us, however. Humanity can only solve these problems and make these reforms as it learns to act as one being, with one united voice. If we sit on the sidelines, we fail to play our appointed role. Even worse, we will find that life simply passes us by.

Let us therefore learn to radiate the light of our skills, our hopes, and our understanding, to dispel the darkness of society and accelerate the emergence of the divine design of human life here on earth. Let us become a living part of the ceaseless flow of spirit that is seeking to redeem the world.

THE LIFE OF SPIRIT

The complete series of 31 essays in The Life of Spirit:

The Spiritual Person
The Spiritual Path
Defeating Evil and Sin
The Power of God: The Mother Aspect
The Power of God: The Son Aspect
The Power of God: The Father Aspect
The Treasures of Spirit
Redeeming Life
Psychic Dimensions of the Life of Spirit
The Role Death Plays in Life
The Trials of Initiation
The Path To Transfiguration
Praying Effectively
Enlightened Confession
The Act of Meditation
Invoking Divine Life
Worshipping God
Making Life Sacred
Finding Heaven on Earth
Linking Earth with Heaven
Harnessing Esoteric Traditions
The Inner Teachings of the Bible
Working with Angels
The Work of the Hierarchy
The Divine Workshop of Education
The Divine Workshop of the Arts
The Divine Workshop of Science
The Divine Workshop of the Commerce
The Divine Workshop of Government
The Divine Workshop of the Healing Arts & Sciences
The Divine Workshop of Religion

The full set of five volumes may be ordered for $69.

THE ART OF LIVING

Robert R. Leichtman, M.D. and Carl Japikse have also written a 30-essay series called The Art of Living:

Enriching the Personality
The Practice of Detachment
Finding Meaning in Life
Building Right Human Relationships
The Spirit of Generosity
Joy
Living Responsibly
The Nature and Purpose of the Emotions
Cultivating Tolerance and Forgiveness
Seeking Intelligent Guidance
The Bridge of Faith
Discerning Reality
Cooperating with Life
The Mind and Its Uses: Parts I and II
Coping with Stress
Enlightened Self-Discipline
Inspired Humility
The Act of Human Creation: Parts I & II
The Work of Patience
The Pursuit of Integrity
The Way to Health: Parts I and II
The Process of Self-Renewal
Filling Life with Beauty
Becoming Graceful
The Importance of Courage
The Noblest Masterpiece: Parts I and II

The full set of five volumes may be ordered for $69. Call 1-770-894-4226 to order individual volumes from either essay series. Orders can be placed by telephone or by sending an order, plus a check for the appropriate amount, to Ariel Press, P.O. Box 297, Marble Hill, GA 30148. Visit our website at www.lightariel.com. Email us at lig201@lightariel.com.